THE BEST FILMS OF OUR YEARS

M. OWEN LEE

Bloomington, IN Milton Keynes, UK

authorHOUSE®

AuthorHouse™
1663 Liberty Drive, Suite 200
Bloomington, IN 47403
www.authorhouse.com
Phone: 1-800-839-8640

AuthorHouse™ UK Ltd.
500 Avebury Boulevard
Central Milton Keynes, MK9 2BE
www.authorhouse.co.uk
Phone: 08001974150

First published by AuthorHouse 3/5/2007

ISBN: 978-1-4259-9621-5 (e)
ISBN: 978-1-4259-9620-8 (sc)

Library of Congress Control Number: 2007901083

Printed in the United States of America
Bloomington, Indiana

This book is printed on acid-free paper.

for

Tom Mohan
Doug Hilmer
Joe O'Regan

my fellow Shakespeareans

CONTENTS

"Everyone acts superior to lists (so arbitrary and invidious!), but the act is a bluff. The fact of the matter is basic and ineluctable: we need these lists. The year would not be complete without them. The year would not *make sense* without them."

Louis Menand in *The New Yorker*
January 12, 2004.

INTRODUCTION

I saw my first movie in 1935, and it was in the thirties that I started compiling an annual list of the top ten pictures – an indulgence I have allowed myself every year since. Most of this book is devoted to those listings, augmented by thumbnail reviews of the pictures that, over the years, made my final cut. There are also preliminary thumbnails on fifty famous films that appeared before my moviegoing began, and a concluding section that discusses in some detail the ten films I regard as the best of all our years.

How does this book differ from hundreds of others on the movies? Well, with the entries arranged chronologically rather than alphabetically, the book can hardly be used for ready reference. It is, I like to think, a volume that can be read straight through - or one year at a time, as its special emphasis is on years. We have been conditioned for too long to think of individual films apart from their times, as part of a star's filmography or of a director's output. Here each film is commented on in the context of nine others that appeared with it in the year of its American release. Each "best film" is seen as part of a period of development or - in some years, alas - as part of a period of decline.

I hope that the book conveys some of the excitement I felt, in the thirties and forties, in following year-by-year the careers of such American directors as John Ford, Frank Capra, George Cukor, and Preston Sturges. Of the excitement, in the fifties, of reading the reviews (in that decade, during my seminary training, I saw very few movies) of the latest successes by Alfred Hitchcock, David Lean, and Billy Wilder. Of the excitement, in the sixties, of waiting year-by-year for the new films of Federico Fellini, Ingmar Bergman, and Akira Kurosawa. And of the excitement, in the seventies, of teaching film courses, of meeting on campus Roberto Rossellini, King Vidor, George Stevens, and Francis Ford Coppola, of inviting Robert Altman to address my class the very week *M*A*S*H* opened, and of spending several late hours talking with young directors and their wives under the surveillance of the remarkable woman who dominated three decades of film criticism, Pauline Kael.

This is perhaps the place to thank the late Miss Kael and the other critics, not all of them still with us, whose writing shaped my responses to movies through the years — Leslie Halliwell, Andrew Sarris, Dwight McDonald, and above all Stanley Kauffmann, who will not approve of many of my opinions in this book, but whose intelligence and taste I respected beyond any measure. I am also indebted, for many details about Hollywood, to that compulsively readable volume, *Inside Oscar*, by Mason Wiley and Damien Bona, to Meredith Usher, and, for expert computer aid, to Doug Hilmer.

For younger readers, a few preliminary words may need to be said about the Hollywood studios. Most books on film treat American movies as almost exclusively the work of their directors. But in the best years of the Hollywood studios, roughly from 1925 to 1955, it was often the producer, and even more the studio, with its pool of professional talent, that stamped a picture with what quality it had. All of the major studios turned out serious dramas, comedies, musicals, westerns, and gangster pictures in those years but, to a degree not always appreciated today, each studio had its own trade-mark characteristics. And in the early pages of this book I have made an effort to profile each studio via the pictures it sent year-by-year to the ten best list.

When I was a boy, I knew that when that lady lifting her torch, the logo of Columbia Pictures, appeared on the screen, I would be watching a comedy that sparkled in its first hour, only to turn serious ("political" and "sociological" were terms that didn't mean much to me at the time) for its last thirty minutes. And no wonder: it was Frank Capra and his populism that turned Columbia, a little studio helmed by the obtuse Harry Cohn, into an award-winning success story, and set it on its course.

When in those days I saw Universal's logo, a planet ringed with satellites, I was usually prepared to see a low-budget drama. none of us then would scarcely have imagined that tiny Universal, founded by Carl Laemmle, would surge ahead of all the other studios when the television era dawned. Universal was smart enough to see early on what could be done with the newer medium, and by the century's end it had become the best-known Hollywood purveyor of commercial entertainment.

Glossiest, wealthiest, and most productive of the studios for many decades (with fifty films a year in its heyday) was Metro-Goldwyn-Mayer. Louis B. Mayer once boasted that his studio had "more stars than there are in the heavens". (Samuel Goldwyn had by then bowed out to form his own independent company.) Glittering among the MGM stars were Greta Garbo, Clark Gable, Judy Garland, and Gene Kelly. Remembered best now for its musicals and its prestigious Irving Thalberg productions, the studio virtually broke up in the late sixties when its assets were invested in a Las Vegas hotel. Most of the films it has produced since, still

3

with the familiar "Ars Gratia Artis" slogan and the roaring lion logo, were released through United Artists. (Ironically, MGM's biggest money-maker, *Gone With the Wind*, was independently produced by David O. Selznick at his own studios - though MGM got the lion's share of the profits by releasing Gable to star in *GWTW* in return for distribution rights.)

The original United Artists were Mary Pickford, Douglas Fairbanks, Charles Chaplin, and D.W. Griffith. The company they formed was not so much a studio as an organization for releasing and distributing films independently of the studio system. When in the fifties and sixties independent films became increasingly the rule rather than the exception, many directors opted to release their films through United Artists. So the logo-less organization stood for quality but can hardly be said to have had the profile of any of the studios themselves.

Lowly RKO, which introduced its pictures with a globe-topping radio tower beaming out an insistent signal, could also release films made by others – by Walt Disney, notably. But RKO could do impressive work on its own, even if Ginger Rogers complained that it was too cost-conscious (not Ginger's word) to film her pictures with Fred Astaire in color.

On the other hand, 20th-Century-Fox usually wallowed in the brightest and most unsubtle technicolor. Founded by garment manufacturer William Fox and headed in its palmy days by Darryl F. Zanuck, 20th introduced its pictures with trumpet fanfares and a searchlight logo. It employed even more people than MGM and enjoyed almost equal box-office success with its galaxy of (somewhat lesser) stars. To compete with television in the fifties, it introduced the wide-screen process called Cinemascope. Since then it has veered and lurched onwards, losing millions with *Cleopatra* in 1963, recouping them with *The Sound of Music* in 1965, and then losing them again.

Paramount, with its familiar mountain-peak logo, was helmed by Adolph Zukor, who managed even in hard times to bankroll the superproductions of Cecil B. DeMille and to bring Joseph von Sternberg, Erich von Stroheim, and Ernst Lubitsch over from Europe. In later years, Paramount meant innocent merriment with Bob Hope and Bing Crosby, uninnocent merriment from Preston Sturges, and acid wit from Billy Wilder. Though its front gate remained standing when most studios started tearing buildings down, Paramount eventually declined like the others, merging with Gulf-Western and releasing pictures made elsewhere. Sometimes, however, the business deals paid off: in the seventies Paramount hit the jackpot, critically and commercially, with *The Godfather*.

But the studio whose pictures stand up best sixty or more years later is Warner Brothers, named for its belligerent founders – Jack, Harry, Albert and Sam Warner. Think Bette Davis, Humphrey Bogart, and James Cagney dominating the screen in the hard-hitting, tightly made vehicles they made, sometimes four per year, early in their careers. Think Max Steiner and Erich Wolfgang Korngold music on the sound track. Think workhorse director Michael Curtiz and the familiar logo of a curved shield inscribed WB. Sadly, the glory days were gone by the late sixties, when the studio was taken over by a conglomerate and, like the others, began financing and releasing films made independently. But the old black-and-white logo was sported proudly in the new millennium, when *Mystic River* marked a welcome return to Warners standards.

In the heyday of these studios, only a few directors could imprint their own personalities on the films turned out. Then independent film-making came into its own in the mid-fifties, and big producers left the back lots of their studios to film *The African Queen*, *The Bridge on the River Kwai*, and many more, "on location" around the world. The end of studio control was by then imminent. When MGM made its last big musical, *Gigi*, in 1958, many of the talented people who knew how to turn out a musical – singers, dancers, designers, musicians, costumiers who had lovingly plied their trade for three decades - were gone. Things change, as one movie title has it. Hollywood films are now made, with considerably more expenditure of time and money than ever before, through deals between directors, producers, and stars, and released through what are largely business firms. Good pictures are still produced, but the special creativeness – and occasional ruthlessness – of the old studio system is now a thing of the past.

I hope, gentle reader, that some of that history will come to life for you as you make your way from year to year in the pages that follow.

Now for some general comments.

On comprehensiveness: Every passing year beings some five hundred films to North American cinemas, and I can hardly claim to have seen anywhere near all of them. I have not yet seen such highly regarded films from abroad as *La Jetée, Charulata, The Story of Late Chrysanthemums*, and *The Life of Oharu*. Nor did I see every one of my choices in the year of its American release. In many cases films that I once thought worthy of inclusion in the annual top ten have had to make way for those I caught up with later in life. In some recent years, I'm afraid to say, it has often been a stretch to find ten films worthy of listing. In other years, in 1939 and in 1962 for example, every one of the final ten was a bell-ringer, and a bumper crop of films competed for tenth place. Finally, I have not included films made for television unless they also received theatrical release. That will explain why *The Forsyte Saga* (1967), *I, Claudius* (1976), *Roots* (1977), *Brideshead Revisited* (1981), and *Wit* (2001) are not included here.

On years: In a book that remembers movies not from their release dates abroad but from the dates of their American openings, there are a few chronological problems that are not easily solved. In 1942, for example, Warner Brothers opened *Casablanca* in a single theater in New York to capitalize on the newsworthy landing of American troops under General Eisenhower in the Moroccan port city. The picture only opened world-wide in 1943, when it was seen by millions, when its song "As Time Goes By" topped the Hit Parade, when it qualified for and won the Oscar for best picture, and when Roosevelt and Churchill agreed to join forces against the Axis at a meeting held in, again, the Moroccan port that gave the movie its title. It seems best to list *Casablanca* here as a 1943 film. There are similar problems fitting *Olympia*, *The Rules of the Game*, *In Which We Serve*, *The Lavender Hill Mob*, and quite a few others into the appropriate years. Generally, I have followed the Academy's decision on these matters.

On awards: Movie awards are now so much with us that I have decided to cite, usually with the abbreviation AA (or, for supporting performances, AAS) each year's winners of the top six Oscars. I have also indicated which of the films were named best of the year at the festivals in Cannes and Venice.

On titles: I have given foreign films the titles they bore in their American releases. In cases where they are also widely known by their original titles, these are cited, with the rubric OT, at the end of the entry.

Finally, an apology on the matter of style. Many sentences in this book are like the one you have just read – that is to say, they are not sentences at all but specimens of the kind of journalese familiar in handbooks of this sort. A style in which a noun trails a string of adjectives and even a subordinate clause or two - replete with parenthetical remarks and asides set off with dashes - with nary an anchoring verb in sight. This is a style sanctioned by generations of critics, commentators, blurb writers, apologists, and publicists in a field where grammatical shorthand is one of the rules of the game. There is also a problem with tenses: generally, I have used the past tense when dealing with the making of a film and its first release, and the present tense when referring to its perennial good, or not so good, features. To those who find such writing difficult to read or otherwise off-putting, I hereby apologize and hope that they will read what follows anyway, and with pleasure.

FIFTY FAMOUS FILMS FROM 1915 TO 1934

(All of these films are in black-and-white.)

The Birth of a Nation (D.W. Griffith). 1915, US, silent. *The Birth of a Nation* was in effect the birth of the movies, sprung like Athena full-grown and armed from the Olympian genius of David Wark Griffith. Of course there had been movies before. Griffith himself had already turned out some four hundred, of varying lengths. But in this epic saga of two families - one Southern, one Northern, weathering the Civil War and Reconstruction - we have, at last, all the grammar and syntax of movie-making put to work in sentences, paragraphs, and narrative chapters, exploding often into symbols, metaphors, and rhythmic cadences. There are moments both great (the Civil War battle scenes that look like Matthew Brady photographs come to life) and small (the hospital sentry sighing after Lillian Gish) that, after almost a hundred years of movies, stay in the memory. There is also, notoriously, the pervasive racism Griffith inherited from his Confederate forebears. Of that, James Agee has rightly written, "Griffith's absolute desire to be fair is written all over the picture. So are degrees of understanding, honesty, and compassion far beyond the capacity of his accusers."

Intolerance (D.W. Griffith). 1916, US, silent. Griffith was so shocked that his *Birth of a Nation* was thought bigoted that he based the whole of his next magnificent folly of a picture on the theme of prejudice, cutting back and forth between four subjects - the fall of Babylon, the conflict of Jesus with the Pharisees, the St. Bartholomew's Day massacre, and a contemporary story of American injustice. It was a spectacle unequaled in size until today's computer-animated epics, and Soviet film-makers of the silent era spent years studying and reassembling it to discover the secrets of the master's editing. (The picture climaxes in excited cross-cutting.) Griffith, who had put up most of the money to make it, was paying debts on it for the rest of his life.

Broken Blossoms (D.W. Griffith). 1919, US, silent. Griffith recouped some of his savings on this low-budget melodrama, the most technically accomplished and beautifully photographed, if not the most important, of his films. And once again he seemed to be trying to refute the old charges of racism: the story tells of a Chinese man in Limehouse London (Richard Barthelmess) defending an English girl (Lillian Gish) from the brutality of her father (Donald Crisp).

The Cabinet of Dr. Caligari (Robert Wiene). 1919, Germany, silent. The famous expressionist film in which the director of a lunatic asylum uses a somnambulist to murder his enemies. The story is told pictorially, in splintered, stylized settings, and enhanced by neurotic performances by Werner Krauss and Conrad Veidt. The surprise ending, fully equal to that of 1999's *The Sixth Sense*, will support the view of Siegfried Kracauer's book *From Caligari to Hitler* that Wiene's film is not an attack on a mad authority figure but an argument in *favor* of (perhaps Hitler-like) authority, which is shown to be wise and humanitarian.

Nosferatu (F.W. Murnau). 1922, Germany, silent. Perhaps the earliest and certainly the best of many film treatments of Bram Stoker's *Dracula*, with Max Schreck as the most grotesque Transylvanian vampire of them all, and with transparent camera work by the great Murnau that not even Murnau was to surpass.

Nanook of the North (Robert Flaherty). 1922, US, silent. The granddaddy of feature-length documentaries, filmed on the northwest coast of Hudson's Bay by the most famous of the early documentarians. As in his later films, Flaherty had to resort occasionally to manipulation in order to record permanently a way of life (Inuit) that was already passing away, but *Nanook*, a world-wide success in its day, remains and brave and beautiful piece of cinema.

The Last Laugh (F.W. Murnau). 1924, Germany, silent. Murnau again, and the high point of camera virtuosity in the silent film. In this simple, sordid story of the downward progress of an Grand Hotel doorman, Karl Freund's camera becomes almost a living organism, following Emil Jannings along the corridors and through the revolving door of the Grand Hotel, down the city streets to his tenement, now gazing up at him affectionately, now peering down at him superciliously. Most of the then-startling effects can be achieved with ordinary equipment today, but few living cameramen have shown anything like Freund's sensitivity. So wide is the range of emotion conveyed by the camera alone that the film needs no intertitles, and has none. NOTE: The film is called *Der Letzte Mann* (*The Last Man*) in Germany. The American title was given the film when, for US distribution, it was equipped with an unfortunate "happy ending".

Variety (E.A. Dupont). 1924, Germany, silent. Almost as stunning as *The Last Laugh* in its use of Karl Freund's camera, Variety also uses the movie devices of a whole decade (iris, dissolve, superimposition, soft focus, angled shots, visual patterns, a 360-degree camera turn) to tell another sordid story, about a trapeze artist (Emil Jannings) and his common-law wife. But it is the telling use of Freudian symbols - hats, windows, mirrors, keys, cigars - that really give *Variety* its special standing as a work of film art. That and the fact that Jannings, as Josef von Sternberg observed, can act with his back. OT: *Vaudeville*.

Die Nibelungen (Fritz Lang). 1924, Germany, silent. An elaborate two-part filming, not of the pagan myths that Wagner used for his *Ring* cycle, but of the twelfth-century Middle High German epic, the *Nibelungenlied* (divided here into two groups of seven cantos each). The ambitious project was part of a movement at UFA's Berlin studios to build up Germany's national identity, after its defeat in World War I, by dramatizing its traditional myths. (Murnau was filming *Faust* at the same time.) Part I, *Siegfried*, is ponderous and oddly paced but has scenes of astonishing beauty; much of Part II, *Kriemhild's Revenge*, is wearying. The architecture and costuming of both parts are famously criss-crossed with angular zigzags. Available only in severely cut versions for several decades, the diptych was restored in 2002 to its original five-hour length and equipped with a Romantic score by Gottfried Huppertz that propels the drama along effectively - with nary a note of Wagner to be heard.

Greed (Erich von Stroheim). 1924, US, silent. A landmark of cinema realism in the face of the German expressionism that was fashionable at the time. Von Stroheim followed Frank Norris' novel *McTeague* page by page, filming every detail, from the (painstakingly reconstructed) street in San Francisco where the novel's protagonist lived to Death Valley, where he met his grisly end. The result was a carefully edited film more than eight hours in length. Stroheim was forced by the Goldwyn Company to cut it to four hours, to be shown in two parts. When even that was unacceptable, MGM took the film out of Stroheim's hands and released it in the version we have - edited down to less than two hours' running time. Even in that form, *Greed* is a film of great power. Though the eight-hour original seems to be lost forever, its screenplay has survived, and was published in 1972. With Gibson Gowland, Zasu Pitts, and Jean Hersholt.

The Thief of Bagdad (Raoul Walsh). 1924, US, silent. No *Greed* problems here. This is the kind of picture that automatically made money in Hollywood's silent era, with massive sets and with Douglas Fairbanks, out to outwit an evil Caliph, leaping about as athletically as he had two years before in *Robin Hood*. He even challenges Fritz Lang's hero Siegfried: in one exuberant scene he slays a dragon. The picture also borrows some good ideas from Lang's 1921 *Destiny* (*Der Müde Tod*).

Sherlock, Jr. (Buster Keaton). 1924, US, silent. A 45- minute feature from MGM in which a movie projectionist (Keaton at his best) falls asleep, slides down the beam of light from his projector, enters the screen, and solves the crime he is falsely accused of. René Clair compared it to Pirandello's *Six Characters in Search of an Author*, and Woody Allen remembered it in his *The Purple Rose of Cairo*.

* **The Gold Rush** (Charles Chaplin). 1925. US, silent. Is this the greatest of all silent comedies? See the essay later in this book.

The Big Parade (King Vidor). 1925, US, silent. The most cinematic of the American anti-war films that followed on World War I, and the biggest money-maker of the whole silent era (from MGM, of course), but rather slow-going today. With John Gilbert as the young enlistee who learns that war is more horrific than heroic, and Renée Adorée as the French girl who, in a famous scene, clings to the army truck that is carrying him off to battle.

Potemkin (Sergei Eisenstein). 1925, USSR, silent. The famous film - named at the Brussels World's Fair in 1958 as the best ever made - about a mutiny aboard a czarist battleship and the slaughter of hundreds of sympathetic citizens in reprisal. That scene of slaughter, filmed on the waterfront steps of Odessa, is probably the most famous single scene in the history of the movies, a brilliant demonstration of the power of film editing - specifically of the quick editing of small bits of film that came to be known as "montage".

Mother (V.I. Pudovkin). 1926. USSR, silent. A demonstration that a novel (in this case, Maxim Gorky's story of a mother betraying her strike-breaking son) can be reconstructed and expanded in silent-movie form through the use of visual motifs, close-ups in montage, parallel sequences that come together at climactic moments, and a pictorial eye that suggests, in rural Russia, compositions by Velasquez, Van Gogh, Dégas, Picasso, and Rouault.

Metropolis (Fritz Lang) 1926, Germany, silent. The story of this early sci-fi melodrama may be preposterous, and the acting not much better, but the architecture - a heaven of thrusting spires and floating highways, a hell of monstrous robotic machinery, with great fluid blocks of men and women massed between - remains one of the lasting achievements of German expressionism on film. It even survived a reissue in the eighties with color and pop music added.

The General (Buster Keaton) 1926, US, silent. A Civil War reject (Keaton) commandeers a train stolen by Union forces and, impervious to all that rages around him, races to the rescue of his lady love. Based on the incident later filmed by the Disney Studios as *The Great Locomotive Chase*, it is Keaton at his most poker-faced and acrobatic, and it has placed highly on the all-time lists of critics who find Chaplin too sentimental.

Napoleon (Abel Gance). 1927, France, silent. A visually impressive four-hour account of the early career of another general, with images from three separate cameras projected on three side-by-side screens, combining at the finish in a single panoramic image. Cut and reassembled many times, equipped on occasion with sound and color, this pioneering film no longer exists in its original version. Imitated in the fifties by the processes called Cinerama and Cinemascope.

October (Sergei Eisenstein). 1927, USSR, silent. Eisenstein applies his "montage" technique to stunning effect in commemorating the Russian revolution on its tenth anniversary. The film ran into censor trouble almost immediately, as regimes changed in the USSR and Eisenstein was forced to remove all the footage in which Trotsky appeared. The version released in Britain and America as *Ten Days That Shook the World* was even more heavily cut. But any print will show you more than you thought the cinema could do.

Sunrise (F.W. Murnau). 1927, US, silent. Murnau, invited to Hollywood after the success of *The Last Laugh*, made in effect a German film that might happen "anywhere and at any time", with dreamlike studio sets (by Rochus Gliese), superb camerawork (by Charles Rosher and Karl Struss), and a luminous performance by Janet Gaynor (AA) as a young wife whose husband (George O'Brien), madly in love with another woman, tries to kill her. The tears Gaynor's performance evokes during the famous scene on the trolley are honest, unsentimental tears. The film lost a mint for the Fox studio but at the first Academy Award ceremony it won the Oscar (discontinued thereafter) for "artistic quality of production". Did that make it better than *Wings*, which won the best picture Oscar? I think so.

The Jazz Singer (Alan Crosland). 1927, US, silent/sound.
Not much of a movie, but there's no denying the thrill that is still there when Al Jolson, playing a cantor's son who goes into show business, breaks the silence barrier to speak, and then to sing. It was the moment when Warner Brothers studio went from the brink of bankruptcy into the big Hollywood money. Special Academy award.

The Crowd (King Vidor). 1928. US, silent. Vidor stayed with the silent film one last time, and produced for MGM a small but enduring, and to some extent Germanic, masterpiece: the camera moves up the side of a New York building, passes through a window into a room filled with office workers, singles out one of them, and follows him through his life of joys and sorrows till he is lost again in the crowd. (Vidor filmed eight different endings, and some prints still show a version where the man lands a better job and celebrates Christmas with his family. Vidor also made a sequel of sorts, *Our Daily Bread*, in the sound era.)

* **The Passion of Joan of Arc** (Carl Dreyer). 1928, France, silent. The great, pivotal film that sums up the silent era even as it cries out for sound. See the essay later in this book.

Un Chien Andalou (Luis Buñuel). 1928, France, silent. A surrealist collage, designed by Salvador Dali, lasting only as long as the destructive fancy of its creators hold out. And that (17 minutes) is too long for some tastes: a man slashing a woman's impassive eyeball, a human hand aswarm with ants, a dead decaying donkey slung on a grand piano, and other images aimed like so many darts at conventional art and morality. Sheer Buñuelesquerie, and relatively harmless. But there was more to come.

Hallelujah! (King Vidor). 1929. US. Vidor shot his first sound film with an all-black cast, and in remote areas of the South. A good deal of his footage was silent until the editing stage, when, in a movie moment that still impresses, he composed a sound track to supplement the dialogue and to underscore the speechless sequences. The depiction of black life - river baptisms, cotton fields, shanty towns, and a flight through a muddy swamp - might strike some as racist today, but in 1929 this was a brave, pioneering work, especially for conservative MGM.

L'Age d'Or (Luis Buñuel). 1930, France. Buñuel is back, badder than before, equipped with a sound track, furious that the provocative images in *Un Chien Andalou* had been thought "beautiful" and "poetic", and determined *pace* Dali to use more explicit symbols in this all-out attack on Church and State. *L'Age d'Or* even has a plot of sorts, and ends with the survivors of the Marquis de Sade's *120 Days of Sodom* staggering out of their orgy, led by de Sade's criminal hero made up to look like Jesus. The film ran *sans incident* for a few weeks in Paris before the reactions, some of them violent, set in. It was banned thereafter for decades, but remains the key work of one of the cinema's undoubted originals, whose subsequent films can seem almost pious by comparison.

Earth (Alexander Dovzhenko). 1930, USSR, silent. As this beautifully photographed film begins, we see vast, sun-drenched, wind-swept wheat fields, close-ups of huge sunflowers, trees luxuriant with apples and pears, and an old man, lying amid this plenty, surrounded by four generations of his family. He bites into an apple, smiles, and slowly dies. Such is the lyrical mode in which Dovzhenko, commissioned to make a propaganda film in support of the Soviet collective farm program in his native Ukraine, tells his simple story. The radiant visuals interact, now gently, now forcibly, almost with the power of symphonic music. This was the last silent film to reach classic status.

Anna Christie (Clarence Brown). 1930, US. "Garbo talks!" the ads proclaimed when the silent star appeared in MGM's uncinematic version of Eugene O'Neill's play, a veritable antique about a sailor and a streetwalker. As it turned out, Garbo's voice - deep, husky, faintly accented - enhanced her on-screen magnetism, and massive Marie Dressler, moving with conspicuous ease from silence to sound, seemed to achieve the impossible: she made us watch *her* while Garbo was on the screen. With Charles Bickford as the sailor.

The Blue Angel (Josef von Sternberg). 1930, Germany. A put-upon but respectable (and very Teutonic) professor becomes infatuated with a provocative cabaret singer and endures utter humiliation from her and her co-workers. What begins as something like a comedy is by the end as shocking a film as any ever made. Conceived as a vehicle for Emil Jannings (and he is marvelous in it), it made a star of the young Marlene Dietrich, whose career was then taken over by her Svengali, director von Sternberg, who promptly took her to Hollywood. This was the first influential European film of the sound era. Each scene was shot in German and then re-shot immediately in English.

All Quiet on the Western Front (Lewis Milestone AA). 1930. US. Milestone began making Erich Maria Remarque's anti-war novel about young Germans in World War I as a silent film, and it is more remarkable for silent moments (the shockingly realistic depiction of trench warfare, the scene where the young German kneels in a bomb crater to beg forgiveness from the staring corpse of the enemy soldier he has killed, the final shot of young Lew

Ayres fatally reaching for a butterfly) than for its rather clunky dialogue sequences. Yet it was so obviously sincere, and retained its power for so many years, that nations preparing for war have often thought it best to ban it. From ambitious Universal studios. Oscar for best picture.

City Lights (Charles Chaplin). 1931, US. Chaplin made his first film in the sound era as a silent with a musical score and a few sound effects. Some have found the tale of the "little fellow" befriending a drunken millionaire and a blind flower girl too sentimental by half. Others - a large majority - have praised its many moments of comic genius.

Frankenstein (James Whale). 1931, US. Universal's famous version of the tale of the monster made of dead parts owes more to German expressionist films that in does to Mary Shelley's novel, and has inspired - if that is the word - some two dozen sequels in America and abroad. Boris Karloff (actually William Pratt, a fairly distinguished English actor) was typed for life, but not allowed to play his look-alike fifteen years later in the screen version of *Arsenic and Old Lace*.

Le Million (René Clair). 1931, France. Clair, the wittiest and most inventive of all the directors of the early sound era, plays endlessly with sound techniques in telling a madcap tale about a lost lottery ticket. Especially inventive are the little songs, some of them used as dialogue, others as interior monologues, still others sung to the characters by offstage voices.

À Nous la Liberté (René Clair). 1932, France. Determined not to let the silent movie succumb completely to sound, Clair uses a lot of his old tricks and some new ones to tell the story of a factory owner (patterned after Charles Pathé) whose assembly line turns out sound equipment and of his change of heart when he sees the dehumanizing effect such industrialization has on its hapless workers. Four years later, Clair's producers wanted to sue Charles Chaplin, whose *Modern Times* was clearly influenced by this film. Clair simply said, "I am honored if he was inspired by my film."

M (Fritz Lang). 1932, Germany. Amid much puffing on cigarettes, a child-murderer is tracked by the police and finally fingered by his fellow criminals (with the letter M chalked on his back) and put on trial by them. Lang's compositional genius (see *Nibelungen* and *Metropolis*) is still in evidence in this, his first sound film, but he shows as well a new and welcome interest in characterization. In the devastating finale Peter Lorre almost makes us understand the pathology of the man who screams, "I can't help myself."

Freaks (Todd Browning). 1932, US. A bizarre and disturbing film (from the man who directed Bela Lugosi in *Dracula*) in which most of the roles are played by circus freaks. Certainly a curious project for a main-line studio like MGM, which later disowned it. Many American exhibitors refused to show it, and it was banned in Britain for thirty years. But twenty-first century audiences sated with phony horror movies might learn something about understanding and compassion from seeing it.

I Am a Fugitive from a Chain Gang (Mervyn LeRoy). 1932, US. Paul Muni as an innocent man brutalized by his prison experience. Typical of Warner Brothers' hard-hitting films of the thirties, it was the first to plead for social reform. Any one who has seen it can tell you the last line of dialogue.

Trouble in Paradise (Ernst Lubitsch). 1932, US). The artfully erotic "Lubitsch touch" can be felt in every scene of this scintillating Paramount comedy about accomplished jewel thieves (Herbert Marshall and Miriam Hopkins) and the rich widow (Kay Francis) who almost comes between them. With C. Aubrey Smith, Charles Ruggles, and Edward Everett Horton.

Love Me Tonight (Rouben Mamoulian). 1932, US. An infectious Paramount musical, reminiscent of the Parisian films of René Clair, with Maurice Chevalier, Jeanette MacDonald, Myrna Loy, and a Rodgers and Hart score that includes "Lover" (which Jeanette sings to her horse!), "Mimi" (which practically everybody gets a chance to sing), and "Isn't It Romantic" (which is charmingly reprised again and again as we move from Chevalier's tailor shop to a taxi to a train to a gypsy camp to princess Jeanette's castle balcony). Why can't they make them like that today? Maybe because today we have no Rodgers and Hart.

Grand Hotel (Edmund Goulding). 1932, US. Though the doctor in the lobby (Lewis Stone) may say "Grand Hotel, always the same, people come, people go, nothing ever happens", almost too much happens when the lives of Greta Garbo ("I want to be alone"), John Barrymore, Lionel Barrymore, Joan Crawford, and Wallace Beery begin to intersect. But what was the last word in MGM star-power entertainment in 1932 can seem forced and dated today. Oscar for best picture.

King Kong (Merian C. Cooper and Ernest Schoedsack). 1933, US. A giant ape escapes his captors and terrorizes Manhattan. Still the most famous monster movie, with some of the best early trick photography, and still, after two massive remakes, the one and only. From fast-rising RKO studios, with Robert Armstrong, Fay Wray, and Bruce Cabot.

Duck Soup (Leo McCarey). 1933, US. A riotously ramshackle semi-musical with the Marx Brothers at their zaniest. Groucho, president of a lilliputian country under siege, says to his minions, apropos of matronly Margaret Dumont: "Remember, you're fighting to defend this woman's honor - which is probably more than *she* ever did." The picture, now regarded as a comedy classic, was too ramshacklely riotous for thirties audiences, and it lost money for Paramount.

42nd Street (Lloyd Bacon). 1933, US. Warner Brothers, the studio that introduced sound, presents *the* archetypal show business musical, with great songs by Harry Warren and Al Dubin, choreography by Busby Berkeley, and with harried producer Warner Baxter telling chorus girl Ruby Keeler as he sends her out to save the show, "You're going out a youngster but you've got to come back a star!"

The Private Life of Henry VIII (Alexander Korda). 1933, UK. The first British film to make its way around the world, with a famous performance by Charles Laughton (AA) as the king who had six wives and seemed not to like any of them very much. With Robert Donat, Merle Oberon as Anne Boleyn, and Elsa Lanchester as Anne of Cleves. I'm afraid that some of it now seems rather perfunctory.

Man of Aran (Robert Flaherty). 1934, UK. Flaherty's best documentary, with unforgettable seascapes. The Irish-American director has been accused of idealizing his Aran islanders and romanticizing his subject - but he was an explorer to start with, and always more poet than sociologist. This is poetry. Best film winner at the Venice Film Festival.

It Happened One Night (Frank Capra AA). 1934, US. Charming comedy about an heiress on the run and a reporter down on his luck. Quickly turned out by the young Capra at what was then a minor studio (Columbia), it was rapturously received by Depression audiences and went on to becomes the first film (there have been only two more to date) to win all four major Academy awards - best picture, director, actor (Clark Gable) and actress (Claudette Colbert). Sales of gentlemen's undershirts plummeted when Gable revealed that, beneath his shirt, he wasn't wearing one.

The Gay Divorcée (Mark Sandrich). 1934, US. The first film to star Fred Astaire and Ginger Rodgers (they played secondary roles in the earlier *Flying Down To Rio*), and perhaps the most enjoyable of all screen musicals. The pair's hushed "Night and Day" (words and music by Cole Porter) is a fascinating study in choreographic seduction, and "The Continental" (by Con Conrad), danced with a hundred others and possibly the longest dance number in the history of the movies, is so good you don't want it to stop - and to your delight it goes on and on. With Edward Everett Horton, Eric Rhodes, and Eric Blore. With this one RKO moved to within hailing distance of the big four studios - MGM, Fox, Warners, and Paramount.

Little Women (George Cukor). 1934, US. An affectionate, faithful rendering, from ambitious RKO, of Louisa Mae Alcott's story about four affectionate sisters, with Katharine Hepburn enchanting as Jo, Joan Bennet as Amy, Frances Dee as Meg, Jean Parker as Beth. Cukor's reputation for bringing out the best in actresses was firmly established with this young quartet. With Paul Lucas and Edna Mae Oliver in support.

Sons of the Desert (William A. Seiter). 1934, US. The Hal Roach studios proudly present Mr. Stanley Laurel and Mr. Oliver Hardy in their finest film, and if you don't think it belongs on a list of fifty famous films there's something the matter with you.

The 1930s

1935

1 **Top Hat** (Mark Sandrich). US, bw. Even without color, this RKO delight comes close to being the essential Hollywood musical. The classic Irving Berlin score, the deliciously dopey Venice set, the inspired silliness of Edward Everett Horton and Eric Blore, and of course the elegant and witty dancing of Fred Astaire and Ginger Rogers - all seem better with every passing year. (But does *Top Hat* really top 1934's *The Gay Divorcée?*)

2 *The Informer* (John Ford AA). US, bw. A predictable story of betrayal in Dublin during "the troubles" is elevated by stylized expressionist cinematography, Ford's toughly sentimental direction, and Victor McLaghlen's unforgettable performace (AA) into what was thought in 1935 the finest achievement of the American sound film. If, in the years since, even Ford's most ardent worshipper, Andrew Sarris, has called it dated, *The Informer* remains one of the most memorable of the Irish-American director's more than 130 films. From RKO.

3 *The 39 Steps* (Alfred Hitchcock). UK, bw. The master of suspense sends an innocent man (Robert Donat) on the run across England and Scotland, handcuffed a good deal of the time to a beautiful woman (Madeleine Carroll) who doesn't like him. Droll, exciting, and full of surprises – especially for readers of John Buchan's novel, to which it (perversely?) bears almost no resemblance. Lovely vignette by Peggy Ashcroft as a selfless Scottish countrywoman.

4 ***A Night at the Opera*** (Sam Wood). US, bw. The Marx Brothers and Margaret Dumont are finally given the big studio treatment (courtesy MGM), and come up with one of their zaniest entertainments, even though the studio demanded love interest (Kitty Carlisle and Allan Jones) complete with love duets, and obligatory scenes of Chico at the piano and Harpo at the harp. Dowager Dumont, always a good sport, faces up hilariously to Groucho's withering wit.

5 ***Mutiny on the Bounty*** (Frank Lloyd). US, bw. Some of this famous MGM saga, filmed "on location" at sea and in Tahiti, may seem patchy and primitive today, though the performances of Charles Laughton as the sadistic Captain Bligh and Clark Gable as the stalwart Mr. Christian stay indelibly in the memory. It cost twenty-five times as much as *The Informer*, and was a big box-office success, so no one was surprised (though some critics were indignant) when it got the Oscar for best picture. Twice remade, but not nearly as well.

6 ***David Copperfield*** (George Cukor). US, bw. MGM again, and a prime example of deluxe Hollywood story-telling in the glory days of the studios. With Freddie Bartholomew, Edna Mae Oliver, W.C. Fields (as Mr. Micawber), and a dozen more Dickensian professionals happily stealing scenes from one another.

7 ***Anna Karenina*** (Clarence Brown). US, bw. MGM again, with almost half of the cast of *David Copperfield* now playing second fiddles to Tolstoy's lovers, enacted by Greta Garbo and Fredric March. Expectedly luxurious, but more romantic than tragic. Voted best film at the Venice Film Festival.

8 *Les Misérables* (Richard Boleslawski). US, bw. An all-out attempt by 20th-Century-Fox to challenge MGM in the literary adaptation department, and quite the best of a dozen attempts to film Victor Hugo's classic novel. Fredric March as Jean Valjean is hounded by Charles Laughton as Inspector Javert. Each of them had a busy year at the top in 1935.

9 *Ruggles of Red Gap* (Leo McCarey). US, bw. Unbelievably, Charles Laughton tops his two other 1935 appearances (see above) playing an English butler comically coping with American frontier society (i.e., Charles Ruggles, Mary Boland, and Zasu Pitts). Laughton even brings off a devout reading of the Gettysburg Address in the midst of the hilarity. From Paramount.

10 *The Bride of Frankenstein* (James Whale). US, bw. Boris Karloff marries Elsa Lanchester. The only regret is that Universal didn't think to get her real-life husband Charles Laughton to appear as the minister – but with three other bell-ringing performances this year, Laughton was clearly busy enough. This low-budget black comedy now has a vocal cult following and is easily the most professional and sophisticated of all thirties horror movies.

Contending for tenth place were *The Man Who Knew Too Much*, *Follow the Fleet*, and *Lives of a Bengal Lancer*.

1936

1 *Modern Times* (Charles Chaplin). US, bw. A silent comedy defiantly produced by Chaplin in the thick of the new sound era.

(The sound track contains one song-and-dance number by the producer-director-star, a sentimental score of his own composing, occasional sound effects, and a few startlingly disembodied industrial voices.) The film is compassionate, concerned, and occasionally anarchic in its view of the depressed thirties, and is often cited as Chaplin's best work. Certainly it contains his funniest single scene - the "little fellow" is selected for a demonstration of how an assembly-line worker can be fed by a machine (complete with mechanically operated napkin) while staying at his job. Some ideas are taken from René Clair's *A Nous la Liberté*, which was also concerned with the dehumanizing effect of industrialization and the limitations that sound was to place on hitherto silent movies. (Clair said he was honored to have Chaplin borrow from his work.) With Paulette Goddard as the gamin, a good comic turn by Chester Conklin, and a closing shot that became a Chaplin trade mark.

2 *La Kermesse Heroique* (Jacques Feyder).   France, bw. Woman's Lib in a seventeenth-century Flemish town invaded by Spaniards: while the men find places to hide, the women, led by the magnificent Françoise Rosay, give the Spaniards what they most want, and in the nicest way. Pauline Kael called it "one of the rare, perfect works of the screen...a fusion of Breughel and Boccaccio".

3 *Show Boat* (James Whale). US, bw. Was Universal's *Frankenstein* director the right man to film Broadway's great pioneering musical? As it turns out, yes. Everything is ship-shape until the ending - but then every *Show Boat*, stage or screen, runs aground at the end. Paul Robeson sings "Ol' Man River", Helen Morgan sings "Bill" and "Can't Help Lovin' Dat Man", and Irene Dunne and Alan Jones sing three more of the greatest songs ever written.

They're by Jerome Kern and Oscar Hammerstein II, in case you didn't know -- and that fabulous team turned out three new tunes for this screen version. (The 1950 MGM technicolor *Show Boat*, often unjustly maligned, is good, but would have been better if it had had Whale at the helm.)

4 **San Francisco** (W. S. Van Dyke). US, bw. An MGM melodrama with everything the movies could provide in 1936 - romance, religion, fist-fights, popular songs, opera, and a climactic earthquake sent to put the fear of God into the wicked but plucky Barbary Coast. With Clark Gable and Jeannette MacDonald, and with Spencer Tracy in the first of his priestly roles. The earthquake scenes owe much to (and have some special effects even better than) the montage sequences pieced together by Eisenstein for the Soviets.

5 **The Great Ziegfeld** (Robert Z. Leonard). US, bw. Another blockbuster from MGM. William Powell plays Broadway producer Florenz Ziegfeld, with Luise Rainer (AA) and Myrna Loy as his two wives. Among the highlights: Rainer on the telephone tearfully congratulating Powell on his second marriage, Fannie Brice singing "My Man", and a truly mammoth wedding-cake finale. Much too long at three hours, it cost two million and made more than twice that at the box office. An unamused Graham Greene, in his days as a critic, called it a "huge inflated gas-blown object". That didn't stop it from winning the Oscar for best picture.

6 **A Tale of Two Cities** (Jack Conway). US, bw. MGM again, and the last picture David O. Selzick made there before going independent and making *Gone With the Wind*. Fast-moving, picturesque, and as respectful of Dickens as last year's *David*

Copperfield had been. In the proverbial cast of thousands swept up in the French Revolution are Ronald Coleman, Edna Mae Oliver, Basil Rathbone, and Blanche Yurka.

7 ***The Green Pastures*** (William Keighley). US, bw. Old Testament stories, and heaven itself, recreated at the Warners studio by an all-black cast. Marc Connelly's Broadway success sits oddly on the screen, but overflows with good humor, tenderness, and childlike faith - qualities one would like to have seen in any number of Hollywood's biblical epics. Despite its good intentions, it was banned as sacrilegious in Canada, held up for a year in Britain, and is still periodically – but quite wrongly - attacked as racist. With Rex Ingram and Eddie Anderson.

8 ***Swing Time*** (George Stevens). US, bw. To more of Jerome Kern's music, Fred Astaire pretends he needs dancing lessons from Ginger Rogers, slips, sings "Pick Yourself Up", woos her with "The Way You Look Tonight" as she washes her hair, and spars with her in the snow in "A Fine Romance". These sequences plus the most exhilarating and impressive dance numbers the duo ever attempted ("Waltz in Swing Time" and "Never Gonna Dance") more than compensate for a tiresome script. From RKO, which never found the money to put Rogers and Astaire on the screen in color. (MGM did it a dozen years later, when it was too late to matter.)

9 ***Mr. Deeds Goes To Town*** (Frank Capra AA). US, bw. Capra's early attempt at honoring the honest man - Gary Cooper in this case - may have dated in a way that the three pictures he made with James Stewart have not, but it did send the words "pixilated" and "doodle" straight into the dictionary, and many people still find it endearing. From Columbia.

10 **My Man Godfrey** (Gregory LaCava). US, bw. Classic screwball comedy with butler William Powell bringing sanity to upper-crust dumbbells Carole Lombard, Eugene Pallette, and Alice Brady. Houseguest Mischa Auer does a startling gorilla imitation. For have-not Depression audiences, nothing matched watching the haves at their silliest. From Universal.

Contending for tenth place were *Fury*, *Dodsworth*, and *The Story of Louis Pasteur*.

1937

1 **Snow White and the Seven Dwarfs** (Walt Disney studios). US, color. Three years in painstaking production, *Snow White* was the first feature-length cartoon and is in many ways still the best. A fairytale atmosphere is charmingly and, when need be, frighteningly evoked. Delightful songs in operetta style move the action along more effectively than the did the songs of most studio musicals of the time. Each of the dwarfs is endowed with individualizing human qualities and yet retains some kinship with the animals and the forest. Best of all are the animals themselves, carefully studied from nature and imaginatively set in motion. On the other hand, Snow White and the Prince, copied from live models, seem curiously less substantial than the other figures. But that doesn't prevent *Snow White* from being one of the brightest, bravest, and most beautiful pictures ever made. Given an honorary Oscar with seven miniature Oscars by the Academy in 1938. Hollywood scuttlebutt predicted disaster but when the film was released (as were all the Disney cartoons for two decades) through RKO it made money as well as history.

2 ***Lost Horizon*** (Frank Capra), US. bw. A small plane full of civilians (including Ronald Coleman, Thomas Mitchell, and Edward Everett Horton) escapes a Chinese revolution but is peremptorily hijacked and flown to a Tibetan paradise presided over by a Belgian priest turned High Lama (Sam Jaffe). The James Hilton story is completely incredible, at least as filmed here (Shangri-La, which President Roosevelt made a household word, looks like a rejected set design for the Emerald City), but there is no denying the effectiveness of the story-telling and the horror of the penultimate scene. Columbia was ready at last to put up some big money for Capra. (The exciting first half-hour, long excised, has now been restored; some later scenes have apparently been lost with the horizon.)

3 ***The Good Earth*** (Sidney Franklin). US, bw. An MGM Irving Thalberg project that, along with *Camille* (see the next entry), was released after his death. Against all odds, the massively expensive production of Pearl Buck's best seller about a Chinese farmer (Paul Muni) was a critical and popular success, thanks largely to the moving performance of Luise Rainer (AA) as O-lan, his wife, and to a climactic swarming of locusts that was as impressive as the earthquake sequence in *San Francisco*.

4 ***Camille*** (George Cukor). US, bw. The younger Dumas' "Lady of the Camelias", Marguerite Gauthier (the Violetta of Verdi's *La Traviata*), enacted by Greta Garbo in a glamorous MGM production, with Lionel Barrymore and Robert Taylor as Duval *père* and *fils* and with Henry Daniell as the Baron de Varville. Garbo's most moving performance. There was audible shock when the best actress Oscar went to Luise Rainer (see the previous entry), who was the first star to win the award in two successive years. Garbo fans have never forgotten or forgiven.

5 *A Star Is Born* (William Wellman). US, color. The Hollywood star of Vickie Lester (Janet Gaynor) rises while that of her husband Norman Maine (Fredric March) sets. The archetypal studio tragi-romance and perhaps the first film to use color creatively. Based on Wellman's 1932 film *What Price Hollywood* and undimmed either by the stupendous re-make with Judy Garland (1954) or the deplorable rock version with Barbra Streisand (1976). From the Selznick studios.

6 *The Life of Emile Zola* (William Dieterle). US, bw. Warner's prestige item for the year, with Joseph Schildkraut (AAS) as the wrongly accused Captain Dreyfus and Paul Muni as the famous writer who comes to his defense. *The New York Times* called it "the finest historical film ever made". Oscar for best picture, two others – but, sadly, all but forgotten now.

7 *Stage Door* (Gregory LaCava). US, bw. The Broadway comedy-drama by Edna Ferber and George Kaufman - about life in a theatrical boarding house for ladies - is still potent on the screen. With Katharine Hepburn rehearsing her "calla lilies" speech for Ginger Rogers, Lucille Ball, Eve Arden, and other femmes under contract to RKO.

8 *Sabotage* (Alfred Hitchcock). UK, bw. Titled *A Woman Alone* on its first American release, this suspenseful Hitchcock treatment of Joseph Conrad's *The Secret Agent* features Oskar Homolka as a saboteur who runs a small London cinema and Sylvia Sydney as his suspicious wife. Hitchcock had already made a picture called *The Secret Agent* (not based on Conrad) in the UK and was soon to make a picture called *Saboteur* in the US. Confusing? Well, Hitch always kept us guessing.

9 ***The Awful Truth*** (Leo McCary AA). US, bw. McCarey's improvisational skills, learned from years of work in silent movies, really pay off in this screwball comedy about a marriage coming apart at the seams. With Cary Grant, Irene Dunne and Ralph Bellamy. Fast moving, frothy, and funny. From Columbia.

10 ***Night Must Fall*** (Richard Thorpe). US, bw. A homicidal psychopath (Robert Montgomery), a rich old lady (Dame May Whitty), a distraught young lady (Rosalind Russell), and an ominous hatbox. This film version of Emlyn Williams' stage success was a box office disaster, publicly disowned by studio head Louis B. Mayer. The National Board of Review didn't care; they proclaimed it the year's best picture. Well, it comes in here as number ten.

Contending for tenth place were *Mayerling* and *Shall We Dance*.

1938

1 ***Grand Illusion**** (Jean Renoir). France, bw. The most perceptive, humane, and hopeful of all films, and my own personal favorite. See the essay later in this book.

2 ***You Can't Take It With You*** (Frank Capra AA). US, bw. The Kaufman and Hart play won a Pulitzer Prize, but the best parts of Capra's screen adaptation, for Columbia, are the additions - the tender, funny scenes where James Stewart woos Jean Arthur in his office, in a park, and in a swank restaurant. In typical Capra fashion, the Broadway eccentricity of the "little people" who do their own thing at the Vanderhof household has been softened,

and the cold-heartedness of big business emphasized - all of which makes the movie more durable and enjoyable than any of the play's many stage revivals. Unforgettable performances by Lionel Barrymore and Edward Arnold. Oscar for best picture.

3 *Pygmalion* (Anthony Asquith). UK, bw. Though it now seems like *My Fair Lady* without the music, this expert filming of Shaw's play about a phoneticist turning a cockney flower girl into a lady has rewards of its own, not least the performances of Wendy Hiller and Leslie Howard (who also had a hand in directing). David Lean did the editing. The British cinema took a leap forward with this prestige item, but Shaw himself was furious when the Academy gave him the award for best screenplay: "It's an insult for them to offer me any honor, as if they had never heard of me before - and it's very likely they never have."

4 *The Lady Vanishes* (Alfred Hitchcock). UK, bw. Even more witty, surprising, and suspenseful than *The 39 Steps*, with Dame May Whitty vanishing on a train crossing Europe, with Michael Redgrave and Margaret Lockwood as the baffled young people, and with Basil Radford and Nauton Wayne as two British twits to whom anything not British is inexplicable, not to say unseemly.

5 *The Adventures of Robin Hood* (Michael Curtiz). US, color. This generous helping of daring-do is second only to 1940's *The Thief of Bagdad* as the best of all little-boy movies. With Errol Flynn as the stalwart Robin, Alan Hale as Little John, Eugene Pallette as Friar Tuck, Claude Rains as nasty Prince John, Basil Rathbone as villainous Guy of Gisbourne, and Olivia De Havilland - very pretty in white - as Maid Marian. Outstanding technicolor and a rousing Warner Brothers score by Erich Wolfgang Korngold.

6 ***Bringing Up Baby*** (Howard Hawks). US, bw. The screwball comedy that was too screwball for some in 1938; now many regard it as the best of all the screwballs. Katharine Hepburn plays an heiress with a pet leopard, and Cary Grant is a paleontologist in desperate search of a lost dinosaur bone. Magnificent mayhem, with a final scene to end all final scenes. From RKO.

7 ***Holiday*** (George Cukor) US, bw. The second filming of Philip Barry's wistful stage play. Katharine Hepburn, who was supposed to be "box-office poison" at this time (see the entry above) is absolutely radiant as a Park Avenue rich girl who falls in love with her sister's fiancée, played by Cary Grant. With a touching performance by Lew Ayres, and funny bits from Binnie Barnes and Edward Everett Horton. Cukor is masterly with this sort of material. From Columbia, by 1938 the studio best known for comedy with a serious edge.

8 ***La Bête Humaine*** (Jean Renoir). France, bw. Jean Gabin wanted to play a railroad engineer on film, and Renoir adapted a Zola novel for him — one from the long series of interrelated works that also gave us *Gervaise* and *Germinal*. Against a virtually continuous background of powerfully atmospheric train scenes, Gabin gives an extraordinary performance as a man who can neither understand nor control the violent impulses he has inherited. Many viewers imagine the final sequence — the train hurtling out of control toward Le Havre — as emblematic of France itself in 1938. With Simone Simon and Fernand Ledoux. Renoir appears in a vivid cameo.

9 ***The Citadel*** (King Vidor). US, bw. High-minded drama about a young doctor (Robert Donat) in England's mining district who is lured away to an easy life treating wealthy hypochondriacs in

London and finally comes to his senses. With Ralph Richardson, Emlyn Williams, and Rosalind Russell. Doctors on both sides of the Atlantic were grateful for it. From MGM's British studios, which produced "quality" films for the next four years.

10 ***The Adventures of Tom Sawyer*** (Norman Taurog). US, color. The newly formed Selznick studio warms up for *Gone With the Wind* with a nostalgic piece of Americana from Mark Twain. Taurog, with ten years' experience in directing children (his *Boy's Town* also came out in 1938) does well by his young cast and gets ideal performances out of oldsters May Robson, Walter Brennan, and Victor Jory. Somebody slipped up badly when Twain's magnificent Jim was turned into an amiable pickaninny; if you can forgive that, this is something to show the kids and watch yourself.

Contending for tenth place were *Jezebel, Four Daughters, Alexander's Ragtime Band*, and *The Dawn Patrol*.

1939

1 ***Gone With the Wind*** (Victor Fleming AA). US, color. Of the year most often cited as Hollywood's greatest, *GWTW*, based on Margaret Mitchell's best seller, is the undisputed champ. Scarlett O'Hara (Vivien Leigh AA) learns, after years of war and reconstruction in the South, that Rhett Butler (Clark Gable) and not Ashley Wilkes (Leslie Howard) is the man she should have loved, though Melanie (Olivia de Havilland) and Mammy (Hattie McDaniel AAS) could have told her as much three and a half hours earlier. Superb production values, lovely opening

half-hour filmed by George Cukor, and another stunning half-hour, Fleming-led, as the Yankees besiege Atlanta. Sam Wood and art director William Cameron Menzies also helped with the direction, and David O. Selznick presided dictatorially over the whole production, securing Gable's services from MGM only by allowing that studio to handle the release (and reap millions with a revival every seven years). With Thomas Mitchell, Butterfly McQueen, and Laura Hope Crews, whose line "Yankees in Georgia! How did they evah get heah?" is only one of many quotable quotes. (It should be said that, six decades on, some hindsighted churls indict *GWTW* for reputed racism; more to the point is that too much plot piles up in the picture's last half hour.) Oscar for best picture, seven others.

2 ***The Wizard of Oz*** (Victor Fleming. US, color. An American fairy tale and a movie legend. It did not clear its costs in 1939, but in subsequent years generations of TV-watching children have taken it to, and learned it by, heart. Heart is the word for Judy Garland's performance, and it is hard to imagine how Ray Bolger, Jack Haley, Bert Lahr, Frank Morgan, Billy Burke, and Margaret Hamilton could ever have been bettered, though most of them were not MGM's first choices for their fantasy roles. Judy's poignant "Over the Rainbow", by Harold Arlen and Yip Harburg, was selected "song of the century" in a survey taken in 2000 by the Recording Industry of America and the National Endowment for the Arts - though the MGM front office at first ordered it cut from the picture. How *could* they have been so brainless, heartless, and cowardly?

3 ***Wuthering Heights*** (William Wyler). US, bw. Emily Bronte's passionate tale of the Yorkshire moors, rather severely tailored to movie length but poetically filmed on studio sets by Gregg

Toland, with Laurence Olivier as Heathcliff and Merle Oberon as Kathy. Geraldine Fitzgerald, as Isabella, has a searing moment that lives in the memory. Olivier claimed that he learned the director's art from Wyler while making this picture. From the Goldwyn studio.

4 *Mr. Smith Goes to Washington* (Frank Capra). US, bw. James Stewart as a greenhorn senator who smartens up and exposes corruption in Washington. JFK's father wired FDR that if shown overseas it would "do inestimable harm to American prestige all over the world", but in the end Capra, Stewart, Jean Arthur, Claude Rains, Edward Arnold, Thomas Mitchell, and Harry Carey covered themselves with glory both here and abroad. Everything about the film is perfectly turned out in Capra's best Columbia style.

5 *Stagecoach* (John Ford). US, bw. Until the fifties brought us *High Noon* and *Shane*, this was *the* Hollywood western: John Ford and his astounding camera crew invade Monument Valley, John Wayne moves from Grade B oaters to the big time, and a motley group of troubled travelers - played by Claire Trevor, John Carradine, Donald Meek, and the ubiquitous Thomas Mitchell (AA) – ride through a climactic Indian attack. Great stunt work by the half-Indian Yakima Canutt compensates for a certain buckboard clumsiness here and there. From United Artists.

6 *Ninotchka* (Ernst Lubitsch). US, bw. An icy Russian emissary (Greta Garbo) thaws out under the intoxicating influence of Paris, and the "Lubitsch touch" learns to live, at MGM, alongside the Billy Wilder wisecrack. Sample: newly arrived commissar Ninotchka says straight-faced to her intimidated Soviet underlings, "The last

mass trials were a great success. There are going to be fewer but better Russians." With Melvyn Douglas and Ina Claire.

7 *Alexander Nevsky* (Sergei Eisenstein). USSR, bw. Even before the USSR banned *Ninotchka*, its darling Eisenstein was busy making spectacular Russian propaganda in the face of a potential German invasion. *Nevsky*, his first sound film, is brazenly operatic in its larger-than-life gestures, its elaborately staged and costumed set pieces, and its carefully worked out symbiosis of visuals and music (by Serge Prokofiev). The battle on the ice between Nevsky's people's army and the Teutonic Knights is a great piece of cinema, and it clearly influenced the Agincourt sequence in Olivier's *Henry V*. Nikolai Cherkassov, later to be Eisenstein's Ivan the Terrible, plays Nevsky.

8 *Goodbye Mr. Chips* (Sam Wood). US/UK, bw. A prestigious product of MGM's British studios, this much-loved film version of James Hilton's novel about a benevolent schoolmaster offered Robert Donat (AA) a role in which he could age from twenty-five to eighty-three. Greer Garson, emerging from the mist on an Austrian Alp, made an impressive movie debut. Sentimental? Yes. Millions in England and America wept.

9 *The Hunchback of Notre Dame* (William Dieterle). US, bw. This expensive remake of the famous silent shocker with Lon Chaney was turned out by a less pecunious studio (RKO) with loving attention to all production details, and in an ordinary year it would have placed near the top of such a list as this. With Cedric Hardwicke, Maureen O'Hara, Edmond O'Brien, and, as Victor Hugo's misshapen bellringer, Charles Laughton - in an unforgettable performance that, amazingly, was not nominated by the Academy.

10 **Harvest** (Marcel Pagnol)   France, bw. The film that first awakened most American moviegoers to movies beyond Hollywood, this simple tale of rustic life in Provence, adapted by Pagnol from a novel by Jean Giono, was startlingly frank at the time and remains quietly disquieting. With Fernandel, Orane Demazis, and Giono himself. Music by Arthur Honneger. OT: *Regain*.

Contending for tenth place were *Of Mice and Men, Gunga Din, The Four Feathers, Beau Geste, Dark Victory, Juarez, The Private Lives of Elizabeth and Essex, The Women, Love Affair, Stanley and Livingstone, Young Mr. Lincoln, Only Angels Have Wings, Drums Along the Mohawk,* and (from abroad) *Port of Shadows* (*Quai des Brumes*). Among all "the best years of our films", it might have been the best.

No wonder that in the United States one-third of the population was going to the movies every week!

ADDENDUM:

Olympia (Leni Riefenstahl). Germany, bw. This historically significant film is not so much a record of the 1936 Berlin competitions by which Hitler hoped to demonstrate Aryan superiority as a long, carefully wrought poem in praise of physical beauty, courage, ambition, failure, and success - and, incidentally, an elegy for all the young men soon to die in Allied and Axis armies. The athletic bodies all but become spirit in the closing sequences, as slow-motion divers soar and veer against a darkling sky in a montage of patterns. Edited by Fräulein Riefenstahl from more than a million feet of film, with different versions sent to different countries. "America's magnificent negroes" figure prominently in all the prints I've seen; Hitler, I'm told, dominates others. The New York opening, in two parts, was early in 1940, but I have not been able to determine in what year *Olympia* officially debuted in the United States.

The 1940s

1940

1 *The Thief of Bagdad* (Michael Powell, Ludwig Berger, and Tim Whelan). UK, color. This Arabian Nights fantasy is the best of all little-boy movies, shot in dazzling color and replete with elegant sets and lovingly executed special effects. Conrad Veidt plays the evil wizard, with Sabu as the thief, Rex Ingram as the genie, and June Duprez and John Justin as the lovers. Amazingly, it was filmed in various parts of the world by six directors (in addition to those cited above, there was considerable input from William Cameron Menzies, Zoltan Korda, and Alexander Korda) at a time when the world was at war. Fifty years later, a new generation of filmmakers, including George Lukas, Steven Spielberg, and Martin Scorsese, acknowledged indebtedness to it, and the Disney people certainly had a look at it when they did their *Aladdin*. But for this little boy, the 1940 *Thief of Bagdad* still tops all subsequent efforts.

2 *The Grapes of Wrath* (John Ford AA). US, bw. John Steinbeck's novel about dust-bowl Oklahomans making a troubled odyssey to a hostile California, memorably filmed by a studio (20th) more noted for cheerful entertainment than for serious subjects. With Henry Fonda, John Carradine, many of Ford's repertory actors, and with Jane Darwell (AA) as Ma Joad. Some of the dialogue is unnaturally folksy (Ma's big "We're the people" speech was written by 20th's head man, Darryl F. Zanuck), but the picture, something of a departure for Ford, is nonetheless a very moving experience.

3 ***Rebecca*** (Alfred Hitchcock). US, bw. David O. Selznick, elated by the success of *Gone With the Wind*, brought Hitchcock over from England to direct this film version of Daphne du Maurier's gothic best seller, and the two gentleman locked horns: Hitch wanted suspense, Selznick wanted world-class gloss. The result was, almost miraculously, an effective blending of both. With Laurence Olivier, Joan Fontaine, George Sanders and, as the two unforgettably domineering women who harass the second Mrs. de Winter, Florence Bates and Judith Anderson. The book's climactic revelation was, however, regrettably softened to suit the Hollywood production code. Oscar for best picture.

4 ***The Philadelphia Story*** (George Cukor). US, bw. The Broadway play, about a spoiled heiress facing her faults on the eve of her second marriage, was written to order by Philip Barrie for Katharine Hepburn, who had been labeled "box office poison" by Hollywood. She faced her presumed real-life faults head-on in the Broadway role, and she was terrific. She then returned to the movie capital, filmed the play at MGM under Cukor's direction, was even more terrific. She never had to look back again. Her luck extended to the rest of the cast - James Stewart (AA), Cary Grant, and Ruth Hussey all gave la Hepburn skilled, perceptive support.

5 ***His Girl Friday*** (Howard Hawks). US, bw. In 1931, *The Front Page* was a fast-paced story about two male reporters. In this riotous remake, one of them, Hildy, becomes a woman's role, and what a woman! - Rosalind Russell, ripping out the rapidest dialogue ever heard in a movie, rattling both husband Cary Grant (the rival reporter) and new suitor Ralph Bellamy. In a recent poll of favorite movies this Columbia feature wound up number 1 of all time. Some people didn't like *Citizen Kane*, some didn't

like *Potemkin*, but nobody didn't like *His Girl Friday*. I thought, when I first saw it, that I even heard Robinson Crusoe roaring approval.

6 ***Pride and Prejudice*** (Robert Z. Leonard). US, bw. "More Dickens than Austen", said *The New Yorker* of this broadly but brilliantly played adaptation of Jane's perennial novel about a family with five daughters who seem destined not to find husbands. Reduced to one third the length of the recent television versions, and sporting costumes hilariously updated from 1810 to 1860, this MGM glossy boasts career-peak performances by Edna Mae Oliver, Mary Boland, Frieda Inescort and - inevitably introduced by his wheezing clarinet leitmotif - Melville Cooper as Mr. Collins. With Laurence Olivier and Greer Garson in fine form as Pride and Prejudice themselves.

7 ***The Letter*** (William Wyler). US, bw. Bette Davis empties a revolverful of bullets into her husband in the opening sequence, and then gives what Pauline Kael has called "very likely the best study of female sexual hypocrisy in film history." It's a Somerset Maugham story, set in sweltering Singapore, with Herbert Marshall and James Stevenson, and with a shiver-inducing Gale Sondergaard as a Eurasian woman intent on revenge. Music by Max Steiner, and direction by Wyler at his most expert. From Warner Brothers.

8 ***The Great Dictator*** (Charles Chaplin). US, bw. With World War II already underway in Europe, Chaplin plays two roles - a barber in a Jewish ghetto and a brush-mustached dictator named Adenoid Hynkel. Jack Oakie plays a strutting, chin-out dictator named Napaloni. The first part of the picture is in the best Chaplin style, with the barber polishing a bald man's head

to a Brahms "Hungarian Dance" and the dictator doing a ballet with a floating globe to the Prelude to Wagner's *Lohengrin*. But inevitably seriousness sets in, and at the end Chaplin makes a six-minute speech about human decency straight into the camera that almost wrecks the picture. With Paulette Goddard as a young Jewess.

9 *Foreign Correspondent* (Alfred Hitchcock). US, bw. The other 1941 film from a happy Hitchcock newly arrived in America. Free for a while from his contract from Selznick, working for another independent, Walter Wanger, he quickly crafted what may be his most enjoyable comedy-suspenser, and even permitted an ending that pleaded for American involvement in Europe's war. Three classic moments: an assassination on the rainy steps of Amsterdam's town hall, with a sea of open umbrellas adding to the confusion; a windmill mysteriously turning against the wind; an attempted murder atop Westminster Cathedral. With Joel McCrae, Laraine Day, Herbert Marshall, George Sanders, Albert Basserman, and Edmund Gwenn.

10 *Pinocchio* (Walt Disney studios). US, color. This careful treatment of the children's classic by Carlo Collodi was an unequivocal critical triumph for Disney, with the best animation of any of his features, but it did not fare nearly as well as *Snow White* had at the box office. Punsters quipped that audiences suspected Disney's puppet might have termites; certainly there was too much footage of the puppet-boy with his donkey tail and ears. But in time, with Disney World, Disneyland, "Walt Disney Presents" and the arrival of VHS and DVD, the film finally found the public it deserved. With the best of all Disney songs, "When You Wish Upon A Star."

Contending for tenth place were *The Sea Hawk*, *The Shop Around the Corner*, *Destry Rides Again*, *The Westerner*, *The Great McGinty*, *Christmas in July*, *The Bank Dick*, *My Little Chickadee*, *Daybreak* (*Le Jour se Lève*), and *The Baker's Wife* (*La Femme du Boulanger*). 1940 is a clear contender for the best of all movie years.

1941

1 ***Citizen Kane**** (Orson Welles). US, bw. Bitterly opposed and little seen in 1941, but voted the best movie ever made in the *Sight and Sound* poll of critics and directors world- wide in 1962 *and* in every decade since. See the chapter later in this book.

2 ***How Green Was My Valley*** (John Ford AA). US, bw. Critics have never forgiven this film for taking the best picture Oscar away from *Citizen Kane*. Some have even poured scorn on it. But in fact, *How Green Was My Valley*, Ford's second film at a studio (20th) eager to treat more serious subjects, is an essential film. Andrew Sarris linked it with *Citizen Kane* as "the beginnings of a cinema of memory", notable for "introducing Ford's visual treatment of the past as a luminous memory more real than the present". The memory in *HGWMV* is the childhood of Huw Morgan (Roddy McDowall), nurtured in a close-knit Welsh coal-mining family, learning through a series of crises about the importance of human relationships and the impermanence of human achievement. With Donald Crisp (AA), Sara Allgood, Walter Pidgeon, Maureen O'Hara, and Anna Lee. Ford often referred to *HGWMV* as his favorite of all his many films. Five Oscars in all.

3 ***The Maltese Falcon*** (John Huston). US, bw. Huston, in his directorial debut, remakes a Dashiell Hammett detective story that had been filmed twice before - and scores a Warner Brothers knock-out. The pacing is so quick, the plot twists so unpredictable, and the lies so convincingly told, that you can watch the picture ten times over and still not remember from previous viewings just who did what to whom and why. Certainly it's impossible to imagine a cast better suited to bring all this delicious nastiness off than Humphrey Bogart, Mary Astor, Sidney Greenstreet, and Peter Lorre. The director's father, Walter Huston, makes a quick appearance in a crucial scene.

4 ***Fantasia*** (Walt Disney studios), US, color. Discussion of the merits and demerits of this most ambitious of all cartoon features seems never to end. Of the eight pieces of "classical" music animated by the studio and served up by Leopold Stokowski in stereophonic "Fantasound", only Dukas' "Sorcerer's Apprentice" and Ponchielli's "Dance of the Hours" are played as originally composed, and not surprisingly they are the most enjoyable bits. Most of the rest has been rearranged to suit the free-wheeling imagination of Disney's remarkably gifted illustrators. All of the sections, however, have vociferous defenders. Confused Disneyacs stayed away in the forties, potheads flocked to see the dance of the mushrooms in "The Nutcracker Suite" and the hallucinatory "Night on Bald Mountain" in the sixties, and a *Fantasia II*, wholly new, was released in the nineties.

5 ***The Little Foxes*** (William Wyler). US, bw. The film version of Lillian Hellman's play about a vicious, self-destructive post-Civil War family on the brink of financial disaster, acted to the hilt by Bette Davis, Herbert Marshall, and several members of the Broadway cast. Slightly marred by unnecessary "opening

up" sequences, the film for most of its length is given the feeling of both cinema and stage by the deep-focus photography that Gregg Toland first used in *Citizen Kane*. "Catch us the little foxes that destroy the vines" is the Biblical motto. From the Goldwyn studios.

6 ***Here Comes Mr. Jordan*** (Alexander Hall). US, bw. A prize piece of Columbia whimsy about a prizefighter who almost dies in a plane crash, finds himself taken prematurely to heaven, returns to earth, discovers that his body has been cremated, and is told by his guardian angel (Edward Everett Horton) that there is nothing to do but find a new one. With Claude Rains as St. Peter in a business suit, Robert Montgomery as the prizefighter, and, in a hilarious performance, James Gleason as his manager. Imitated many times since 1941, but never bettered.

7 ***The Lady Eve*** (Preston Sturges). US, bw. A double-edged, cruel-only-to-be-kind comedy about the always uneven battle of the sexes, with Henry Fonda as the turkey and Barbara Stanwyck as the axe. One of the seven idiosyncratic, roaringly satirical pieces turned out in four years at Paramount by immensely talented writer-director Sturges. (The first two were last year's *The Great McGinty* and *Christmas in July*.) With Charles Coburn, Eugene Pallette, and several members of Sturges' own repertory company of movie crazies. *Citizen Kane* devotees should know that *The New York Times* named *this* as the best picture of 1941.

8 ***That Hamilton Woman*** (Alexander Korda), UK, bw. Laurence Olivier and his wife Vivien Leigh as Lord Nelson and Lady Hamilton in a drama climaxing in the Battle of Trafalgar. Elaborately filmed in Hollywood by Korda, the dean of British producer-directors, who hoped it would enlist U.S. support

for a Britain once again in danger of invasion. (It was Winston Churchill's favorite movie.) Top laurels are almost stolen from the very professional Oliviers by Gladys Cooper as Lady Nelson.

9 ***All That Money Can Buy*** (William Dieterle), US, bw. Stephen Vincent Benet's story "The Devil and Daniel Webster", which transfers the Faust legend from Germany to New England, is given something of a German expressionist production by veteran Dieterle, who had played Valentin in Murnau's *Faust* some twenty years earlier. With James Craig as a young Yankee selling his soul, Edward Arnold as Daniel Webster, and, in an extraordinary performance, Walter Huston as the Devil aka Mr. Scratch. Predictably good musical score from Bernard Herrmann. From RKO.

10 ***The Strawberry Blonde*** (Raoul Walsh). US, bw. The second of three filmings of James Hagen's play *One Sunday Afternoon*, and easily the best. With James Cagney as a dentist with a score to settle, Olivia De Havilland as the girl he marries, Rita Hayworth as the strawberry blonde he thinks he really wants, Jack Carson as the cad who almost wrecks his life, and Alan Hale as his charm-a-mile-thick Irish father. Loads of studio-set Gay Nineties atmosphere. Irresistible. From Warner Brothers.

Contending for tenth place were *Major Barbara, Suspicion, Sergeant York, Dumbo, Tom, Dick, and Harry, The Devil and Miss Jones, Man Hunt, Meet John Doe, The Flame of New Orleans,* and *Pepe le Moko*. One of our best years.

1942

1 ***The Magnificent Ambersons*** (Orson Welles). US, bw. The first and best of Orson Welles' unlucky post-*Citizen Kane* projects, taken out of his hands by the studio (RKO), cut from a reported three hours to 88 minutes, equipped with a phony ending, and released on a double bill with *Mexican Spitfire Sees a Ghost*. Even in its mutilated form, Welles' retelling of a familiar tale by Booth Tarkington shows much of the cinematic brilliance that had enlivened *Kane*. With Joseph Cotton, Tim Holt, Dolores Costello, and Anne Baxter. The scene in which Agnes Moorehead as a spinster aunt teeters on the brink of madness is harrowing - and by report was doubly harrowing before the cuts were made. The sadly truncated *Ambersons* still finds its way on many critics all-time ten best lists.

2 ***Mrs. Miniver*** (William Wyler AA). US. bw. MGM's glossy tribute to the British home front at the time of German bombing is not always believeable: Mrs. Miniver (Greer Garson AA) holds off a Nazi flyer who has parachuted into her garden while Mr. Miniver (Walter Pidgeon) is away helping to evacuate the British forces at Dunkirk. But much of it is stirring, especially the final scene in a bombed-out church where the minister tells his congregation that World War II is a new kind of war - a people's war, with civilian casualties. F.D.R. ordered that speech to be printed on millions of leaflets and dropped on Nazi-occupied Europe. Winston Churchill told Louis B. Mayer that *Mrs. Miniver* was "propanganda worth a hundred battleships". With

Teresa Wright, Henry Travers, and Dame May Whitty. Oscar for best picture, five others.

3 **Yankee Doodle Dandy** (Michael Curtiz). US, bw. Flag-waving wartime Warner Brothers bio of Broadway actor-composer George M. Cohan, with James Cagney (AA) dancing up a storm in the musical numbers and strutting like a peacock through the rest. FDR, with only a year left to live, asked Cagney to perform some of the numbers at the White House for his birthday. Still immensely popular on DVD. With Walter Huston and Joan Leslie.

4 *Kings Row* (Sam Wood). US, bw. Melodramatic, often gripping, sometimes less-than-credible saga of four children growing up at the turn of the nineteenth century in a town that advertises itself as "a good place to raise your children" but beneath the surface is anything but. Originally released with an intermission to relieve the tension. With one of the great Hollywood scores (by Erich Wolfgang Korngold) and good performances by Claude Rains, Betty Field, and - better than anyone expected them to be - Warner Brothers contract players Ann Sheridan, Robert Cummings, and Ronald Reagan.

5 *The Palm Beach Story* (Preston Sturges). US, bw. The fourth of Sturges' seven madcap Paramount comedies, often cited as the best. Inspired nonsense about four people (husband Joel McCrae and winsome wife Claudette Colbert, millionaire playgirl Mary Astor and bumbling brother Rudy Vallee) in marital mixups. The overdone scene of the "Ale and Quail" shoot-up is more than compensated for by a hilarious performance earlier in the film by Robert Dudley as "the Weenie King". "Screwball" is really the word.

6 ***Sullivan's Travels*** (Preston Sturges). US, bw. A change of pace for the hectic Sturges, and something of an *apologia pro vita sua*. Joel McCrae plays a director of cinema comedy who has to be convinced of comedy's importance in a world full of human misery; Veronica Lake plays the muse-like waif who accompanies him on his odyssey. In 2000, the Coen brothers *may* have intended to make the movie Sullivan wanted to make - in their *Odyssey*-based *O Brother, Where Art Thou*.

7 ***To Be Or Not To Be*** (Ernest Lubitsch). US, bw. Jack Benny gets to play Hamlet in wartime Warsaw, but only up to a point. Not only is his theatrical troupe forced to turn its attention to espionage but, whenever he comes to his big soliloquy, his wife (Carole Lombard in her last film) entertains a soldier (Robert Stack) from the audience in her dressing room. Lots of comedy, suspense, "Lubitsch touches", and laughs at the expense of one Adolph Hitler. Produced by Alexander Korda.

8 ***Holiday Inn*** (Mark Sandrich). US, bw. It was Irving Berlin's idea to write a musical about an inn that would be open for business, and a floor show, only on holidays. The result worked like a charm, with Bing Crosby, Fred Astaire, and a Berlin song for each of eight holidays. "Easter Parade", an oldie, was a natural for one holiday, but new songs, including "White Christmas", were composed for the other days. Avoid the 1954 partial remake in color called *White* (it should have been called trite) *Christmas*, with Crosby and Danny Kaye. Both are from Paramount.

9 ***Woman of the Year*** (George Stevens). US, bw. The first of the MGM Katharine Hepburn-Spencer Tracy vehicles, and one of the best. She's a super-smart political commentator, he's a regular-guy sports columnist. Some feminists churlishly object

to the penultimate scene where *she* proves completely inept in *his* kitchen. The point is that both she and he are inept in some rooms, very compatible in one.

10 **Bambi** (Walt Disney studios) US, color. Disney's beloved, beautifully animated story of a woodland fawn, years in preparation and watched by utterly fascinated children throughout three quarters of a century. The forest fire is genuinely exciting, and the death of the young deer's mother has been known to make strong men, even members of the NRA, weep.

Contending for tenth place were *The Major and the Minor, Ball of Fire, The Talk of the Town, Random Harvest, Saboteur, Reap the Wild Wind*, and *The Road to Morocco*. (During this and the next three years, virtually no foreign language films made it to America.)

1943

1 **Casablanca** (Michael Curtiz AA). US, bw. What promised at first to be little more than a project on which to keep contract players at Warner Brothers busy became, after cast and other changes, the most timely and entertaining film made in Hollywood during World War II, one of the great screen romances - between Humphrey Bogart and Ingrid Bergman - and a more-than-cult classic for over sixty years. Its troubled birthing, with day-to-day changes in the script (is it by Julius G. and Philip J. Epstein or by Howard Koch?) has become legend. With Warners workhorse Curtiz directing Claude Rains, Paul Henreid, Conrad Veidt, Sidney Greenstreet, and Peter Lorre, and with Dooley Wilson as

Sam playing "As Time Goes By" by special request. Oscar for best picture, two others.

2 ***Cabin In the Sky*** (Vincente Minnelli) US, bw. Ethel Waters, my patron saint, puts this all-black MGM musical in her pocket from the very start, and even though the cast includes Eddie "Rochester" Anderson, Duke Ellington, Lena Horne, Butterfly McQueen, Rex Ingram, John Bubbles, and (seen all too briefly) Louis Armstrong, it's Ethel singing "Takin' A Chance On Love" and "Happiness is Just a Thing Called Joe" that you remember for the rest of your born days. The script, a Faustian fantasy, may be stagebound, but Minnelli, in his directorial debut, keeps the visuals fluid.

3 ***The Song of Bernadette*** (Henry King). US, bw. 20th-Century-Fox's annual bid for prestige. John Ford wasn't around this time, or possibly wasn't as interested in this religious subject as he had been in *The Grapes of Wrath* and *How Green Was My Valley*, but the studio proceeded apace (even converting the big *HGWMV* set from a Welsh to a French village). The results were impressive: a record number of Oscar nominations (13), massive box office returns, and a picture that even unbelievers worshipped. With Jennifer Jones (AA) as the peasant girl who saw visions of the Virgin Mary at Lourdes, and with Charles Bickford, Gladys Cooper, and Anne Revere solid in support.

4 ***Heaven Can Wait*** (Ernst Lubitsch). US, color. While the war raged in Europe, and heroism and sacrifice were virtues striven for by home-front Americans, the German-born Lubitsch, master of sophisticated innuendo, perversely had a decidedly unheroic and selfish bon vivant (Don Ameche) tell his life's story to the devil (Laird Cregar) and win audiences' sympathy and understanding.

The nifty cast also included Gene Tierney, Eugene Pallette, Marjorie Main, Charles Coburn and - all too briefly before she is hilariously consigned to Hell - Florence Bates. From 20th-Century-Fox. (Not to be confused with an inferior picture of the same name from 1978, which is actually a botched remake of another 40's classic, *Here Comes Mr. Jordan*.)

5 ***The Human Comedy*** (Clarence Brown). US, bw. Though MGM's prestige item for the year was a too respectful bio, *Madame Curie*, most critics found this wartime drama written for the screen by William Saroyan (and later turned by him into a novel) matter more attractive. Others thought it terribly pretentious and sentimental. Among the homespun inhabitants of Ithaca, California are Homer (Mickey Rooney) and Ulysses (Jackie Jenkins). Grown-ups in the cast, all of them gifted by nature with goodness, are Ray Collins, Fay Bainter, Van Johnson, Donna Reed, James Craig, and Frank Morgan.

6 ***Shadow of a Doubt*** (Alfred Hitchcock). US, bw. Hitch made sure that there were far more sinister goings on in another small American town, far away from innocent Ithaca, California. This Universal picture was only a modest success until, in the sixties, French New Wave directors rediscovered it and found "visual rhymes" down to the smallest detail in the relationship between a nice girl called Charlie (Teresa Wright) and her uncle, also named Charlie (Joseph Cotton), who comes to town to lie low.

7 ***For Whom the Bell Tolls*** (Sam Wood). US, color. Heavily touted by Paramount as *their* prestige item for 1943, this expensive and ponderously slow adaptation of Hemingway's novel about the Spanish Civil War had Gary Cooper and a close-cropped Ingrid Bergman together in a sleeping bag, a fierce performance

by Katina Paxinou (AA), and an impressively staged climax. That was about all the excitement there was, but it was enough for most audiences.

8 *The Ox-Bow Incident* (William Wellman). US, bw. A Western with a subject - a lynch mob taking the law into its own hands – that was unusual, even daring, for a time when a nation at war was reasonably sure of its moral rightness. Studioesque sets lend an almost expressionist feel to the grim goings on. With Dana Andrews, Anthony Quinn, and Francis Ford as the victims, Frank Conroy and Jane Darwell prominent among the mobsters, and Henry Fonda and Henry Morgan as shocked onlookers. A box-office failure for 20th, a cult favorite today.

9 **Watch on the Rhine** (Herman Schumlin), US, bw. Dashiell Hammett's screenplay of Lillian Hellman's stage play about a family of German refugees in Washington has a lot of talk about issues that can now seem dated (and let's hope they stay that way), but it has a famous performance by Paul Lucas (AA) and a smaller but intense one from Bette Davis. From Warner Brothers.

10 **In Which We Serve** (Noel Coward and David Lean). UK, bw. A film with great propaganda value in the forties, and still impressive in some ways. English survivors of a torpedoed destroyer recall their past lives as they cling to a life raft during the Battle of Crete. Based on the experiences of Lord Mountbatten. Coward wrote, directed, composed the musical score, and starred - and only in the latter capacity, as the ship's commander giving endless pep talks, does he disappoint. In the large cast are John Mills, Bernard Miles, and, in their screen debuts, Celia Johnson and Richard Attenborough. This was also David Lean's first credit as director. There was much more to come. NOTE: Both *In*

Which We Serve and *Casablanca* had limited US releases in 1942, but qualified for Oscars only in 1943. For reasons best known to the Academy Coward received a special award for *In Which We Serve* in '42, then the film itself got two nominations, including one for best picture, in '43.

Contending for tenth place were *The More the Merrier*, *Five Graves to Cairo*, and *Sahara*.

1944

1 *Going My Way* (Leo McCarey AA). US, bw. Though any one of the top four pictures of 1944 might well have been called best, both the Academy and millions of moviegoers opted for Paramount's *Going My Way*, and so shall I. Jean Renoir, working in Hollywood during the war years, rightly observed that writer/ director McCarey knew more about human nature than anyone else in American movies, and with Barry Fitzgerald (AAS) as the loveable but old-line pastor of a poor parish and Bing Crosby (AA) as a more up-to-date curate equally good at golf and popular songs, the devout, playful McCarey had the most congenial material of his career to work with. Insightful, tender, and amusing, it was in its unassuming way a great morale booster during war time. With opera star Risë Stevens singing *Carmen* at the Met years before she actually got to sing the role there, and with Bing and his choir boys singing "Swinging on a Star". Six Oscars in all, and one of the few films to win five of the top seven awards.

2 *Double Indemnity* (Billy Wilder). US, bw. This story of a husband done in by his wife and an insurance agent would have

been the best picture choice of twenty-first century critics if they had had a vote in 1944. Billy Wilder, working at Paramount but no fan of Paramount's *Going My Way*, was determined to take the Oscar away from Leo McCarey the next year and - with *The Lost Weekend* - he did. His 1944 *film noir* was, however, even better than *The Lost Weekend* – a James Cain novel honed to a cutting edge by Raymond Chandler and Wilder himself, brilliantly filmed, with performances by Barbara Stanwyck, Fred MacMurray, and Edward G. Robinson that are still talked about. And yet, not an Oscar in sight.

3 ***Meet Me In St. Louis*** (Vincente Minnelli). US, color. The only color picture of any significance in this wartime year, and what color! Renoir again! His "Two Girls at the Piano" and several other paintings are a palpable influence on MGM director Minnelli, who limns his wife-to-be, Judy Garland, in luminous hues as the seasons change in a turn-of-the-century city preparing for a world's fair. The Hugh Martin/Ralph Blaine songs ("The Boy Next Door", "Have Yourself a Merry Little Christmas" and "The Trolley Song") are integrated into the story in the manner Rodgers and Hammerstein had just initiated on Broadway. With seven-year-old Margaret O'Brien in an almost hallucinatory Hallowe'en sequence, and with Mary Astor and Leon Ames as mother and father.

4 ***Laura*** (Otto Preminger). US, bw. A Park Avenue murder mystery with a haunting musical theme, a riveting twist half-way through, and dozens of smart one-liners from Clifton Webb as a waspish columnist ("In my case, self-absorption is completely justified"). Judith Anderson plays a society dame infatuated with a gigolo played by Vincent Price ("He's no good but he's what I want"). Dana Andrews plays the detective who falls in love with

the portrait of the beautiful Laura (Gene Tierney). From 20th. Pure pleasure.

5 *Gaslight* (George Cukor). US, bw. When Ingrid Bergman (AA) picked up her Oscar for this one, at the ceremony where *Going My Way* was cleaning up, she said, disarmingly, "Tomorrow I go to work in a picture with Bing and Mr. McCarey, and I'm afraid that if I didn't have an Oscar too, they wouldn't speak to me." The award was for playing a Victorian wife being slowly driven mad by her husband. MGM made an attempt to buy up and destroy the negative of an earlier, and to some extent superior, British filming of the same subject. This version had Charles Boyer, Joseph Cotton, Dame May Whitty, and, in her first movie, Angela Lansbury.

6 *The Miracle of Morgan's Creek* (Preston Sturges). US, bw. Madcap comedy about a rowdy but good natured bobby-soxer (Betty Hutton) who wakes up the morning after a wild night at a GI party to find a ring on her finger but remembers little or nothing about what happened - and with whom. Sturges, master of the uninnocent innuendo, makes an it's-bad-taste-but-who-the-hell-cares attack on motherhood, family life, Christmas, the armed forces, and other things sacred to an America at war. With a classic performance by William Demarest as Officer Kockenlocker, and with typical turns by Eddie Bracken, Diana Lynn, and other assorted oddballs from Sturges' Paramount repertory company.

7 *Hail the Conquering Hero* (Preston Sturges). US, bw. Scarcely had audiences recovered from *The Miracle of Morgan's Creek* when Sturges was back with another brash but brilliant patriot-bashing comedy from Paramount. A despondent home town boy rejected by the Marines (Eddie Bracken) is mistaken

for a war hero. With William Demarest, Franklin Pangborn, and Ella Raines. It was the writer/director's last worthy effort before his comic muse mysteriously deserted him.

8 *Lifeboat* (Alfred Hitchcock). US, bw. Hitch's wartime effort for 20th-Century-Fox places eight survivors of a torpedoed ship in a lifeboat, has them rescue the Nazi who had almost sent them to the depths, sets them all talking in John Steinbeck language about moral issues, and never moves the camera any farther away than a few feet. It was an unusual challenge for the resourceful director, and most Hitchcockians today agree with critic John Russell Taylor, who called it "a worthy failure". With Tallulah Bankhead, who certainly makes an impression, and with Walter Slezak, cast very much against type.

9 *Since You Went Away* (John Cromwell). US, bw. David O. Selznick was hoping for another *Gone With the Wind* with this professionally done but overlong story of a mother (Claudette Colbert) and her two daughters (Jennifer Jones and Shirley Temple) coping on the home front while the man of the family was away at war. Audiences wept. Some scenes still register strongly today. With Joseph Cotton, Robert Walker, Agnes Moorehead, and Monty Wooley.

10 *The Uninvited* (Lewis Allen). US, bw. Forget about the war! Surrender to a Paramount cliff-hanger, a chillingly ectoplasmic ghost story with spooky studioesque sets, Broadway veterans Cornelia Otis Skinner and Dorothy Stickney in supporting roles, a scary seance scene, a surprising whiff of Lesbianism in the plot solution, and plenty of whole-tone scales on the sound track! The critic in *The Nation* reported that while watching it he experienced "thirty-five first-class jolts, not to mention a well

calculated texture of minor frissons". With Ray Milland, Ruth Hussey, Donald Crisp, and Gail Russell.

Contending for tenth place were *None But the Lonely Heart*, *Jane Eyre*, and *The Mask of Dimitrios*.

1945

1 ***Anchors Aweigh*** (George Sidney). US, color. The war was over at last, and the movie that most matched our jubilant mood was this MGM musical with Gene Kelly and Frank Sinatra as a couple of sailors on leave in a peacetime Los Angeles. Kelly dancing with Jerry the MGM cartoon mouse, Kelly cheering up a glum little Spanish waif by a wishing well, Kelly imitating a floozy coming down the street, Kelly and Sinatra leaping from cot to cot at the USO, Sinatra warbling those beautiful Jules Styne and Sammy Cahn songs "What Makes the Sun Set" and "I Fall In Love Too Easily" - it was the best celebration imaginable. All right, it was too long, too predictable, and Kathryn Grayson got to sing at least two songs too many. And four years later *On The Town*, with Kelly and Sinatra as sailors again, was more inventive. So what? The war was over!

2 ***The Lost Weekend*** (Billy Wilder AA). US, bw. The cynical director of *Double Indemnity* got his Oscar at last - two of them, in fact, as his screenplay with Charles Bracket also beat out the competition. And Ray Milland (AA) took best actor honors, playing a dipsomaniac writer wandering the streets of New York, hallucinating in his room, and escaping from a DDT sick room. It was heady stuff in 1945. With Jane Wyman, Howard da Silva,

and a weird resonating instrument called the theremin haunting the sound track. From the studio Wilder was turning on its ear, Paramount. Oscar for best picture, plus the three cited above.

3 *Mildred Pierce* (Michael Curtiz). US, bw. Joan Crawford (AA), abandoned by MGM and regarded as washed up, made a stunning comeback at Warners in this J.M. Caine melodrama about a divorcee who is manipulated by her lover (Zachary Scott) and abandoned by her shockingly ungrateful daughter (Ann Blyth). What might, in lesser hands, have been soap opera becomes *film noir* at a studio unmatched in the genre. With Jack Carson and Eve Arden. Compulsively watchable many times over.

4 *State Fair* (Henry King). US, color. Rodgers and Hammerstein apply their patented *Oklahoma!* style to the 20th-Century-Fox musical and come up with another winner. The Strake family goes to the Iowa state fair, where Mom (Fay Bainter) and Dad (Charles Winninger, in the old Will Rogers role) hit it big at the rural awards ceremonies. But the kids (Jeanne Crain and Dick Haymes) have more trouble in their romantic encounters. Dana Andrews gamely joins in on "It's A Grand Night For Singing", and Vivian Blaine, without a chance to show what she can really do, settles for "That's For Me". The classic moment in the new score is "It Might As Well Be Spring", as effective a piece of musical characterization as anything the famous musical team wrote for Broadway. With Donald Meek, Percy Kilbride, and, as an impossibly stuck-up pickle champion, Josephine Whittell.

5 *The Picture of Dorian Grey* (Albert Lewin). US, bw. Oscar Wilde's story of a depraved sensualist who stays young while his portrait ages becomes a strangely elegant horror story on the screen. Waxen-faced Hurd Hatfield victimizes innocent cockney

warbler Angela Lansbury, George Sanders tosses off decadent Wildean epigrams with indecent aplomb, the portrait (by one Ivan le Lorraine Albright) turns ever more frighteningly hideous via color insets, director Levin indulges his strange taste for cats and Omar Khayyam, and Chopin has never sounded so sinister. From MGM.

6 *Spellbound* (Alfred Hitchcock), US, bw. A Hitchcock piece that is more spellbinding, and also more fun, than the standard reference works on Hitch would give you to believe. Gregory Peck has a Salvador Dali dream that Ingrid Bergman, using primer-simple Freud, uses to solve the mystery. The murderer (we'd better keep him nameless) decides that suicide is the best solution, turns the gun on himself - that is to say, on us in the theater - and the screen goes red. And that eerie *Lost Weekend* theremin is back vibrating on the sound track again. The original novel, *The House of Dr. Edwardes*, was a good deal nastier - closer to the film version of *The Picture of Dorian Gray*. But Hitch was still fulfilling his part of the contract with Selznick, and could only get away with so much.

7 *A Tree Grows in Brooklyn* (Elia Kazan). US, bw. Peggy Ann Garner gives one of the most touching screen performances ever given by a child in this beautifully realized 20th-Century-Fox adaptation of Betty Smith's novel about a poor Irish-American family. With Dorothy Maguire, Joan Blondell, and James Dunn (AAS). An auspicious film debut for director Kazan.

8 *National Velvet* (Clarence Brown). US, color. Velvet Brown (the twelve-year-old Elizabeth Taylor) poses as a boy and rides her own horse in the Grand National. A much loved film despite a heavy overlay of MGM gloss. (Herbert Stothart's treacly score is

a persistent irritant.) Mickey Rooney, Anne Revere (AAS), and Donald Crisp are all fine, and Miss Taylor, who does much of her own riding, is radiant.

9 *The Bells of St. Mary's* (Leo McCarey). US, bw. This sequel to *Going My Way*, with last year's Oscar winners Bing Crosby as Father O'Malley and Ingrid Bergman as Sister Benedict, was another box-office bonanza, but audiences kept waiting for Barry Fitzgerald to come shuffling around the corner of the parochial school, and he never did. McCarey's famed improvisational skills are, however, still very much in evidence: he allows the first-grade kids to do their own Christmas pageant, and lets Bergman at the piano sing a charming song in Swedish. Bergman was a triple threat in 1945, as a nun (here), a psychiatrist (in *Spellbound*) and a nineteenth-century vamp (in *Saratoga Trunk*). From RKO.

10 *To Have and Have Not* (Howard Hawks), US, bw. This is the film that brought Humphrey Bogart and Lauren Bacall together for the first time, and their scenes really sizzle. But the rest of it is *Casablanca* without the magic, an old Hemingway story about skullduggery in Martinique updated to World War II. With Walter Brennan at his scruffiest, and with Hoagy Carmichael at the piano singing "Hong Kong Blues". Despite rumors that she was dubbed, Bacall does her own sultry singing in the Johnny Mercer-Hoagy Carmichael song "How Little We Know." From Warner Brothers.

Contending for tenth place were *The Life and Death of Colonel Blimp, Blithe Spirit, On Approval, The Southerner, The Woman in the Window, And Then There Were None, Where Do We Go From Here?, The Corn Is Green, Hangover Square, The Story of G.I. Joe,* and *The True Glory*. It was a good year. 1946 was even better.

1946

1 ***Henry V*** (Laurence Olivier), UK. color. The best of all Shakespearean films, and the best film of a year in which long-delayed movies from abroad began arriving in American cinemas. Olivier handily solves the problem of filming the Bard by beginning with a performance full of mishaps at the Globe theater, then responding to Chorus' invitation "On your imaginary forces work" by dissolving from a scrim of towers and landscape to a painted sea, and then panning left to the massive set for Southampton and the sailing of the fleet for France. And who will forget the subsequent settings patterned after the Book of Hours and the Bayeux tapestry, the audible twang and arched flight of the arrows at Agincourt, the many moods of William Walton's musical score, and the finest screen performance of the best actor on the English-speaking stage - Olivier, warring for, wooing, and winning with kingly authority all that was the king's by right, most particularly the king's sweet English? (Olivier also appears, without speaking, as a French equerry.) With Renée Asherson, Robert Newton, Leslie Banks, Felix Aylmer, Robert Helpman, Leo Genn, Esmond Knight, and Niall MacGinnis. The spectacular film was actually made, with inventive economy, to boost wartime morale in 1944. It still makes the spirit soar.

2 ***Brief Encounter*** (David Lean). UK, bw. Poignant, perceptive, much-loved film of an unconsummated but nonetheless guilt-ridden love affair carried on against a background of speeding trains. Adapted by Noel Coward from his one-act radio play *Still Life*, sensitively acted by Trevor Howard and (in one of the

screen's great performances) Celia Johnson, and filmed by David Lean with masterly control. There is a heart-stopping moment where Johnson's character tries to throw herself in front of an express train; by the subtlest of means the camera records not just her sudden desperation but her return to sanity. (Trains figure significantly in most of Lean's subsequent films.) The realism is heightened by one of the most inventive sound tracks ever - the clanging noises of a busy provincial railroad station, the controlled passion of Rachmaninoff's second piano concerto, the rueful, restless voice of Johnson remembering the long flashback that brings us so heart-stoppingly back to the present.

3 *It's A Wonderful Life* (Frank Capra). US, bw. Another much-loved film, but one that took a quarter-century to win its vast cult following. During the war there had been a spate of what were dubbed "metaphysical" American films (the spirits of soldiers killed in battle returning to comfort their families, etc.), and by 1946 the public did not need another one, especially one the critics called as "preachy" as this. So Capra's story of a good man contemplating suicide and allowed by his guardian angel to see what the world would be like if he had never been born was at best a middling critical and financial success. But during the Vietnam War cultists rediscovered it, and younger critics took notice. Andrew Sarris, auteurist guardian of a private pantheon, actually wrote, "*It's a Wonderful Life* has become manifestly an all-time masterpiece." He was right. With James Stewart, Donna Reed, Henry Travers, Thomas Mitchell, and Lionel Barrymore. Released through RKO.

4 *Les Enfants du Paradis* (Marcel Carné). France, bw. The "children of paradise" are the noisy scamps in the top balcony (*paradis*) of a nineteenth-century Parisian theater; the actors

73

miming on the stage below are the famous Jean-Louis Barrault, Arletty, and Pierre Brasseur; the dialogue, about the strange symbiosis of life and art, is by Carné's long-time collaborator Jacques Prévert; the depiction of the Paris of Alexandre Dumas and Victor Hugo is lavish and memorable, and the film, made in Nice while the Gestapo watched, has been seen as a sly subversion of the Nazi occupation. Carné himself has not pressed that point, but there is no doubt that his complex and compelling *Les Enfants du Paradis* is a timeless chef d'ouvre.

5 ***The Best Years of Our Lives*** (William Wyler AA). US, bw. In 1946, we saw *ourselves* on the screen in Wyler's story of three service men returning home to their families. In the years since, post-war generations have found less in the film to respond to personally, but there is no denying its professionalism - in Gregg Toland's cinematography, in Robert Sherwood's writing, and in the performances of Fredric March (AA), Myrna Loy, Dana Andrews, Teresa Wright, and, as a sailor who has lost his hands in the war, Harold Russell (AAS and a separate honorary Oscar). The award for best picture was stubbornly claimed as his own achievement by producer Samuel Goldwyn, but Billy Wilder, handing the best director's Oscar to Wyler, knew where the praise should go, and said *The Best Years of Our Lives* was "the best *directed* picture I've seen in my life." Eight Academy Awards in all.

6 ***Open City*** (Roberto Rossellini). Italy, bw. Shooting began on this early neo-realist film while the Nazi occupation forces were still in control of Rome, and the tense atmosphere is palpable. Today the story may seem melodramatic, but the film is still memorable for the director's passionate sincerity and for the performance, all too brief, of the volcanic Anna Magnani, shot down in the street while running after the Gestapo truck that is

carrying her man away. That scene, at least, is not melodramatic. It is real. Italian neo-realism had arrived.

7 ***Notorious*** (Alfred Hitchcock). US, bw. Ingrid Bergman is notorious, Cary Grant is cynical, Claude Rains is caught in a web of his own making, and the audience is dazzled by Hitchcock's slyly manipulative techniques and Ted Tetzlaf's camera work, which is gritty here, luminous there - as the situation demands. From RKO.

8 ***The Big Sleep*** (Howard Hawks). US, bw. Even author Raymond Chandler couldn't explain everything that happens in this moody mystery scripted by William Faulkner and a crew of Hollywood writers. But no *film noir* is more fun to watch, and the flip, innuendo-laden dialogue is as quotable as anything this side of Preston Sturges. With Humphrey Bogart, Lauren Bacall, Dorothy Malone, and, most memorably, Charles Waldron as General Sternwood, a man who speaks his mind. From Warners, naturally.

9 ***The Killers*** (Robert Siodmak). US, bw. One of Hemingway's best-known stories is expanded into a taut, noirish drama that explains the psychological question Hemingway had left unanswered. John Huston is probably responsible for the venturesome screenplay (there are eleven flashbacks), though the credit went to one Anthony Veiler. From Universal-International, with Burt Lancaster in his movie debut, Ava Gardner very early in her career, and Edmund O'Brien. (The story was remade in 1964, in un-noirish color and with several new twists, by Don Siegel, who had originally been slated to direct in 1946.)

10 **My Darling Clementine** (John Ford). US, bw. The best of several movie treatments of the legendary gunfight at the O.K. Corral. The photography of Monument Valley is poetry itself, and Ford, virtually creating the myth of the American West, is introspective, even rueful, and yet keenly alive to the action. With Henry Fonda as Wyatt Earp and Victor Mature as Doc Halliday, and with Walter Brennan, Alan Mobray, Tim Holt, and that great Ford veteran, Ward Bond. The women, as often with Ford, are inadequate. From 20th.

Contending for tenth place were *Une Partie de Campagne, The Postman Always Rings Twice, The Yearling, The Spiral Staircase, The Razor's Edge, Cluny Brown, Anna and the King of Siam, The Road to Utopia, Duel in the Sun*, and *Caesar and Cleopatra*. One of the best years of our lives: a new post-war Hollywood and a backlog of great films from abroad.

1947

1 **Great Expectations** (David Lean). UK, bw. The finest of all screen adaptations of Dickens, with an opening sequence that, once seen, is never forgotten. It could be objected that what in Dickens is reflective and nostalgic becomes theatrical, mysterious, and even hallucinatory on the screen, but such is the nature of the film medium - and the strength of Lean's control of, and daring with, the opportunities it offers. With Anthony Wager and Jean Simmons perfect as the young Pip and Estella, and John Mills and Valerie Hobson less convincing as the same pair grown up. Alec Guinness makes his screen debut as Herbert Pocket, and Francis L. Sullivan is frighteningly efficient as Jaggers. As for

the unforgettable Finlay Currie as Magwich and Martita Hunt as Miss Havisham - well, I'm sure I'll remember them till, and perhaps on, my dying day.

2 *Ivan the Terrible* (Sergei Eisenstein). USSR, bw. Many of the best films to reach America in 1947 were long delayed because of the war or for censorship reasons. Part I of Eisenstein's great paranoidal epic on the most notorious of the czars was made in war-torn Russia in 1944. The acting takes stylization to new heights of exaggeration, the sets are jaw-droppingly grandiose and, with its studied visual motifs, the cinematography seems graphically to rewrite the cinema – while reducing history to a series of grotesque incidents in which, as Pauline Kael observed, "the figures are like giant spiders and rodents". The less impressive Part II, which experiments unsuccessfully with color, was made in 1946, banned by Stalin (who began to see himself in Nikolai Cherkassov's Ivan), and released only in 1958. Eisenstein didn't live to complete the proposed Part III. The music by Prokofiev is carefully keyed to the visuals, as it had been in *Alexander Nevsky*.

3 *L'Atalante* (Jean Vigo). France, bw. The real and the surreal make a strange sort of poetry in this unashamed tale of the young owner of a barge on the Seine (Jean Dasté), his bride (Dita Parlo), and their crude, lavishly tattooed mate (Michel Simon). A film much loved by international critics. Made in 1934, it opened in Paris on the day Vigo, a filmmaker of unique vision and promise, died of leukemia, aged twenty-nine.

4 *Zero de Conduit* (Jean Vigo). France, bw. The same Vigo's almost surreal 45-minute film about conspiracy and revolution in a boys' school. Partly autobiographical, perhaps blasphemous,

certainly shocking, sometimes funny, and very influential. Made in 1932.

5 **La Belle et La Bête** (Jean Cocteau). France, bw. A fairy tale for adults conjured up by France's least innocent and most volatile genius, with Josette Day as the Beauty and Jean Marais as the Beast. Remarkable for its elaborate sets and costumes, for the glittering music by Georges Auric, for any number of Cocteauesque special effects, and above all for the expressive mask that seems to distill very essence of the Beast's tender, anguished feelings. (When Marais was transformed into Prince Charming at the end, Greta Garbo said, "Give me back my Beast!") The film clearly left its mark on the 1991 Disney cartoon feature and, along with Cocteau's *Orphée* and *Les Enfants Terribles*, was equipped with a new, operatic sound track in the nineties by minimalist composer Philip Glass.

6 **Shoeshine** (Vittorio de Sica). Italy, bw. Two street urchins in Rome unwittingly become involved in the black market, are caught, sent to prison, separated, and betray each other. A gritty neo-realist film worthy to follow Rossellini's *Open City*, if not quite on a level with De Sica's upcoming *The Bicycle Thief*. It was a plea for reform more effective than any documentary could be. Given a special award by the Academy. OT: *Sciuscià*.

7 **Black Narcissus** (Michael Powell and Emeric Pressburger). UK, color. This account of the physical and emotional problems faced by five Anglican nuns attempting to run a mission high in the Himalayas ran into censor problems in the United States: while the novel by Rumer Godden was sympathetic to the women's plight, the film version sank relentlessly into gothic melodrama. (Hitchcock seems to have remembered its almost hallucinatory

penultimate scene when he made *Vertigo*.) Nonetheless the skilled duo (Powell and Pressburger) that dubbed itself "The Archers" recreated an India at Pinewood studios that, with color photography by Jack Cardiff and art direction by Alfred Junge is still the classic instance of Technicolor used to convey mood. With Deborah Kerr, Flora Robson, Jean Simmons, and Sabu.

8 *I Know Where I'm Going* (Michael Powell and Emeric Pressburger). UK, bw. Another picture from The Archers, as fresh and charming in black and white as *Black Narcissus* was troubled and neurotic in color. An English girl determined to marry for money (Wendy Hiller) is stranded in Scotland and decides to marry for love. With Roger Livesey and Finlay Currie.

9 *Odd Man Out* (Carol Reed). UK, bw. The flight of a wounded revolutionary through the streets of an unidentified Irish city. This is the atmospheric if somewhat pretentious morality play in which director Reed and actor James Mason came to world attention. Most of the characters encountered by the fugitive are played by veterans of the Abbey Theater. People compared the film, not unfavorably, to John Ford's *The Informer*. Reed and his cameraman Robert Krasker were poised to make their masterpiece, *The Third Man*.

10 *Out of the Past* (Jacques Tourneur). US, bw. A *film noir* with Robert Mitchum, Jane Greer, and Kirk Douglas that attracted little attention at the time but has become a cult classic since. The only American film on our 1947 list – and it's from tiny RKO. The big guns in Hollywood were temporarily silenced by the post-war invasion of quality films from abroad. Even *Out of the Past* is the work of a French-born director, and indebted to the films of Marcel Carné and Luchino Visconti.

Contending for tenth place were *To Live in Peace, Miracle on 34th Street, Song of Love*, and *The Macomber Affair*. The Oscar went to *Gentleman's Agreement*.

1948

1 *The Treasure of the Sierra Madre* (John Huston AA). US, bw. Three prospectors (Humphrey Bogart, Tim Holt, and Walter Huston) find gold in Mexico and face attacks from marauding bandits and, eventually, from each other. A now-classic moral fable that in 1948 brought the critics to their feet but left the public, unaccustomed to seeing Bogart as a loser, unenchanted. Expensively filmed on location, yet surprisingly studioesque at several points, it seems better with each viewing. Walter Huston (AAS) gleefully chortles, snorts, dances, and laughs off the ironic outcome in an almost legendary performance, and his director son appears briefly as an American giving Bogart handouts on the streets of Tampico. From Warners.

2 *Marius / Fanny / César* (Alexander Korda, Marc Allegret, and Marcel Pagnol). France, bw. A long-delayed American release in which Pierre Fresnay, Orane Demazis, Raimu, and Charpin provide the finest ensemble acting in the history of the movies. Living proof that stage plays - even stage plays adapted from novels - can be transferred virtually intact to the screen and be effective, even without adequate editing and production values. All you need are actors who know everything about acting and a story (by Pagnol) about life in the Marseilles harbor that tells practically all there is to know about living. The three parts of the "Pagnol trilogy" were filmed in 1931, 1932, and 1936.

3 ***Hamlet*** (Laurence Olivier). UK, bw. Shakespeare in brooding German expressionist sets, costumes, and hair styles, with a camera tracking the Elsinore ramparts à la Murnau, and a text pared almost to the bone. A disappointment after the stylistically assured *Henry V*, but notable for another bravura Olivier performance (AA). With Jean Simmons, Felix Aylmer, and with Stanley Holloway as the grave digger. The score by William Walton stands in in place of a soliloquy or two. The film won the International Grand Prize at Venice. When it also won four Oscars, including best picture, eight indignant Hollywood studios withdrew their financial support for the Academy – briefly, as it turned out.

4 ***Day of Wrath*** (Carl Dreyer). Denmark, bw. The burning of a witch and its terrible aftermath in seventeenth-century Denmark. What Pauline Kael described as "a fusion of Hawthorne and Kafka" is often, in its pictorial compositions, reminiscent of Rembrandt as well. American critics dismissed it as they were to dismiss Dreyer's *Ordet* years later. Today the director's complex aims and artistry are acknowledged and admired. Made in 1943 during the Nazi occupation of Denmark, and something of a comment on it.

5 ***Paisan*** (Roberto Rossellini). Italy, bw. Six episodes about American soldiers in Italy during World War II, shot on location in Sicily, Naples, Rome, Florence, a northern Italian monastery, and the Po valley, with mostly non-professional actors. The Florence story, perhaps the best of the lot, was protested in Britain because it gave the impression that the British had deliberately abandoned the city. Still admired for its improvisational neo-realist style, though not every episode is dramatically compelling. Partially scripted by Federico Fellini.

6 ***The Search*** (Fred Zinnemann). US, bw. A refugee child in post-war Germany is befriended by an American soldier and eventually found by his Czech mother. There was no attempt to sentimentalize the story, yet audiences wept profusely. The screen debut of Montgomery Clift. Opera lovers remember it for preserving a beautiful (non-singing) performance by Jarmila Novotna, a beloved Met Octavian and Cherubino, as the mother. An untypical piece of work for MGM.

7 ***The Red Shoes*** (Michael Powell, Emeric Pressburger). UK, color. The Archers score another bull's eye with this story of a ballerina (Moira Shearer) whose backstage life becomes confused with her onstage role in a fairy tale ballet. Powell and Pressburger make sure that the stage sequences are as opulent and imaginative as all get-out. With Anton Walbrook, Marius Goring, and Robert Helpman.

8 ***Letter from an Unknown Woman*** (Max Ophuls). US, bw. In a year when Olivia de Havilland was expected to win a second Oscar for her work in the sensational *The Snake Pit*, her younger sister Joan Fontaine quietly won attention in this fragile romantic story, lovingly directed in a Universal Studio Vienna by Vienna's master of elegant camera movement. Decades later, critics who have forgotten *The Snake Pit* regard this film as Hollywood at its best. With Louis Jourdan.

9 ***Monsieur Vincent*** (Maurice Cloche). France, bw. Reverent biography of the seventeenth-century saint Vincent de Paul, with Pierre Fresnay in one of his best performances. The last line of the script by Jean-Bernard Luc and Jean Anouilh pretty well says it all: "It is only when he can see your love that a poor man will

forgive you for your gift of bread." Honorary award from the Academy.

10 ***Joan of Arc*** (Victor Fleming). US, color. A failure at its premiere, cut thereafter by almost a third, and long issued in mutilated prints with inept voiceovers, this independently made, close-to-the-facts epic on the fifteenth-century saint has reemerged, complete and in often astonishing color, on DVD, and Victor Fleming's ambition to make a *Gone With the Wind* independently of David O. Selznick now seems to have been at least partially realized. Ingrid Bergman (whose worshipful fans deserted her when, during the film's initial run, she bore a child out of wedlock to Roberto Rossellini) gives a radiant performance, and there is solid support from José Ferrer, Francis L. Sullivan, and J. Caroll Naish.

Contending for tenth place were *Red River*, *A Foreign Affair*, *I Remember Mama*, *Louisiana Story*, *The Snake Pit*, *Johnny Belinda*, *Sitting Pretty*, *Easter Parade*, and *Rope*.

1949

1 ***The Bicycle Thief*** (Vittorio de Sica). Italy, bw. The finest and most moving of all Italian neo-realist films. See the essay later in this book.

2 ***The Heiress*** (William Wyler). US, bw. Wyler searched for three years to find a project that could follow his all-but-worshipped *The Best Years of Our Lives*, and finally opted for Henry James' *Washington Square*, which had been recently done on Broadway

as *The Heiress*. The result was a critical but not a popular success for Paramount. Olivia de Havilland won her second Oscar as a homely spinster harassed by her father (Ralph Richardson) and deceived by a young fortune hunter (Montgomery Clift). Musical score by Aaron Copeland.

3 ***A Letter to Three Wives*** (Joseph Mankiewicz AA). US, bw. Three women receive a letter from a friend informing them that she has run off with one of their husbands - but doesn't say which one. Mankiewicz's highly original screenplay forecasts the wit and wisecracks of the scintillating *All About Eve*, which was to follow from the same studio (20th) the next year. With wives Jeanne Crain, Linda Darnell, and Ann Sothern and husbands Kirk Douglas, Jeffrey Lynn, and Paul Douglas.

4 ***All the King's Men*** (Robert Rossen), US, bw. A political drama based on the careening career of Louisiana governor Huey Long as treated in Robert Penn Warren's roman à clef. Independently made (released through Columbia), with Broderick Crawford (AA), Mercedes McCambridge (AA), and John Ireland. Its once-vaunted realism seems dated now, but the performances continue to impress. Oscar for best picture.

5 ***The Fallen Idol*** (Carol Reed). UK, bw. Skillful adaptation of a Graham Greene short story about a small boy, left virtually parentless in an embassy, who innocently causes the one man he admires to be suspected of murder. With Ralph Richardson, Michele Morgan, and Jack Hawkins.

6 ***Intruder in the Dust*** (Clarence Brown). US, bw. Atypical MGM filming of William Faulkner's novel about a Southern boy and a widow saving a black man from a lynch mob. A tough

subject for audiences then, it should be seen more widely now, just as Brown's status as a director should be reassessed. With Claude Jarman, Jr., Elizabeth Patterson, and Juano Hernandez.

7 *Adam's Rib* (George Stevens). US, bw. Generally thought the best of the MGM comedies in which Katharine Hepburn and Spencer Tracey starred and sparred - this time as rival lawyers in an attempted murder case. The film introduced four new personalities to movie audiences - Judy Holliday, Jean Hagen, David Wayne, and Tom Ewell - but except for some memorable scenes between the two celebs it seems oddly paced and labored today.

8 *She Wore A Yellow Ribbon* (John Ford). US, color. The second of Ford's US cavalry trio, following *Fort Apache* and followed in turn by *Rio Grande*. An affectionate tribute to the horse soldiers, with John Wayne, Victor McLaglen, Ben Johnson, and other familiar Ford ingredients. From RKO.

9 *Quartet* (Ralph Smart, Harold French, Arthur Crabtree, and Ken Annakin). UK, bw. Four wry, perceptive short stories - "The Facts of Life", "The Alien Corn", "The Kite" and "The Colonel's Lady" - introduced by their author, Somerset Maugham, and engagingly acted by Naunton Wayne, Françoise Rosay, George Cole, and Cecil Parker.

10 *On the Town* (Gene Kelly and Stanley Donen). US, color. Inventively filmed on location all over "New York, New York", this lively MGM musical about three sailors on a day's leave (Kelly, Frank Sinatra, and Jules Munshin) was rapturously received by critics. Leslie Halliwell cited it as "Among the best things ever to come out of Hollywood". The only problem is that the best

Leonard Bernstein songs from the original Broadway show are missing. While Kelly gets an opportunity to strut his stuff (in a poor substitute for the original "Fancy Free" ballet), Sinatra has terrible studio songs to sing, and never gets a crack at Bernstein's original "Lucky To Be Me' or "Some Other Time". Vera-Ellen, Ann Miller, and Betty Garrett make enthusiastic, partly compensating contributions.

Contending for tenth place were *White Heat, Twelve O'Clock High, The Fountainhead,* and *Germany, Year Zero.*

The 1950s

1950

1 *The Third Man* (Carol Reed). UK, bw. In an ordinary year, any one of the first four films of 1950 would have placed first. My own favorite of the four is this wonderfully atmospheric adaptation of a characteristically ambivalent Graham Greene story set in cold-war Vienna. Robert Krasker's inventively angled camerawork captures and conveys the feel of a desperate city riddled with intrigue, and all of the music is provided, famously, by a single zither. (The tunes may be banal but the effect is almost surreal). With Joseph Cotton, Alida Valli, Trevor Howard, and, as the elusive Harry Lime, Orson Welles, who wrote his own oft-quoted speech about the superiority of villainous Renaissance Italy to centuries of Swiss decency, democracy and peace. Long stretches of untranslated German (still thought a sinister language in 1950) enhance the viewer's mood of uneasiness and alienation. Palme d'Or at Cannes.

2 *The Rules of the Game* (Jean Renoir). France, bw. Renoir's complex tragicomedy was too acerbic for France's sensibilities in 1939, temporarily banned there as demoralizing, partially destroyed in an air raid, eligible for an Oscar in 1950 but not deemed worthy of a single nomination, and memorably savaged by the *New York Times* ("really one for the buzzards"). Restored to its original length in 1958, it has since then run second only to *Citizen Kane* in international "best films of all time" polls. Something of a twentieth-century *Marriage of Figaro*, and also something of a sequel to Renoir's own *Grand Illusion*, it shows the society that the survivors of that film hoped to create merely playing at life

89

according to its own selfish "rules" - on the eve of another war. In a large cast, Marcel Dalio and other players from *Grand Illusion* – as well as Renoir himself - have prominent parts. No film so generously repays repeated viewings. OT: *La Règle du Jeu.*

3 ***All About Eve*** (Joseph Mankiewicz AA). US, bw. Eve is the worm in the Broadway apple in this scintillating 20th-Century-Fox comedy-drama, quite the best movie Hollywood ever made about the theater. Upwards of a hundred quotable, smartly cynical lines are tossed off by Bette Davis and George Sanders (AA) at their bitchiest best. With Anne Baxter as the insidious Eve, and with Thelma Ritter, Celeste Holm, Gary Merrill, Hugh Marlowe and (briefly) Marilyn Monroe as assorted theater people. Oscar for best picture, and a record fourteen nominations in all.

4 ***Sunset Boulevard*** (Billy Wilder). US, bw. Quite the best movie Hollywood ever made about itself. Here is Louis B. Mayer to Paramount's Billy Wilder at the preview: "You bastard! You should be tarred and feathered and run out of here." Wilder had the nerve to show a faded silent screen star (Gloria Swanson) teetering on the verge of madness, clinging to old memories, and desperately hoping for a comeback. Worse, Wilder had the ingenuity to tell the tale via the corpse of a gunned-down gigolo (William Holden) floating face down in the silent star's swimming pool. He also had Cecil B. DeMille playing himself, Erich von Stroheim all but playing himself, and, briefly, Buster Keaton, Anna Q. Nilsson (who had played Hamlet in a silent movie) and H.B. Warner (who had played Jesus for DeMille) actually playing themselves as has-beens. So how could Wilder expect to get the Oscar for best picture? (He and Charles Bracket picked up one for writing.)

5 *Kind Hearts and Coronets* (Robert Hamer). UK, bw. All eight of the snobbish D'Ascoyne heirs are murdered by the snubbed ninth-in-line. And all eight done-in D'Ascoynes are played by the amazing Alec Guinness! Heartless hilarity of a high order. With Dennis Price, Joan Greenwood, and Valerie Hobson.

6 *Born Yesterday* (George Cukor). US, bw. Boorish Broderick Crawford hires bookish William Holden to give his dumbbell doll Judy Holliday (AA) some couth. She smartens up fast, and bullying Broderick doesn't like it one bit. Garson Kanin's Broadway comedy about Washington simply lights up the screen. Unhappily it also marked the end of two decades of sophisticated comedy from Columbia.

7 *Harvey* (Henry Koster). US, bw. On Broadway, by the time *Harvey* reached its third act, people in the audience happily claimed that *they* could see the "big white rabbit" that befriended one Elwood P. Dowd. That doesn't quite happen in the movie, but otherwise the screen version is a very successful transfer that over the years has attracted a cult following. With James Stewart as the amiable toper and Josephine Hull (AAS) as his dotty sister. From Universal-International.

8 *The Asphalt Jungle* (John Huston). UK, bw. Louis B. Mayer sputtered, about a film made at his own studio (MGM), "That asphalt pavement thing... I wouldn't walk across the room to see something like that." But Huston's archetypal heist film, with its pointed character studies, has been imitated for over a half-century and never quite surpassed. With Sterling Haydn, Louis Calhern, Sam Jaffe, Jean Hagen, and (briefly again) Marilyn Monroe.

9 *The Winslow Boy* (Anthony Asquith). UK, bw. Terence Rattigan's play about a boy wrongly dismissed from military school seems even better on the screen. The scene in which barrister Robert Donat, persuaded to take up the case, relentlessly questions the boy is unforgettably tense. With Margaret Leighton, Cedric Hardwicke, and Francis L. Sullivan.

10 *Tight Little Island* (Alexander Mackendrick). UK, bw. Scottish islanders fighting fast and furious for a cache of whiskey washed up from a Second World War shipwreck. What do you suppose the *London Sunday Chronicle* meant when they called it "wholly plausible"? Titled *Whiskey Galore* in the UK.

Contending for tenth place were *Father of the Bride*, *The Men*, and *Treasure Island*.

1951

1 *Rashomon** (Akira Kurosawa). Japan, bw. The film that first made the world aware of Japanese cinema, and arguably the best film of the fifties. See the essay at the back of this book.

2 *The African Queen* (John Huston). US, bw. A gin-soaked Canadian loner (Humphrey Bogart AA) and a virginal English missionary (Katharine Hepburn) travel through an African jungle on a broken-down riverboat during World War I to do what they can in support of the Royal Navy. Huston has said that the infectious humor and touching humanity of their performances were not in the original novel by C.S. Forster, or in the script by James Agee, but sprang spontaneously from the two stars playing

beautifully against each other. There were many difficulties with the shooting, done mainly on location in the Congo with Jack Cardiff lensing. Hepburn wrote a book about the experience, and Clint Eastwood made a film of a another, darker book, mostly about Huston during the filming, called *White Hunter, Black Heart*. As for *The African Queen* itself, audiences for a half century have exclaimed, with spinster Hepburn, "I never dreamed that any mere physical experience could be so stimulating!"

3 *A Streetcar Named Desire* (Elia Kazan). US, bw. Sweltering screen version of Tennessee Williams' most famous play, with Marlon Brando recreating his stage role as the loutish Stanley Kowalski and with Vivien Leigh (AA) as the repressed Blanche Dubois. Oscars also went to Broadwayites Kim Hunter and Karl Malden in support, leaving only Brando, whose performance burns up the screen, shut out by the Academy in the acting awards - but then didn't they *have* to reward Bogart for *The African Queen*?

4 *Oliver Twist* (David Lean). UK, bw. Lean follows his *Great Expectations* with another atmospheric adaptation of Dickens, so unsubtle and terrifying that it was bound to be controversial, and it was. The 1948 film's American release was delayed for almost three years by pressure groups, and seven minutes of Alec Guinness' too-Semitic Fagin were excised. With Robert Newton, Francis L. Sullivan, Peter Bull (briefly but memorably), and, as the orphan boys, John Howard Davies and Anthony Newley.

5 *An American in Paris* (Vincente Minnelli). US, color. Gene Kelly plays the American and, in an elaborately choreographed closing sequence, an MGM back lot plays Paris in the styles of Utrillo, Dufy, Renoir, and Van Gogh. The music is, of course,

by George Gershwin. The film debut of Leslie Caron. Surprise Oscar for best picture.

6 *A Place in the Sun* (George Stevens AA). US, bw. Meticulously crafted adaptation of Theodore Dreiser's *An American Tragedy*, with Montgomery Clift as the poor boy who falls for a rich debutante (Elizabeth Taylor) and is driven to drown, perhaps accidentally, his mistress (Shelley Winters). With immense close-ups, a sound track that uses bird cries to haunting effect, and a musical score that finally answers the question the trial scenes do not. But Stevens's careful pacing, much admired in 1951, seems overdeliberate today.

7 *Strangers on a Train* (Alfred Hitchcock). US, bw. Hitch cheerfully films Patricia Highsmith's neurotic novel about a psychopath (Robert Walker) and a tennis star (Farley Granger) who swap murders. The murder seen from within the lens of a pair of glasses and the tennis match at which only one face in the crowd stares straight ahead are famous touches. The merry-go-round out of control is a gleefully horrifying climax.

8 *Detective Story* (William Wyler). US, bw. A pathologically upright New York detective (Kirk Douglas) finds in his own life what he most hates in the criminals he rounds up. Sidney Kingsley's tightly written play has some of the ironic inevitability of Greek tragedy, and Wyler's direction daringly transfers it from stage to screen by breaking all the Hollywood rules: he keeps all the talk, permits no music, and provides very little by way of "opening up". Joseph Wiseman and Lee Grant recreate their Broadway roles. Amazing result: the stagebound play becomes real cinema.

9 **Orpheus** (Jean Cocteau). France, bw. Cocteau overlays the Greek myth with a wealth of idiosyncratic symbols (Death as a woman escorted by motorcyclists), visual sleights-of-hand (passing through mirrors) and oracular utterances ("The bird sings with its fingers"). With Jean Marais and Maria Casarès. OT: *Orphée*

10 **La Ronde** (Max Ophuls). France, bw. Viennese streetwalker meets soldier meets chambermaid meets youth - and so on till "the round" is completed. Anton Walbrook provides cynical comment, without ever stating explicitly that *au fond* the film, based on a rueful play by Arthur Schnitzler, is about the transmission of venereal disease. Of course it ran into censorship problems. In the starry cast are Simone Signoret, Danielle Darrieux, Jean-Louis Barrault, and Gérard Philipe. But the real star is director Ophuls' omniscient, ever-gliding camera.

Contending for tenth place were *The River*, *Miracle in Milan*, *The Steel Helmet*, *The Red Badge of Courage*, and *A Christmas Carol*.

1952

1 **Singin' in the Rain** (Gene Kelly and Stanley Donen). US, color. A hilarious and endlessly inventive satire on Hollywood converting from silence to sound, often cited as the best musical ever made, and certainly the most colorful. From MGM, of course. Two standout scenes: a smiling Kelly singing and dancing the title song in a street showered with studio rain, and Donald O'Connor wrecking a studio set - and hardly sparing himself - in the astonishing "Make 'Em Laugh" sequence. With Debbie Reynolds, Cyd Charisse, and, as the all-time dumbest of dumb

blondes, Jean Hagen. The period songs by Arthur Freed and Nacio Herb Brown actually determined the story line, and there are any number of MGM in-jokes for the cognoscenti.

2 ***High Noon*** (Fred Zinnemann) US, bw. An independently produced, low-budget western that moves in "real time" from minute to minute and uses oblique shots of railroad tracks to suggest the angle of the minute hand on a great clock. The film is also a parable, scripted by Carl Foreman, about the McCarthy era: a principled man is abandoned by cowards and left to defend himself. It is still potent stuff. With Gary Cooper (AA), Grace Kelly, Katy Jurado, Lloyd Bridges, and a highly effective theme song by Dimitri Tiomkin and Ned Washington.

3 ***Forbidden Games*** (René Clement). France, bw. The incomprensibility of death and the human need for love as seen through the eyes of children. The film begins as Nazi strafing cuts down the parents of a little Parisienne (the five-year-old Brigitte Fossey), continues through her experiences with a slightly older peasant boy, and ends as she vanishes into the crowd at a refugee center. Obstinately unsentimental, many-leveled, and memorably scored for solo guitar by Narciso Yepes. Winner of the Golden Lion at Venice and the Oscar for best foreign film. OT: *Jeux Interdits*.

4 ***The Importance of Being Ernest*** (Anthony Asquith). UK, color. By frankly acknowledging at the start that his film is determined to be self-consciously stagy, Asquith is able to preserve for posterity the expert and unsurpassedly silly performances of Edith Evans, Margaret Rutherford, Michael Redgrave, Joan Greenwood, Dorothy Tutin, and Miles Malleson in one of the

wittiest plays ever written. Some good lines, probably deemed *too* witty for movie audiences, have unfortunately been excised.

5 *The Quiet Man* (John Ford AA). US, color. Ford's affectionate, beautifully photographed tribute to the land of his ancestors, with the biggest assemblage of blarney-speaking Irishmen imaginable and with John Wayne as the not-so-quiet American rough-handling his battling bride-to-be Maureen O'Hara. Amazingly, Ford had to sue to a minor studio (Republic) to bankroll filming this Irish greenery in Ireland.

6 *The Lavender Hill Mob* (Charles Chrichton). UK, bw. Alec Guinness, at the top of his form, plays a dutiful bank clerk who ingeniously steals millions in gold bullion and then runs into a series of hilarious crises, including one on the Eiffel Tower. With Stanley Holloway playing an "artistic" thief, and much droll observation of English life. The first screen appearance of Audrey Hepburn - briefly, in the opening scene.

7 *Breaking Through the Sound Barrier* (David Lean). UK, bw. A tense drama, scripted by Terence Rattigan, about the first plane to fly faster than sound. Attention is riveted even before the credits roll, as a Spitfire goes out of control over the cliffs of Dover. With Ralph Richardson, Nigel Patrick, Ann Todd, John Justin, and Denholm Elliott. OT: *The Sound Barrier*.

8 *The Member of the Wedding* (Fred Zinnemann). US, bw. Sensitive filming of the play by Carson McCullers, with Julie Harris, Brandon de Wilde, and Ethel Waters recreating their Broadway roles. Movie audiences were indifferent and even hostile, but the film, marred only by a few "opening up" sequences, now preserves three cherishable performances and a depth of human

feeling that a hundred financially successful 1952 releases knew or cared nothing about.

9 *Moulin Rouge* (John Huston). US, color. José Ferrer on his knees playing Toulouse Lautrec. With a marvelous opening sequence in which the stunted artist's famous figures come to life amid a whirling can-can, and a good closing bit when they return as dream images to visit him on his death bed. What's in between is of minimal interest. The first Hollywood film to break the Technicolor ban on filters. Georges Auric's "The Song from Moulin Rouge" is sung in its non-commercial version by Zsa Zsa Gabor.

10 *Outcast of the Islands* (Carol Reed). UK, bw. Director Reed's follow-up to *The Third Man* is an atmospheric, truly unsettling film version of Joseph Conrad's study of a white man's descent into depravity in Malaya. With memorable performances by Trevor Howard and Robert Morley, and good ones by Wendy Hiller and Ralph Richardson.

Contending for tenth place were *Casque d'Or*, *Limelight*, and *Pat and Mike*. The best picture Oscar went to *The Greatest Show on Earth*.

1953

1 *Shane* (George Stevens). US, color. Paramount's high-styled, panoramic, mythic Western in which Shane (Alan Ladd) is the archetypal knight who comes to the aid of those in trouble and then must leave as mysteriously as he came. The final scene,

in which the hero-worshipping boy (Brandon de Wilde) runs after Shane calling his name, still affects audiences deeply. With Van Heflin, Elisha Cook, Jr., and, in an unforgettably creepy performance, Jack Palance. Unfortunately Jean Arthur, who rode the range convincingly a dozen years earlier, seems lost in this, her last screen appearance.

2 *From Here To Eternity* (Fred Zinnemann AA). US, bw. Columbia's sanitized but still potent adaptation of James Jones' novel about army life at Pearl Harbor in December, 1941, with Burt Lancaster and Deborah Kerr making out on the beach as Pacific waves crash over them, and with Montgomery Clift, Ernest Borgnine, and Donna Reed (AA). Frank Sinatra (AA), who begged for his small part, played it for a pittance and turned his then-fading career around. Oscar for best picture, seven others.

3 *The Earrings of Madame de...* (Max Ophuls). France/Italy, bw. The director of *La Ronde* does another, wiser, sadder variation on his theme: the earrings given by Monsieur D... (Charles Boyer) to his wife (Danielle Darrieux) eventually pass to his mistress, to Madame's lover (Vittorio de Sica), and back to Madame - with tragic consequences. Again the real star is the gliding camera of director Ophuls, which seems to comment omnisciently on the vanity of human wishes. OT: *Madame de...*

4 *Julius Caesar* (Joseph Mankewicz). US, bw. The writer-director of *All About Eve* films Shakespeare in Roman sets left over at MGM from their recent *Quo Vadis*. Marlon Brando, coached by co-star John Gielgud, is a riveting method-actor Marc Antony, Gielgud soldiers on in Old Vic fashion as Cassius, James Mason plays Brutus with the restraint familiar from his British films, and Louis Calhern plays Caesar much as he played high-

toned gangsters in any number of American movies. Somehow the mixture of styles actually enhances the drama. With Greer Garson, Deborah Kerr, and Edmund O'Brien.

5 *Roman Holiday* (William Wyler). US, bw. Audrey Hepburn (AA), after her bit part in *The Lavender Hill Mob*, gives one of the screen's most radiant starring performances as a visiting princess who slips away from her official duties in Rome and falls in love with American newspaperman Gregory Peck. Director Wyler, in his twenty-fifth year of movie-making, paces the charming but lightweight tale rather deliberately, but many scenes stay in the memory. From Paramount.

6 *The Band Wagon* (Vincente Minnelli). US, color. Highly regarded MGM musical scripted by Betty Comden and Adolph Green - who are played on screen by Nanette Fabray and Oscar Levant. Much of the original Broadway score by Arthur Schwartz and Howard Dietz is retained, "That's Entertainment" is added, and Fred Astaire and Cyd Charisse spoof the tough-guy potboilers of Mickey Spillane in a terrific extended dance sequence. On the other hand, Jack Buchanan is tiresome in a tiresome role.

7 *Lili* (Charles Walters). US, color. MGM thinks smaller, takes a chance on a whimsical Paul Gallico story, and comes up lucky with another musical. Leslie Caron plays a French orphan girl who falls in love with despondent puppeteer Mel Ferrer while chatting and singing with his puppets. But it's all a little long at a mere 81 minutes. MGM had better material but less luck with yet a third 1959 musical - Cole Porter's *Kiss Me Kate*.

8 *Call Me Madam* (Walter Lang). US, color. 20th-Century- Fox, no slouch with musicals in the fifties, almost trumped MGM by

presenting Ethel Merman on the screen in her Broadway spoof of Washington's "hostess with the mostes' on the ball", Perle Mesta. Unfortunately, only big-city audiences responded. Merman's brassy star quality was too big to be contained in a mere movie, even this exuberant one. George Sanders gamely tries a song from the Irving Berlin score, and Donald O'Connor doesn't seem to mind being drowned out in a Merman duet that's supposed to be comforting.

9 *Stalag 17* (Billy Wilder). US, bw. William Holden (AA) as a wheeler-dealer American POW in Germany, Otto Preminger as the Nazi camp commander, and Sig Ruman as flustered Sgt. Schultz. Wilder, still at Paramount, adroitly mixes humor and heroics.

10 *The Captain's Paradise* (Anthony Kimmins). UK, bw. Alec Guinness as a ship captain with a wife in both of the ports he plies. A plot as old as Plautus, served with a twist: prim Celia Johnson would like to be someone like sultry Yvonne de Carlo, and sulty Yvonne would like to be someone like prim Celia. Now if they were ever run into each other...

Contending for tenth place were *Kiss Me Kate* and *The Man Between*.

1954

1 *On the Waterfront* (Elia Kazan, AA). US, bw. Independently shot in Hoboken for a fraction of the cost of most fifties studio productions, this hard-hitting, partly factual, brilliantly told

story about corruption in the longshoremen's union boasted ensemble acting of the highest order from Rod Steiger, Lee J. Cobb, Karl Malden, Eva Marie Saint (AA), and, in his finest screen performance, Marlon Brando (AA). It also seemed to some (Arthur Miller, for one) to be an unsavory defense of informing by two well-known Hollywood informers (Kazan and writer Budd Schulberg) during the McCarthy hearings. Music by Leonard Bernstein. Oscar for best picture, seven others.

2 *Diary of a Country Priest* (Robert Bresson). France, bw. A saintly young cleric faces hostility and hatred in his first parish. Probably *the* masterpiece of the austerely spiritual Bresson, who meticulously conveys both the harshness and the beauty of Georges Bernanos' novel. Pauline Kael called it "one of the most profound emotional experiences in the history of film". But even dedicated art-house viewers, invited to share the young priest's suffering, have found the picture oppressively bleak: one mis-led essayist called this transcendent work of art "a film about imprisonment".

3 *A Star is Born* (George Cukor). US, color. A showcase for the formidable musical and dramatic talents of the mature Judy Garland, this remake of the 1937 Janet Gaynor vehicle was overlong, troubled in production, mercilessly cut, and eventually all but abandoned by its studio (Warner Brothers). Now, partially restored, it looks like one of the three or four greatest Hollywood musicals. Cukor got heart-breaking performances out of both Garland and James Mason, and Garland's warbling of the Harold Arlen-Ira Gershwin song "The Man That Got Away" is a pop-meets-blues-meets-jazz moment any musician would love to be able to claim as his, or in this case her, own.

4 ***Rear Window*** (Alfred Hitchcock). US, color. James Stewart, as a photojournalist laid up in his apartment with a broken leg, thinks he sees a murderer at work in the apartment building across the court and, with the aid of Grace Kelly and Thelma Ritter, plays detective from his wheelchair. A directorial tour de force (the camera never moves from the room and its view of the living quarters opposite) and the ultimate Hitchcock voyeur movie. The not-so-private lives of a dozen apartment dwellers comment in ironic ways on one another (witness the action that transpires in a first floor flat during a drunken version of "Mona Lisa" sung at a party upstairs), and the whole set-up is a kind of movie-maker's manifesto: Raymond Burr, as the murderer glimpsed from afar, is made to look like Hitch's old enemy David O. Selznick. From Paramount.

5 ***Romeo and Juliet*** (Renato Castellani) UK/Italy, color. Laurence Harvey and Susan Shentall may not give classic Shakespearean readings as the lovers but, lovingly photographed against beautiful backgrounds in Siena, Assisi, Mantegnana, and Venice, they evoke the spirit of Shakespeare's play more than all the Romeos and Juliets in a dozen other versions. With Flora Robson as the nurse and Mervyn Johns as Friar Laurence. The Italians in the cast are poorly dubbed, but the music, by Roman Vlad, is astonishingly beautiful. Winner of the Golden Lion at Venice (over *On the Waterfront*, *The Seven Samurai*, and *La Strada*).

6 ***Ugetsu*** (Kenju Mizoguchi). Japan, bw. Two interlocking "Tales of the Pale and Silvery Moon After the Rain" about piracy, seduction, war, and the supernatural, told in images that recall classical Japanese paintings. In 1954, Japan's gorgeously colored *Gate of Hell* won an honorary best foreign film Oscar. Today the subtler monochrome *Ugetsu* is regarded as the real masterpiece.

7 **Seven Brides for Seven Brothers** (Stanley Donen). US, color. Though we were promised an amusing Western based on the legendary Roman rape of the Sabine women, nobody really expected much from an MGM musical with Jane Powell and Howard Keel - but what we got was an explosively entertaining film that spread the seven brothers and their "sobbin' women" across a wide cinemascope screen and set them dancing with an athletic vigor such as the movies had never, till 1954, seen. With charmingly foursquare songs by Johnny Mercer and Gene de Paul.

8 **Sabrina** (Billy Wilder). US, bw. A Long Island Cinderella story told with Wilder's usual cynicism (casting Humphrey Bogart in a role he was twenty years too old to play), and with scene after scene of uncynical charm (allowing Audrey Hepburn to make us all fall in love with her, just in case we might have been foolish enough not to do so before). With William Holden as the playboy she pines for and John Williams as the father who ruefully wishes she knew her own place in the social scheme of things. From Paramount.

9 **Mr. Hulot's Holiday** (Jacques Tati). France, bw. Inspired nonsense by everyone's favorite accident-prone pipe-smoker, who stoically maintains perfect silence while his audience roars with laughter. (This *must* be seen in a theater.) OT: *Les Vacances de Monsieur Hulot.*

10 **The Golden Coach** (Jean Renoir). Italy, color. Anna Magnani plays the "perichole" of Prosper Merimée's one-act play and of Jacques Offenbach's operetta for director Renoir, who clearly inherited his father's penchant for stunning colors. This is the rarest of the screen's tributes to the magic of the stage – in this

case, of the commedia dell' arte stage, with music by Vivaldi. Unfortunately, made in separate English, French, and Italian versions and poorly dubbed (Magnani had to learn all her English lines phonetically), it was too exotic and imperfectly executed for both critics and public in 1954. Later, Truffaut called it "the noblest and most refined film ever made... absolutely beautiful". It remains an acquired taste. OT: *Le Carrosse d'Or*.

Contending for tenth place were *Le Plaisir*, *The Caine Mutiny*, *The Country Girl*, and *Executive Suite*.

1955

1 ***The Wages of Fear*** (Henri-Georges Clouzot). France, bw. Breathtaking suspense story of four European drifters driving two trucks loaded with nitroglycerine through the jungles and over the mountains of a Latin American country controlled by US oil interests. Clouzot screws the tension almost to the breaking point. Now shown complete, it was cut by forty minutes in its US distribution in 1955 to spare American sensibilities and perhaps also to mute a homosexual subtext. With Yves Montand, Charles Vanel, and Véra (Mrs.) Clouzot. Palme d'Or at Cannes. OT: *Le Salaire de la Peur*.

2 ***Diabolique*** (Henri-Georges Clouzot). France, bw. The headmaster of a boarding school is murdered by his wife and his mistress but keeps turning up in surprising ways. It's Clouzot again, out-Hitchcocking Hitchcock - who promptly secured the rights to another story by the same authors (Pierre Boileau and Thomas Narcejac) and made *Vertigo*. With Simone Signoret and,

once again, Véra Clouzot. Oscar for best foreign film. OT: *Les Diaboliques*.

3 **Summertime** (David Lean). US, color. An unexceptional Broadway play (Arthur Laurents' *The Time of the Cuckoo*) utterly transformed by director Lean's cinematic eye and Katharine Hepburn's commanding presence - commanding even though she plays a self-conscious spinster overawed by the beauty of Venice. A superior screen event.

4 **East of Eden** (Elia Kazan). US, color. John Steinbeck's Cain and Abel story, given an inventive-as-all-get-out cinemascope treatment by Kazan and powered by an emotionally charged performance by James Dean in his first starring role. With Jo Van Fleet (AA) as the boys' mother, Raymond Massey as the father for whose love they compete, and Julie Harris as the only one who understands. Teen-agers who identified with Dean and were overwhelmed by his emoting went overboard when he appeared later in the year in a much inferior movie, the hysterical *Rebel Without A Cause*.

5 **Marty** (Delbert Mann AA). US, bw. Paddy Chayevsky's TV play, effectively transferred to the screen, with Ernest Borgnine (AA) replacing TV's Rod Steiger as the ugly but tender-hearted Bronx butcher who finally finds love. Audiences liked the slice-of-life situations and dialogue so much (and it cost so little to make) that independent film-making came into its own in Hollywood. We tend to forget that *Marty* actually opened in art houses, and was the first American movie to win the Palme d'Or at the film festival in Cannes. Oscar for best picture, three others.

6 ***Night of the Hunter*** (Charles Laughton). US, bw. The great Laughton's only attempt at directing is ungainly in its early scenes and was indifferently received in 1955, probably because Laughton knew too much about silent-movie techniques to appeal to an age of cinemascope "realism". Now it causes regret that he never got a chance to do more work behind the camera. Robert Mitchum's psychopathic preacher is perhaps his best performance, and the flight of the two children to their protectress (the wonderful Lillian Gish) is a sequence of imaginative genius. Scripted by James Agee.

7 ***Umberto D.*** (Vittorio De Sica). Italy, bw. Italian neo-realism reaches another high point in this moving story, close in style and feeling to *The Bicycle Thief*, about a retired and impoverished civil servant all but driven out of his lodgings and saved from suicide by his little dog. De Sica based the character on his own father and dedicated the film to him.

8 ***Picnic*** (Joshua Logan). US, color. William Inge's play about small-town America, transferred from stage to screen by Broadway writer-director Logan. No one expected cinematic success (and Logan never really achieved it again), but the picture packed a real wallop. Arthur O'Connell and Rosalind Russell steal it away from William Holden (who was too mature to play a young hustler) and Kim Novak - though the sultry dance the two of them do to "Moonglow" is a high-water mark in screen eroticism.

9 ***Mister Roberts*** (John Ford and Mervyn LeRoy). US, color. Seriocomic drama set on a World War II cargo ship waiting to do battle. Henry Fonda recreates his fondly remembered stage role, with good support from James Cagney, Jack Lemmon (AAS), and, in his last screen performance, William Powell. Joshua

Logan adapted the stage play he wrote with Thomas Heggen. The direction is both studio-efficient (LeRoy) and humanistic (Ford).

10 **Oklahoma!** (Fred Zinnemann). US, color. 1955 was a year for big screen adaptations of successful stage pieces, and Rodgers and Hammerstein's landmark 1943 musical made the transfer more convincingly than did, say, Frank Loesser's *Guys and Dolls*. Some of the freshness and inventiveness of the Broadway original had evaporated over the twelve years we waited to see the movie version, but the score, one of the best ever, really sang on the wide, wide screen - in the new process called Todd-AO. With Gordon McRae, Shirley Jones, and Rod Steiger, and with Charlotte Greenwood, who had been R&H's original choice for Aunt Eller on Broadway.

Contending for tenth place were *Bad Day at Black Rock*, *Kiss Me Deadly*, *Guys and Dolls*, *The Rose Tattoo*, and *Les Grandes Manoeuvres*.

1956

1 **Seven Samurai** (Akira Kurosawa). Japan, bw. This epic tale of a farming village that hires professional warriors to defend it from marauding bandits attracted little attention in a severely cut version (variously titled) in 1956, but since its reissue at almost *Gone With the Wind* length it has been rightly hailed as the most complex and rewarding of all action films, awesome in its scope. With the versatile Toshiro Mifune as the clownish seventh and with Takashi Shimura as the magisterial first samurai. Remade

with considerable success as an American western (*The Magnificent Seven*).

2 *La Strada* (Federico Fellini). Italy, bw. The film that introduced Fellini to the wide world. Millions of moviegoers were touched by Chaplinesque Giulietta Masina (Mrs. Fellini) playing a carnival waif mercilessly bullied by a strong man (Anthony Quinn) but assured by a saintly clown (Richard Basehart) that her life served some purpose in the world. With a haunting score by Nino Rota. Winner of the first Academy Award for best foreign film. (Previous foreign film Oscars had been honorary only.)

3 *Richard III* (Laurence Olivier). UK, color. Not the best or the most lavish of Olivier's four Shakespeare movies, but it has the most stellar cast (including John Gielgud and Ralph Richardson) and the most multi-faceted Olivier performance. William Walton's score is stirring; the climactic battle scene is not.

4 *The King and I* (Walter Lang). US, color. Though three Rodgers and Hammerstein songs are cut, this may be the best of all film musicals adapted from the Broadway stage. There is a palpable chemistry between Deborah Kerr as Anna and Yul Brynner (AA) as the king of Siam, and the familiar story's message of tolerance comes through with unexpected force. From 20th-Century-Fox. (R&H's finest musical, *Carousel*, was also filmed at Fox in 1956, but with less success.)

5 *War and Peace* (King Vidor). US, Italy, color. This brave attempt at filming Tolstoy has been grossly underrated. Its ballroom scene, battle of Borodino, and retreat of Napoleon through the snow stay in the memory more vividly than do the corresponding scenes in the mammoth 1968 Soviet version. Henry Fonda is

miscast as Pierre and Mel Ferrer's Prince Andrei is uninteresting, but Audrey Hepburn is a radiant Natasha, and Herbert Lom and Oskar Homolka give strikingly effective performances as the two confronting generals.

6 *Giant* (George Stevens AA). US, color. Long, uneven Texas family saga with some stunning sequences early on. James Dean goes over the top in his last performance - a car crash was soon to take his life. Elizabeth Taylor, Rock Hudson, and Mercedes McCambridge do good work, but the real star of the picture is the great Gothic homestead that weathers cultural changes through three generations. Texans themselves were not altogether charmed by Edna Ferber's novelistic view of their recent history.

7 *Moby Dick* (John Huston). US, color. Huston seemed the best man in Hollywood to film Melville, and much of his sea saga is splendidly atmospheric. But Gregory Peck is miscast as Captain Ahab, and Moby Dick himself is unconvincing.

8 *Lust for Life* (Vincente Minnelli). US, color. A generally effective film biography of Vincent van Gogh, capably played by Kirk Douglas, with Anthony Quinn (AA) as Gauguin. Director Minnelli's exquisite sense of color is somewhat disadvantaged by the Metrocolor process, but his camera pans lovingly across many of the famous paintings, and a few scenes (the black crows suddenly rising from a yellow Provençal cornfield) startlingly capture the excitement of an artist's moment of tortured inspiration.

9 *The Searchers* (John Ford). US, color. One of the most influential of all American movies, and a real curate's egg. The story - a racist Confederate loner searches for his niece, intent on killing her because, kidnapped by Comanches, she has "mated

with a squalid savage" - is the strongest Ford ever filmed, but it is interlarded with lame attempts at humor and cornball character studies. Ford's beloved Monument Valley looks less impressive in color than it did in dusty black-and-white, but the framing scenes of John Wayne in a homestead doorway have become classics, and the film has a vociferous cult following, especially among directors.

10 *Around the World in 80 Days* (Michael Anderson). US, color. Ballyhooing showman Mike Todd assembled some fifty international stars to do "cameo roles" in this wide-screen filming of Jules Verne's familiar tale of Phineas Fogg's globe-circling adventures, and he showed the result on a reserved-seat basis – in Todd-AO, of course. It shouldn't have worked but it did, and the box office ballooned. Oscar for best picture.

Contending for tenth place were *Anastasia*, *High Society*, *The Ladykillers*, *Rififi*, and *Yang Kwei Fei*.

1957

1 *The Bridge on the River Kwai* (David Lean AA). UK/US, color. In this first of his famous panoramic epics, Lean tells an ironic, psychologically probing, fact-based but sometimes implausible story of British POWs building a bridge for the Japanese while British-led commandos trek through the jungle to destroy it. Most impressively filmed (in Ceylon), with a classic performance by Alec Guinness (AA), and with William Holden, Jack Hawkins, and Sessue Hayakawa in other roles. Whether or not the film is marred by a tense but confusing quasi-existentialist

climax is perhaps best left up to the viewer. Oscar for best picture, six others.

2 ***Paths of Glory*** (Stanley Kubrick). US, bw. Compact, independently produced, anguished examination of the callous incompetence of the French high command during the First World War. Under the young Kubrick's direction, Kirk Douglas, Adolphe Menjou, George Macready and, notably, Ralph Meeker give the performances of their careers. Banned in France in 1957, and largely ignored then in the US, it has since grown in critical esteem throughout the world.

3 ***Smiles of a Summer Night*** (Ingmar Bergman). Sweden, bw. A weekend in the country when the midsummer night grants three wishes. Bergman's repertory company in an elegant comedy of manners that is reminiscent, now of Beaumarchais, now of Pirandello, now of Renoir's *Rules of the Game.* The basis of Steven Sondheim's musical *A Little Night Music.*

4 ***Nights of Cabiria*** (Federico Fellini). Italy, bw. Giulietta Masina, fresh from her triumph in *La Strada,* plays another Fellini waif, abused but hopeful and, this time around, a survivor. The basis of the musical *Sweet Charity.* Oscar for best foreign film. OT: *Le Notti di Cabiria.*

5 *I **Vitelloni*** (Federico Fellini). Italy, bw. Fellini remembers, not without affection, the five grown-up mama's boys (*vitelloni*) he associated with in his adolescence. An earlier work than *La Strada* and *Cabiria,* it is indispensable for understanding much of Fellini's subsequent work. Some even say it is indispensable for understanding contemporary Italian life. Fellini often called it his favorite among his films.

6 *A Man Escaped* (Robert Bresson). France, bw. A French prisoner of the Gestapo (François Leterrier) meticulously plans his escape, aided by a series of circumstances that come as unexpectedly as God's graces come to the believer. Not by any means an action picture, this is a demonstration of cinematic technique whose original title, *The Spirit Breathes Where It Will* (words of Jesus from St. John's Gospel), indicates its oneness with Bresson's more patently religious films. On the almost wordless sound track a recurrent fragment from the "Kyrie" from Mozart's C-Minor Mass hints at significances beyond the events we see. François Truffaut called it "the most crucial French film of the past ten years". Like all of Bresson's work, its appeal was limited to art houses. OT: *Un Condamné à Mort S'est Èchappé.*

7 *Ordet (The Word)* (Carl Dreyer). Denmark, BW. A slow-moving, strangely compelling dramatization of the conflict between organized Christianity and private mystical experience. Luminously filmed in rural Jutland. No great film is easier to satirize (not since *Kings Row* had so many crises been met by warming up the coffee pot), but *Ordet* has grown in stature over the years, and clearly forecasts the great Bergman films to come. Winner of the Golden Lion in Venice.

8 *The Sweet Smell of Success* (Alexander Mackendrick). US, bw. A melodramatic study of sleazy journalism and big-city decadence, with Burt Lancaster unforgettable as J.J. Hunsecker, a egomaniacal Walter Winchell-like columnist, and with Tony Curtis, in his best performance, as Sidney Falco, Hunsecker's sniveling toady. Scripted by Clifford Odets and Ernest Lehman. A box-office disaster in 1956, highly regarded today.

9 *Twelve Angry Men* (Sidney Lumet). US, bw. A jury room under glass. The second television play (after *Marty*) to make it big in a big-screen adaptation, and a riveting if stagy hour and a half. Shot for a pittance in just twenty days. With Henry Fonda, Lee J. Cobb, E.G. Marshall, Ed Begley, Jack Warden, Martin Balsam and six other angry men. Director Lumet's auspicious debut.

10 *Funny Face* (Stanley Donen). US, color. A chic, vibrantly colored musical about the fashion world. Indefatigable Kay Thompson sets the tone early with "Think Pink". Debonair Fred Astaire woos delectable Audrey Hepburn with "He Loves and She Loves" and other vintage Gershwin songs. Who could ask for anything more?

Contending for tenth place were *The Enemy Below*, *Gervaise*, and *Witness for the Prosecution*.

1958

1 *The Seventh Seal* (Ingmar Bergman). Sweden, bw. Audiences charmed by Bergman's elegant *Smiles of a Summer Night* were hardly prepared for this inelegantly apocalyptic tale of a brutal world living in fear of the Plague and the Last Judgement, a world in which a war-weary knight (Max von Sydow) plays a game of chess with Death and defeats him by saving a "holy family" of strolling players from the impending disaster. Few viewers in 1959 saw any parallel between this parable and their own bomb-threatened existences, but Bergman instantly became an internationally known director whose films kept art houses going for two decades.

2 ***Pather Panchali*** (Satajit Ray). India, bw. Bengali director Ray, thought by many to be insular, actually grew up in India watching films from other lands (he saw the Rodgers/Astaire musicals over and over to learn the songs of Jerome Kern and Irving Berlin by heart). And he admitted that he planned *Pather Panchali* after *The Bicycle Thief*, filming it in city streets with unknown actors, because "a great many notions about our country and our people have to be dispelled, even though it may be easier... to sustain the existing myths than to demolish them." There is no exoticism in this first installment of his Apu Trilogy, no plot twisting, no villainy, no saintliness - only life lived and accepted, mostly in poverty and generosity of spirit.

3 ***Vertigo*** (Alfred Hitchcock). US, color. The hypnotic Hitchcock film that was greeted with scorn in 1959 and now appears on many critics' lists of all-time bests. (Even amateur Hitchcockians have discovered layers on layers in it.) With James Stewart as a detective suffering from vertigo, Barbara Bel Geddes as the girl who wants to help him, and Kim Novak as the all-but-possessed blonde woman he is haunted by and tries, when he loses her, to recreate. (Yes, the film is partly about its director's neurotic fascination with his leading ladies.) A predictably great score by Bernard Herrmann propels the story onwards.

4 ***Touch of Evil*** (Orson Welles). US, bw. Greeted in 1959 with even more scorn than *Vertigo* received, now a cult classic, this harrowing tale of corruption in a Mexican border town boasts a one-take opening shot that, since the film's 1998 re-release, has been hailed as a peak of cinematic story-telling. Director Peter Bogdanovich called *Touch of Evil* "a Goya-like vision of an infected universe" - which might help explain the grotesque performances

of Welles and Marlene Dietrich. With Charleton Heston, Janet Leigh, and Akim Tamiroff.

5 *Gigi* (Vincente Minnelli AA). US, color. Surprisingly frank and often delectable Lerner and Loewe confection adapted from the Colette novel, with Leslie Caron, Louis Jourdan, Maurice Chevalier, and Hermione Gingold. The Broadway composer-librettist team, with designer Cecil Beaton, opted to follow their stage success, *My Fair Lady*, with an original screen musical and they almost - almost - passed another miracle. MGM no longer had all the skilled personnel needed to make a great musical, but Minnelli, of course, had long since learned how to photograph Paris for maximum effect. Oscar for best picture, eight others. This was the last MGM musical of any consequence.

6 *The Defiant Ones* (Stanley Kramer). US, bw. The most effective of Kramer's obvious "message" pictures: a black man (Sidney Poitier) and a white man (Tony Curtis) escape from a chain gang while handcuffed together, flee from their pursuers, and learn mutual respect. Lots of excitement and uplift, but how did the two guys keep their cigarettes dry in those flood waters?

7 *My Uncle Mr. Hulot* (Jacques Tati). France, color. Tati fans found this satire on ultramodern suburban living, with its hilarious fish-fountain, even funnier than *Mr. Hulot's Holiday*. Though there was hardly a word of French in it, by the time it won the Oscar for best foreign film everybody in the world was calling it by its original title, *Mon Oncle*.

8 *A Night To Remember* (Roy Baker). UK, bw. The second and far the best of the three major film treatments of the sinking of

the Titanic, almost documentary in style, with many touching moments. Kenneth More is the stalwart second officer.

9 *Separate Tables* (Delbert Mann). US, bw. Terence Rattigan's West End play featured a single actor and actress in two separate stories. For the screen, he ran the two stories together to accommodate four stars - David Niven (AA), Deborah Kerr, Burt Lancaster, and Rita Hayworth. Strangely, one remembers best Wendy Hiller (AAS), Felix Aylmer, and Gladys Cooper in supporting roles. In any case, this is a feast of good acting. (But someone ought to have scrapped the dreadful title song.)

10 *The Horse's Mouth* (Ronald Neame). UK, color. Alec Guinness as an anarchic artist eking out a bohemian existence in London. Occasionally moving, often amusing, with one moment of inspired hilarity, and lots of provoking Prokofiev on the sound track.

Contending for tenth place were *Auntie Mame* and *The Young Lions*.

1959

1 *North By Northwest* (Alfred Hitchcock). US, color. In what is possibly the master's best film, a dapper advertising man (Cary Grant) is mistaken for a CIA agent and pursued by the minions of a foreign spy (James Mason) across the landscape of America. This exhilaratingly witty and suspenseful combination of elements culled by scriptwriter Ernest Lehman from several of Hitchcock's past films has two classic sequences - the crop-dusting airplane

that suddenly turns on the fugitive hero, and the cliff-hanging escape across the presidential faces on Mount Rushmore. With Eva Marie Saint as an ambivalent heroine, Martin Landau as a saurian villain, and a kettledrum-thumping score by Bernard Herrmann.

2 ***Some Like It Hot*** (Billy Wilder). US, bw. More chases. Two down-on-their-luck jazz musicians (Jack Lemmon and Tony Curtis), disguised as women to escape the St. Valentine's Day massacre, join an all-girl band with a songstress named Sugar Kane (Marilyn Monroe). Critics have called it the best comedy of the sound era. Would that most cheerful of cynics, Billy Wilder, mind my saying that it is a little sweeter than his other films?

3 ***Wild Strawberries*** (Ingmar Bergman). Sweden, bw. A retired professor of science (Victor Seastrom), haunted by nightmares and the consciousness of his personal failings, travels by car with his daughter-in-law (Ingrid Thulin) to his old university to receive an honorary doctorate, and on the way picks up various travelers who unwittingly help him to understand what his life has meant. An essential work of cinema, beautifully realized.

4 ***Aparajito*** (Satyajit Ray). India, bw. Part two of Ray's Apu trilogy (see the entry on *Pather Panchali* in 1958), memorably tracing the boy's relationship with his mother (Karuna Banerjee). Winner of the Golden Lion at the Venice film festival.

5 ***The Nun's Story*** (Fred Zinnemann). US, color. Audrey Hepburn, usually gowned by Givenchy, was never so beautiful to watch as when she played a chaste Belgian nun sent to the Congo in this serious examination of religious life and its rigorous demands. A beautifully photographed film with a score by Franz

Waxman derived from Gregorian chant, and with Peter Finch, Edith Evans, and Peggy Ashcroft.

6 *The 400 Blows* (François Truffaut). France, bw. The New Wave director remembers his own troubled adolescence in Paris - in the streets and under detention. A lyrical but unsentimental memoir, with a final freeze-frame of the boy's face that drives the whole picture forcefully home. OT: *Les Quatre-Cent Coups*.

7 *Anatomy of a Murder* (Otto Preminger). US, bw. A superior courtroom melodrama with much clinical discussion of what constitutes rape. Briefly banned in, of all places, Chicago! Good performances by James Stewart, Arthur O'Connell, George C. Scott and Lee Remick. The judge is played by Joseph E. Welch, who had represented the US Army at the McCarthy hearings. Great jazz score by Duke Ellington.

8 *Room at the Top* (Jack Clayton). UK, bw. Gritty, hard-hitting story of a young man on the make (Laurence Harvey) in England's industrial north. The most influential of Britain's realistic "kitchen sink" dramas. Thought daring at the time, and still worth seeing for the womanly performance of Simone Signoret (AA).

9 *Black Orpheus* (Marcel Camus). Brazil, color. The Greek myth of Orpheus and Eurydice, retold in the favelas and the streets of Rio before, during, and after carnival time. Some of the myth-making is forced, but the whole film is enlivened by infectious Brazilian rhythms. Surprise winner of the Palme d'Or at Cannes. Oscar for best foreign film.

10 *Ben-Hur* (William Wyler AA). US, color. Massive remake of the 1925 silent movie based on General Lew Wallace's best

seller. Charleton Heston (AA) plays the Jewish hero who suffers manfully for three hours and comes to believe that Jesus is the son of God. The treatment is generally tasteful (MGM did a survey to determine how much religion, sex, violence, and leprosy the public wanted) and literate (Christopher Fry and Maxwell Anderson both had a hand in the writing). But the best parts are, as they had been in 1925, the sea battle and the stupendous chariot race. Oscar for best picture, ten others - a record still unsurpassed, though those other superspectacles *Titanic* (1997) and the third installment of *The Lord of the Rings* (2003) were eventually to equal it.

Contending for tenth place were *The Magician, The Diary of Anne Frank*, and *Suddenly, Last Summer.*

The 1960s

1960

1 *The Apartment* (Billy Wilder). US, bw. A Manhattan tragicomedy: an office jerk rises up the company ladder (and almost qualifies for the key to the executive washroom) by making his apartment available to higher-ups for their extra-marital affairs. Then he discovers that the elevator operator he wistfully loves has tried to kill herself in the apartment. Wilder wrote the script with long-time collaborator I.A.L. Diamond, and it is perhaps their most representative work - shrewdly observant and cheerfully cynical. Expert performances by Shirley MacLaine and Wilder regulars Jack Lemmon and Fred MacMurray. Plays even better now than it did in 1960. Oscar for best picture, four others.

2 *Psycho* (Alfred Hitchcock). US, bw. The master of suspense tries his hand at a low-budget shocker and comes up with his biggest popular and - with the passage of years - critical success. This grisly tale of murder in a roadside cabana is reported to have scared millions of people away from motel showers. Marred only by a psychiatrist's "analysis" at the close - no doubt thought necessary in 1960. Anthony Perkins gives a really spooked-out performance. Composer Bernard Herrmann actually tips us off to every violent attack of the bird-loving murderer with a veritable fusillade of screeching violins – which only adds to the deliciousness of the horror.

3 *The World of Apu* (Satyajit Ray). India, bw. The final installment of the Apu trilogy, mildly disappointing because, with a script that is largely Ray's own work, it turns personal and

even sentimental where *Pather Panchali* and *Aparajito* had been depictions of Bengali life that were resonant with the rhythms of life the world over. Here we get plot devices - Apu's surprising last-minute marriage, the death of his wife in childbirth, his estrangement from and final reconciliation with his son - that might have come from a European novel. None of this really diminishes Ray's stature as a great film-maker. The trilogy as a whole is one of the treasures of world cinema.

4 *The Virgin Spring* (Ingmar Bergman). Sweden, bw. A violent medieval miracle play filmed with great purity by the screen's most outspoken agnostic. Possibly a declaration, in advance of his trilogy on the silence of God, that faith has its claims. With Max von Sydow as the father who exacts a ritual vengeance on the despoilers of his daughter and with Gunnel Lindblom as a fearsome, unregenerate pagan woman. Oscar for best foreign film.

5 *Ikiru* (Akira Kurosawa). Japan, bw. A petty official (Takashi Shimura), dying of cancer after a life that has had no meaning, quietly achieves a measure of true humanity. The film, overlong and almost excruciatingly deliberate in its last half hour, took nine years to cross the Pacific. But for us in 1960 it was a Kurosawa film the like of which we had never seen. It had introspection, compassion, and rage against the dying of the light where in the director's other films there had been self-interest, reckless heroism, and samurai swords. Eventually, Shimura's face became almost as familiar world-wide as Toshiro Mifune's, and critics looked for and found new subtleties in the performances he had given in *Rashomon* and *The Seven Samurai*.

6 ***Hiroshima Mon Amour*** (Alain Resnais). France, bw. Possibly the earliest film of the French *nouvelle vague*, hailed at its premiere as a revolutionary moment in world cinema, with its juxtaposition of eroticism and destruction, its flood of poetic dialogue on the soundtrack, its obliquely told tale of a two-day affair between a Japanese man who lost his parents in the bombing of Hiroshima and a French woman who loved a German soldier in Nevers during the occupation. The once celebrated *Hiroshima* has now been neglected for decades, not least by other New Wave directors Francois Truffaut, Jean-Luc Godard, Louis Malle. It nonetheless remains a strangely moving statement about the inevitable fading of memories that once had deep personal meaning. With Emmanuelle Riva as Elle and Eiji Okuda as Lui.

7 ***Ballad of a Soldier*** (Grigori Chukrai) USSR, bw. After an astonishing opening scene in which a young soldier flees before a German tank, the film settles down to charting the course of the youth's chaste love affair when granted a two-day furlough. There are some good vignettes of life on the Russian home front, and there is no propaganda to speak of. The predictable ending reduced even hardened Cold War hawks to tears. But critic Stanley Kauffmann, remembering the great innovative works of Eisenstein, Pudovkin, and Dovzhenko, ruefully asked, "What has happened to Soviet films?"

8 ***The Sundowners*** (Fred Zinnemann) UK/Australia, color. Slow-moving but nicely realized saga of an Aussie sheep-herding family. Zinnemann, who excels at silent moments, never surpassed the brief scene where Deborah Kerr, parched and sunburned, halts her herd of sheep before a stalled train and sees a woman far less beautiful than she casually applying make-up in her first-class

compartment. With Robert Mitchum, Peter Ustinov, and Glynis Johns.

9 *The Entertainer* (Tony Richardson) UK, bw. Laurence Olivier recreates one of his most famous stage roles - Archie Rice, a seedy seaside vaudevillian facing his failures. Alfred Finney makes a brief but unforgettable debut as his soldier son. With Alan Bates (also debuting), Joan Plowright, Roger Livesey, and Brenda de Banzie. The film seems more depressing than John Osborne's stage play had been; Richardson may have loaded it down with too much of the then-fashionable "kitchen sink" realism.

10 *I'm All Right, Jack* (John Boulting). UK, bw. Why lazy olde Britain had such a hard time of it economically in the fifties. Ian Carmichael, fresh from his hapless experience with the army in *Private's Progress*, now plays a silly-ass aristocrat turned factory worker whose naiveté exposes the inane pretensions of both capital and labor. With Peter Sellers in a performance to set beside his *Dr. Strangelove* roles, and with Terry-Thomas, Margaret Rutherford, Miles Malleson, and a host of others in support. Hilarity waives the rules.

Contending for tenth place were *Sons and Lovers*, *Tunes of Glory*, and *Ashes and Diamonds*.

1961

1 *L'Avventura* (Michelangelo Antonioni). Italy, bw. A woman on a yachting weekend in the Aeolian Sea vanishes on a volcanic island and is never seen again. The first and best part of an Antonioni

trilogy, with *La Notte* and *L'Eclisse*, all of them featuring Monica Vitti. The slowly paced, luminously photographed, enigmatic film made Antonioni's name a household word in the sixties, and still places highly on critics' all-time-best lists. One of many studied effects: black-on-white patterns predominate until, when the couple who have long since given up the search for the girl reach a kind of self-discovery, the pattern is memorably reversed to white-on-black. Baffled audiences booed the film at the 1960 Cannes film festival but the jury rightly voted it a special prize "for a new movie language and the beauty of its images."

2 *La Dolce Vita* (Federico Fellini). Italy, bw. A gutter journalist (Marcello Mastroianni) finds decadence, fakery, despair, and lost innocence in Rome - most famously along the Via Veneto. The first of several vast Fellini frescoes wherein human nature is observed in all its weakness but not despaired of. A great international success, with many scenes - from the helicopter carrying a statue of Christ over the rooftops of Rome to the monstrous sea creature washed up on the beach - that stay in the memory. With Anita Ekberg and Anouk Aimée. Winner of the Palme d'Or at Cannes.

3 *The Hustler* (Robert Rossen). US, bw. A relentlessly downbeat but compulsively watchable pool-room saga in which "Fast Eddie" Felson (Paul Newman) takes on the legendary Minnesota Fats (Jackie Gleason) and faces the terrible wrath of Bert Gordon (someone ought to have thought up a more demonic name for George C. Scott's character). With Piper Laurie as the neurotic but perceptive woman who is the pivot of the story, and Jake LaMotta (the "Raging Bull" himself) as the bartender. In a year in which foreign films dominated critics' list, *The Hustler* was almost the only American film with a thought in its head and artistry to burn.

4 **Breathless** (Jean-Luc Godard). France, bw. The famous, cheaply made, elliptically told New Wave film about a young Paris anti-hero (Jean-Paul Belmondo) who styles himself after Humphrey Bogart and goes on the run with an American waif (Jean Seberg). Godard's hand-held camera, idiosyncratic jump-cutting, and "hommages" to American B-movies (the film is dedicated to Monogram Studios) made for heady viewing in the existentialist sixties. Godard's first feature film. He never made a more exhilarating one.

5 **Rocco and his Brothers** (Luchino Visconti). Italy, bw. Five brothers and their mother migrate from the rural *mezzogiorno* to Milan. Each of the brothers dominates a segment of the continuing story, and each provides a different perspective on the tragic events. Memorably photographed (by Giuseppe Rotunno) but melodramatically overstated in its closing scenes. The acting too is uneven: Alain Renais convinces as the saintly Rocco but not as the champion boxer Rocco becomes, and Katina Paxinou overemotes intolerably as the mother - but there is a great tragic performance by Renato Salvatore as her erring son. With Annie Girardot and, briefly, Claudia Cardinale.

6 **Two Women** (Vittorio De Sica). Italy, bw. An Italian mother (Sophia Loren AA) and her daughter flee from the Allied advance on Rome, are violated in a bombed out church by a troop of Moroccan soldiers, and survive the trauma together. Based on the novel by Alberto Moravia. With Jean-Paul Belmondo and Raf Vallone. (Loren's was the first Oscar ever awarded for a performance in a foreign-language film.) Harrowing.

7 **West Side Story** (Robert Wise AA). US, color. Faithful screen version of the Leonard Bernstein musical which sets the story of

Romeo and Juliet in the slums of New York. (The filming was done in the area of New York's upper West Side that was being torn down to make way for the present Lincoln Center). The romantic leads are unconvincing, but the street-wise dancing is exhilarating and the innovative score is preserved practically intact. Oscar for best picture, nine others.

8 *Saturday Night and Sunday Morning* (Karel Reisz). UK, bw. A young buck from the working class (Albert Finney) defies every convention that keeps him trapped in the system but cannot escape the bleak future that awaits him in industrialized Britain. *Look Back in Anger* may have introduced the "angry young man" to the stage, but this was the film that broke all the rules of earlier British cinema and introduced a decade of gritty low-life dramas far removed from the J. Arthur Rank and Ealing Studio products that had previously meant British cinema to the world. Finney has terrific impact in all his scenes.

9 *El Cid* (Anthony Mann), US/Spain, color. A three-hour epic impressive in its scope, with stunning scenes of warfare. Charleton Heston plays the storied hero who drove the Moors from Spain, and Sophia Loren is his Jimena. (The script could have used some Corneillean passion, but then the movie does movie things that the Comédie Française could never do.) With Genevieve Page, Raf Vallone, Herbert Lom, and Hurd Hatfield.

10 *The Bridge* (Bernhard Wicki). Germany, bw. Poignant tale of a band of pathetically armed Hitlerjugend attempting to defend a bridge in a German town in the last days of World War II. Unpretentious, unsentimental and unforgettable.

Contending for tenth place was *The Innocents*.

1962

1 *Lawrence of Arabia* * (David Lean), UK, color. The most intelligent and overwhelming of all screen epics. See the essay at the back of this book.

2 *Jules and Jim* (François Truffaut). France, bw. A key film in the French New Wave movement, and possibly Truffaut's masterpiece. With a variety of cinematic devices new and old, he tells the tale of a bohemian ménage à trois that begins before the First World War and ends on the eve of the Second. The relationship, insouciant at first, is inevitably doomed, with the woman an impulsive and inscrutable free spirit and the men - one French, one German - gradually reverting to their separate cultures. With poetic photography by Raoul Coutard, career peak performances by Jeanne Moreau and Oscar Werner, and a very good one by Henri Serre.

3 *Last Year at Marienbad* (Alain Resnais). France, bw. The tormented awakening of memory in a baroque world of the dead (assembled from Vaux-le-Vicomte near Paris and the Nymphenburg Palace in Munich). The ultimate art-house film, as elusive today as it was when it won the Golden Lion at the Venice Film Festival. No one has succeeded in explaining Alain Robbe-Grillet's prismatic script (Renais insisted that it had no meaning), though in many details it depicts the myth of Orpheus, Eurydice, and Hermes — especially Rilke's poetic treatment thereof. But this is a film to be experienced rather than analyzed. Its icily elegant tracking shots are unforgettable, and there is one astonishing

overview of the palace gardens where the symmetrical trees cast no shadows but the walking dead do. The film itself has cast a long shadow — over the closing scenes in *2001* and onwards to *The Draughtsman's Contract, Memento, Mulholland Drive*, and beyond. OT: *L'Année Derniere à Marienbad.*

4 **Yojimbo** (Akira Kurosawa. Japan, bw. A samurai (Toshiro Mifune) hired by a town to defend it against two warring factions induces the factions to destroy each other. Action-packed, elegantly photographed, and witty, it was followed by a sequel, *Sanjuro*, served as the basis for *A Fist Full of Dollars* (the first of the new-styled "spaghetti Westerns" Sergio Leone did with Clint Eastwood), and eventually influenced Leone's whole Italian-American cycle. It is nonetheless superior in almost every way to its progeny.

5 *The Manchurian Candidate* (John Frankenheimer). US, bw. In this dazzlingly unpredictable, deftly paranoid thriller, a war veteran (Laurence Harvey), brainwashed in Korea, is manipulated by his own mother (Angela Lansbury) to murder her liberal political opponents. Frank Sinatra, who co-produced and starred, had the film withdrawn for twenty-five years after the assassination of President John Kennedy. Re-released in 1987, it proved Hitchcockingly harrowing all over again.

6 *To Kill a Mockingbird* (Robert Mulligan). US, bw. Sensitive and much-loved film version of Harper Lee's novel. A Depression-era lawyer in a small Southern town (Gregory Peck AA) defends a black man falsely accused of rape, and gently teaches his children, charmingly enacted by Mary Badham and Philip Alford, about racial intolerance and justice. Robert Duvall makes his film debut as the all-but-invisible guardian angel Boo Radley.

7 ***The Miracle Worker*** (Arthur Penn). US, bw. More Americana. The true story of the partially blind Annie Sullivan (Anne Bancroft AA) teaching the young Helen Keller (Patty Duke AAS), born without sight, speech and hearing, to use her remaining senses to awake to the world around her. The two actresses had perfected their roles in a long Broadway run. Commendably unsentimental and often surprisingly violent. With Victor Jory and Inga Swenson.

8 ***Divorce - Italian Style*** (Pietro Germi). Italy, bw. Only in Italy? In a society where divorce is taboo but crimes of passion overlooked, a nobleman (Marcello Mastroianni), after considering various fantastic schemes to rid himself of his tiresome wife, finally arranges for her to be seduced, shoots her to defend his honor, receives a light sentence, and (almost) marries the woman of his choice. Five years later, *Marriage American Style* commandeered the title but nothing more, and certainly lacked Germi's sardonic touch.

9 ***The Lady with the Little Dog*** (Josef Heifitz). USSR, bw. In nineteenth-century Yalta, a brief encounter is the prelude to years of quiet desperation. An exquisite depiction of aristocratic life in Czarist Russia, and simply the finest Chekhov ever put on the screen.

10 ***Der Rosenkavalier*** (Paul Czinner) Austria, bw. More continental sentiment and sensibility. This first full-length filmed opera to have mass distribution in theaters was a revelation at the time. Today's opera DVDs are more polished, but this pioneering effort - Herbert von Karajan conducting the Vienna Philharmonic at the Salzburg Festival, with Elisabeth Schwarzkopf's famous Marschallin - remains a true landmark.

Contending for tenth place were *L'Eclisse*, *Through a Glass Darkly*, *Sundays and Cybele*, *My Name Is Ivan*, *Viridiana*, and *Long Day's Journey into Night*. It was a remarkable year for movies.

1963

1 *8½**(Federico Fellini). Italy, bw. The director films his own astonishing psychobiography. See the essay at the back of this book.

2 ***The Leopard*** (Luchino Visconti). Italy, color. Visconti's filming of Giuseppe de Lampedusa's extraordinary novel about a nineteenth-century Sicilian prince coming to terms with inevitable change was, in its 1963 American release, poorly processed, heavily cut, and execrably dubbed, and it failed with both critics and public. Now available in all its complexity and splendor, it can be clearly seen as Visconti's masterpiece and one of the great films of the sixties. The climactic forty-minute Ponteleone ball in Palermo, where a whole aristocracy waltzes through its last hour, is perhaps the finest set-piece in any film. With Burt Lancaster, Claudia Cardinale, Alain Delon, and Serge Reggiani. Winner of the Palme d'Or at Cannes.

3 ***Pickpocket*** (Robert Bresson). France, bw. Perhaps the best of Bresson's taut yet quietly powerful pieces, with a debt (unacknowledged by Bresson) to *Crime and Punishment*. This tale of a thief who may or may not walk deliberately to his imprisonment, and may or may not find redemption, seems to have grown in stature through the decades. Certainly it has had a pronounced influence on scriptwriters (notably Paul Schrader

in *Taxi Driver*) and directors (notably Louis Malle, who said "*Pickpocket* is a film of dazzling originality. On its first viewing it risks burning your eyes, so do like me - go back to see it again every day.")

4 **Tom Jones** (Tony Richardson AA). UK, color. Fielding's picaresque novel certainly comes to life here, thanks largely to its cast - Albert Finney (Tom Jones to the life), Susannah York (Sophie Western right off the page), Joyce Redmond (her suggestive eating scene with Finney achieved instant notoriety), Hugh Griffith (flamboyant, to say the least), and Edith Evans (enough said). Richardson's attempts to imitate Fielding's affectionate use of Homer via silent movie techniques are, however, often clumsy and sometimes desperate, and for some reason he tacked on an ending swiped from *The Beggar's Opera*. Oscar for best picture, three others.

5 **Winter Light** (Ingmar Bergman). Sweden, bw. A pastor (Gunnar Björnstrand) who has lost his faith engages in a series of conversations with his troubled parishioners. This is the second, and best, film in Berman's "crisis of faith" trilogy that began with *Through A Glass Darkly* and ended with *The Silence*. The Euripidean, Manichean questions asked in the first part ("What is God? Does He exist? If He exists, is He good or evil?") are here reduced to more manageable, believable, human proportions, and though no answers are provided, the film ends - starkly but unironically - as the pastor begins his evening service with one lone parishioner in attendance, praying the psalm "The earth is filled with the glory of God". Wonderful photography by Sven Nikvist. With Max von Sydow, Gunnel Lindblom and the magnificent Ingrid Thulin.

6 **Hud** (Martin Ritt). US, bw. A raw moral fable in which an arrogant, amoral Texas rancher (Paul Newman) alienates his stern father (Melvyn Douglas AAS), his adoring nephew (Brandon de Wilde), and their understanding housekeeper (Patricia Neal, AA). Fairly familiar stuff, but impressively done.

7 **The Great Escape** (John Sturges). US, color. Allied prisoners of war plan and execute their escape from a Nazi prison camp. Sturges is a past master of this sort of thing, so long as there are no *Grand Illusion* complexities to deal with. Based on fact and propelled by a rousing Elmer Bernstein theme, it has had perhaps the longest TV rerun life of recent times. With Steve McQueen, James Garner, Charles Bronson, Richard Attenborough, Donald Pleasance, and James Coburn.

8 **The Sound of Trumpets** (Ermanno Olmi). Italy, bw. A shy young man from the rural outskirts of Milan progresses from office boy to clerk in the big city. Olmi, a humanist working on a small scale, draws on his own youthful experience and gives his audience hundreds of rueful, droll, telling details about his characters, none of whom is played by a professional actor. (The charming girl became Mrs. Olmi.) John Simon called the film "as full a picture of the human show as the moving pictures have tendered." Unfortunately this sensitive little film was saddled by an insensitive American distributor with a hopelessly grandiloquent title (its Italian title, *Il Posto*, means simply *The Job*), and the public, to its loss, stayed away.

9 **America, America** (Elia Kazan). US, bw. Kazan indulged himself filming this three-hour saga of one of his Greek ancestors leaving Turkey for the land of his dreams, and what might have been the immigrant story America was waiting to see on the

screen became, in the viewing, something of a trial. A few critics lambasted it, but the Academy gave it three top nominations. A true estimate of its worth lies somewhere in between. Many scenes, photographed by Haskell Wexler, stay in the memory even after the passing of four decades.

10 *Charade* (Stanley Donen). US, color. No problems here. Musical director Donen wanted to direct a Hitchcock suspenser in his own way, and gave Cary Grant, Audrey Hepburn, and Walter Matthau roles that were tailor-made. Composer Henry Mancini even provided a "Drip-Dry Waltz" when Grant takes a shower in his suit.

Contending for tenth place was *Knife in the Water*.

1964

1 *Dr. Strangelove* (Stanley Kubrick). UK, bw. One deluded US general launches a nuclear attack on the USSR, the Soviet Doomsday machine is detonated, and the entire world is destroyed. A comedy, subtitled *How I Learned To Stop Worrying and Love the Bomb*. Kubrick clearly thought that the sane way out of the impasse we were faced with in 1964 was to laugh at ourselves. And we did, though some gentle souls among the critics held up their hands in horror. With Peter Sellers tripling as Merkin Muffley (President of the United States), Captain Mandrake (British exchange officer), and top scientist and ex-Nazi Dr. Merkwürdigliebe. Carrying on in a comic tradition as old as Aristophanes, Kubrick cast George C. Scott as Gen. "Buck" Turgidson, Sterling Hayden as Brig. Gen. Jack D. Ripper, Keenan Wynn as Col. "Bat" Guano, Slim Pickens

as Maj. "King" Kong, and Peter Bull as Russian Ambassador de Sadesky. Predictably there were no Oscars.

2 *The Umbrellas of Cherbourg* (Jacques Demy). France, color. A sweet, disarming tale of young lovers (Catherine Deneuve and Nino Castelnuovo) who are separated when he is sent away to fight in Algiers. They pledge, to a mini-Tchaikovskian tune by Michael Legrand, that they will wait for each other if it takes forever. In fact, every blessed syllable in the movie is sung, the color scheme is so carefully calculated that the lipstick matches the wallpaper, and the girl does not - in fact, cannot - wait for the boy forever. There's not a dry eye in the house when the snow whirls around the twirling Esso sign in the last scene. Charles De Gaulle took a print of this winner of the Palme d'Or at Cannes around the world to show what the French could do. For two other kinds of movie musical see the third- and fourth-place entries below.

3 *My Fair Lady* (George Cukor AA). US, color. So much first-rate talent was assembled for the filming of what was then Broadway's longest running musical (based on Shaw's *Pygmalion*) that the result - too respectful by half and occasionally even a little routine - disconcerted Jack Warner, who had been sure that replacing Julie Andrews with Audrey Hepburn would be the absobloomin'lutely loverly cherry on the top of the cake. Well, Audrey almost was. And for the rest, everyone who should be here was here - Rex Harrison (AA), Stanley Holloway, Cecil Beaton, and Lerner and Loewe – and the result was a winner in the homestretch: Oscar for best picture, seven others.

4 *Mary Poppins* (Robert Stevenson). US, color. Here, and not in *My Fair Lady*, is where Julie Andrews (AA) finally landed, umbrella in hand and Oscar within reach. Hollywood's first

original musical of any note in five years (and Disney's best in something like twenty), *Mary Poppins* was based on the English-nanny stories of P.L. Travers, and set cartoon figures infectiously interacting with Miss Andrews (who is practically perfect in every way) and Dick Van Dyke (whose Cockney accent is far from perfect, but no one on this side of the Atlantic seemed much to mind). Yes, it does run on too long, but the songs are unfailingly right, and the dance of chimney sweeps on the rooftops of London outdoes anything of its kind since René Clair took his camera across the rooftops of Paris in 1929.

5 *Zorba the Greek* (Michael Cacoyannis). US/UK, bw. A young English writer of half-Greek parentage (Alan Bates), sexless and abandoned by his muse, is converted on the island of Crete to the exuberant primitivism of a full-blooded Greek (Anthony Quinn) who spits at book-learning, dances with animal abandon, and considers it a great sin not to share the bed of any woman who wants him. An episodic but fiercely acted rendering of the novel by Nikos Kazantzakis, with an Oscar-winning performance by Lila Kedrova as an old French prostitute, a very good one from Irene Pappas as a young widow, and a famous musical score by Mikis Theodorakis.

6 *Topkapi* (Jules Dassin). US, color. From Greece to Turkey, and to one of the best caper movies ever made. An international group of thieves - including Melina Mercouri, Peter Ustinov (AAS), and Maximilian Schell - attempt to steal a jeweled dagger from the Topkapi museum in Istanbul. Fun for all, with a great end-of-career cameo by Akim Tamirov. The music this time is by Manos Hadjidakis.

7 *Marriage, Italian Style* (Vittorio de Sica) Italy, color. From Turkey to Italy, and to one of Eduardo De Filippo's much-loved Neapolitan plays (*Filamena*) got up in fine style and retitled to trade in on last year's unexpected success by Pietro Germi. With Marcello Mastroianni as the reluctant man and Sophia Loren as the prostitute determined to get him, and with de Sica directing, this was an almost guaranteed crowd-pleaser, and that is what it became.

8 *From Russia With Love* (Terence Young). UK, color. From Naples back to Istanbul. This second of the James Bond adventures to reach the screen is quite the best of the Ian Fleming lot. With Sean Connery's Mr. Bond battling with a sinister blond assassin (Robert Shaw) on a train speeding through Yugoslavia, and with Lotte Lenya, in the Venice finale, playing a spy with a really mean-spirited kick.

9 *Becket* (Peter Glenville). Henry II of England loses the love of Thomas à Becket, who has fallen in love with God. Jean Anouilh's play was filmed in and around Canterbury Cathedral and acted to the hilt by Peter O'Toole, Richard Burton, and a cast of Old Vic veterans - including John Gielgud. In essence, however, the tragic story dramatized by T.S. Eliot in *Murder in the Cathedral* is here reduced to an "end of the affair" affair between another pair of Anouilh's beautifully spoken, death-doomed lovers – a king and a meddlesome priest.

10 *The Silence* (Ingmar Bergman). Sweden, bw. The third installment of Bergman's "crisis of faith" trilogy was originally titled "God's Silence": a young boy, his mother (Gunnel Lindblom) and his aunt (Ingrid Thulin) spend a night in a strange, stifling grand hotel in an utterly foreign country where mysterious armies

marshal around them. Some of the content was shocking in 1964, and Stanley Kauffmann, detecting nine "metaphors of alienation" and sure that there were many more, added this comment: "That the film is a rebus, with clues to be hunted in it, indicates its limitations". It remains a pivotal film in the Bergman oeuvre.

Contending for tenth place were *Le Trou*, *The Fiancées*, *Night of the Iguana*, and *The Pink Panther*.

1965

1 ***Juliet of the Spirits*** (Federico Fellini). Italy, color. *8½* in color for women, and only half as impressive as its predecessor. But that leaves it with enough surreal extravagance, astonishing symbolism, visual elegance, and cinematic virtuosity to land it at the top of the list for 1965. Giulietta Masina - the real-life Mrs. Fellini and a good sport to say the least - is put on the psychiatrist's couch where her husband had lain, in *8½*, two years previously. An infectious Nino Rota score catches the spirit of it all.

2 ***The Pawnbroker*** (Sidney Lumet). US, bw. The first American film to deal in any depth with the Holocaust and its aftermath, with Rod Steiger as a concentration camp survivor in Spanish Harlem living off human misery and unable to feel any compassion after the death of his wife and children. Critics in 1965 gave the film marks for good intentions but found it melodramatic and obvious, especially when Sol Nazerman forced himself to feel pain by impaling his hand on his pawnbroker's spike - as Jesus of Nazareth was nailed to the cross. But the subliminal flashbacks of Nazi cruelty, filmed more than a third of a century before

Schindler's List and *The Pianist*, are still searingly painful, and many of the performances stay in the memory.

3 **Doctor Zhivago** (David Lean). UK/US, color. Lean's epic treatment of Boris Pasternak's novel reduces the major characters from twenty-four to eight, romanticizes its eponymous doctor almost beyond recognition, and tries, via voice-over and flashbacks, to explain much of what the original left deliberately unexplained. In addition, a starry British cast is curiously ineffective playing Russians. But, thanks to Freddie Young's extraordinary cinematography and Maurice Jarre's poetic score, there are set pieces now regarded as classic - the ice-bound journey by train across the steppes and through the mountains, the white-jacketed choir boys shot and killed in a field of waving wheat, the wolves howling at the forest edge where Yuri (Omar Sharif) hides away with Lara (Julie Christie). The first reviews, including a notorious one in *Time*, said "disaster". Eventually, though, the film made pots of money for MGM, and is fondly remembered by the millions who saw it over and over.

4 **Red Desert** (Michelangelo Antonioni). Italy, color. More Angst from Antonioni, this time not in the black-and-white patterns of *L'Avventura* but in colors suited to the city in which it is set - Ravenna, famous for its mosaics. We see gray trees and purple-rust grass, lurid red walls, puffs of poisonous yellow flame - colors patterned to express fear, desire and neurosis. With Monica Vitti and Richard Harris. Winner of the Golden Lion at Venice. OT: *Il Deserto Rosso*.

5 **Kwaidan** (Masaki Kobayashi). Japan, Color. Four ghost stories set in medieval Japan, filmed in stunningly beautiful colors. Addicts of western-style gothics may feel that the colors, stylization, and

deliberate pacing undercut the horror. The second story, deleted in the first North American release, is restored on DVD.

6 **Woman in the Dunes** (Hiroshi Teshigahara). Japan, bw. A horror story from contemporary Japan: a vacationing entomologist stumbles on a remote fishing village, spends the night with a mysterious widow in a huge sandpit, and finds in the morning that he is a prisoner there. His and our initial disquiet turns to panicky fear. The outstanding cinematography, capturing the textures of human flesh and shifting sand in extreme close-ups, may suggest a number of readings about the nature of freedom, but in the end the film seems determined to defy analysis.

7 **Darling** (John Schlesinger). UK, bw. The rise of an ambitious, constitutionally unhappy fashion model (Julie Christie AA) in London's swinging sixties. Expertly done and a big commercial success, it's a matter of "flashy then, faded now." With Dirk Bogarde and Laurence Harvey.

8 **Ship of Fools** (Stanley Kramer). US, bw. Drastically simplified but still overlong film version of Katherine Anne Porter's heavily symbolic shipboard novel, with remarkable performances by Oscar Werner and Simone Signoret and very good ones by Vivien Leigh and Lee Marvin, each of them characters sailing towards uncertain futures in 1933 Germany.

9 **The Ipcress File** (Sidney J. Furie). UK, color. Michael Caine plays a secret agent, a bespectacled, working-class James Bond, whose name, Harry Palmer, became for a time even as well known as Mr. Bond's. Funny, twisty, and filmed as inventively as all get out.

10 ***The Sound of Music*** (Robert Wise). US, color. On Broadway, this melodious Rodgers and Hammerstein musical about the singing von Trapp family benefited from professional pacing. On the screen, you sometimes want to get out and push. Fortunately, director Wise remembered how effective his overhead camera was in *West Side Story*, and his opening scene here, with Julie Andrews caroling the title song, has become a classic. The picture was and remains a top-grossing crowd-pleaser. Ask Mr. von Trapp, glum Christopher Plummer. He'll tell you.

Contending for tenth place were *Repulsion*, *Gertrud*, and *The Knack*.

1966

1 ***A Man for All Seasons*** (Fred Zinnemann AA). UK, color. In adapting his successful play for the screen, Robert Bolt eliminated his stage commentator, the Common Man, and expanded the imagery - ships, currents, tides, navigation - that he said "no one noticed" in the play. So the lordly Thames, with its swans and willows, its fresh lawns and old Tudor houses, and its boats great and small, becomes the all-encompassing visual image of the film. Paul Scofield (AA) repeats his celebrated portrayal of Sir Thomas More, and Robert Shaw plays a handsome young Henry VIII. With Orson Welles, Wendy Hiller, Leo McKern, and, in another of director Zinnemann's patented wordless scenes, Vanessa Redgrave as Anne Boleyn. Oscar for best picture, five others.

2 ***Who's Afraid of Virginia Woolf?*** (Mike Nichols). US, bw. Edward Albee's four-character play was less successful than *A Man*

For All Seasons in its transfer to film, but cynics who said it was nothing more than a breakthrough for four-letter words on the screen were wrong. Richard Burton and Elizabeth Taylor (AA) are brazenly, bitterly effective in their all-night shouting match, and we cringe and cower with George Segal and Sandy Dennis (AAS) as we watch. An auspicious debut for director Nichols.

3 **Blow-Up** (Michelangelo Antonioni). UK, Italy, color. Less Angst from Antonioni this time, and more enigma. A swinging London photographer (David Hemmings) thinks he may have found evidence for a murder in some pictures he has taken of a fashion model (Vanessa Redgrave). This is the only one of the director's films to reach a wide audience. Perhaps it was the Hitchcockian surface that drew viewers, perhaps it was the then-shocking nudity, perhaps it was even some interest in puzzling out the meanings. (The mystery is never solved.) Palm d'Or at Cannes.

4 **Morgan!** (Karel Reisz). UK, bw. A Cockney bohemian (David Warner), fascinated with gorillas and Karl Marx, tries to win back the wife (Vanessa Redgrave) who has had quite enough of his oafish ways. (The subtitle calls Morgan "a suitable case for treatment.") Critics were divided, but young people, especially swinging Londoners, thought it screamingly funny, and much of it is: When Morgan threatens to run off to Greece, his mother asks in bewilderment, "I mean, what is there *in* Greece?"

5 **Georgy Girl** (Silvio Narizzano), UK, bw. Still more from swinging London, this time with Vanessa Redgrave's sister, Lynn, as a childlike, not-very-slim girl attracted to her roommate's boy friend (Alan Bates) but pursued instead by her aging employer (James Mason). Obviously trendy, almost as madcap as *Morgan!*,

and as troublesome to the censor as was *Who's Afraid of Virginia Woolf.*

6 *Alfie* (Lewis Gilbert). UK, color. Michael Caine plays yet another swinging Londoner, boasting of his sexual savvy straight into the camera, but finally, in a brutally real moment, learning humility and compassion. With Vivien Merchant, Shelley Winters, Denholm Elliott, and a title tune that announced the arrival of songwriter Burt Bacharach. The picture, thought tawdry and off-putting by some in 1966, is fondly remembered today, even after an ineffective re-filming in 2004.

7 *The Gospel According to Matthew* (Pier-Paulo Pasolini). Italy, bw. A doctrinaire though unquestionably sincere life of Christ by an Italian communist. Jesus is a slim and steely-eyed student preaching only the revolutionary elements of the gospel and all but identified with Eisenstein's Alexander Nevsky. There is just as much phony artiness - tableaux that simulate Renaissance paintings, great music played at curiously inappropriate times - as in any Hollywood epic. But there are many good homely touches - Joseph's bristly face drawn in anxiety as he realizes that his bride is with Child; barefoot fishermen running, too fast for the camera, to follow their Master; wind, sand, and flies everywhere - even on Christ's body in the tomb. Dedicated by Pasolini to "the dear, familiar memory of John XXIII".

8 *The Bible* (John Huston). US, color. While it only fitfully touches on the power and beauty of the archetypal tales of *Genesis*, some of Huston's film has the requisite storybook sense of wonder, and he himself is irresistible as Noah, pied-piping the animals two-by-two into the Ark, puckishly splashing milk down the yawning maw of a lazy hippo, and bidding good-by to his

animals after the flood, as prancing giraffes and lumbering turtles make off into a rainbow-arched landscape. In a largely ineffective cast, Richard Harris and Franco Nero are Cain and Abel, and George C. Scott and Ava Gardner are Abraham and Sarah.

9 ***The Shop on Main Street*** (Jan Kadar). Czechoslovakia, bw. Widely cited as the best foreign language film shown in America in 1966 (the Academy agreed), this bittersweet parable is both an affectionate portrait of life in a provincial Slovak town and an indictment of those who did not oppose the fascist deportation of Jews. Some of the first half is clompingly pedestrian; Ida Kaminska, as an old Jewess who comes to a tragic end, illuminates the rest.

10 ***Shakespeare Wallah*** (James Ivory). India, bw. Desultory tale of a down-at-the-heel Shakespearean troupe touring India after the Raj. This first collaboration of the Ismael Merchant/James Ivory/Ruth Prawer Jhabvala team already has some of the special qualities that mark their later work - literacy, understatement, and close observation of a culture undergoing change. The musical score, people are always surprised to note, is by Satyajit Ray. Hardly a masterpiece, although *Newsweek*, perhaps weary of religious movies, swinging London, and four-letter-words, thought it the best film of 1966 – which was, in the end, a rather ordinary year.

Contending for tenth place were *A Man and a Woman, Grand Prix*, and *The Good, the Bad, and the Ugly*.

1967

1 ***Persona*** (Ingmar Bergman). Sweden, bw. A famous actress (Liv Ullman) who has lost the will to speak is tended by a nurse (Bibi Anderson) who begins to reveal her own emotional problems, discovers from a letter that the actress is studying her with amusement, grows violent, and suffers a breakdown herself. In a series of surprising emotional and psychological twists, Bergman, assisted by his masterly cameraman, Sven Nykvist, all but makes Ullman and Anderson into one *persona*. Both performances are superb. Self-awareness is perhaps the main subject of this challenging film, which begins and ends with images that indicate that the film is itself aware that it is a film. Virtual quotations from *The Seventh Seal*, *Wild Strawberries*, and *Through A Glass Darkly* assure us that it is a film by Ingmar Bergman.

2 ***The Battle of Algiers*** (Gillo Pontercorvo). Algiers/ Italy, bw. An astonishingly detailed reconstruction of the terrorist uprising against the French in Algiers in 1954, combining the immediacy of a newsreel with the excitement of an adventure film while all the time remaining completely *sui generis*. Winner of the Golden Lion at Venice even though its showing there was protested by the French, who had banned it in their own country. It has become something of a textbook for revolutionary – and terrorist - movements ever since. The Pentagon, on the *qui vive*, screened it after 9/11.

3 ***Bonnie and Clyde*** (Arthur Penn). US, color. Innovative, trend-setting filming of the desperate career of the Depression's

most notorious bank robbers, with Warren Beatty as Clyde and with a trio of promising newcomers - Faye Dunaway as Bonnie, and Gene Hackman and Estelle Parsons (AAS) as partners in crime. The film's slow-motion shots of the couple writhing under a hail of bullets began a new vogue for violence on the screen. Some prominent scribes were initially hostile but changed their minds and publicly recanted when the film was enthusiastically received by younger critics and audiences. Bosley Crowther of *The New York Times* wrote two scathing reviews, was invited to retire, and did. Things were changing.

4 ***The Graduate*** (Mike Nichols AA). US, color. The film that, perhaps more than any other, summed up the feelings of young people in the sixties. Naïve Benjamin (Dustin Hoffman in his first major role), insecure and uncertain of his future, is seduced by a family friend, Mrs. Robinson (Anne Bancroft), and finally throws off all allegiances and rejects all conformist values when he falls in love with, and marries, her daughter. The picture has survived its time, and is remembered fondly by the aging baby boomers to whom it originally spoke. The songs by Simon and Garfinkel, carefully worked into the picture, now have enormous nostalgic appeal.

5 ***In the Heat of the Night*** (Norman Jewison). US, color. In this effective statement against racial prejudice, a black police officer from Philadelphia (Sidney Poitier) grudgingly helps a red-neck sheriff in Mississippi (Rod Steiger AA) to solve a murder. The two actors gave their characters such dimension that, even after a variety of sequels, imitations, and rip-offs, their performances – iconic performances of the sixties - stay vividly in the memory. Oscar for best picture, three others.

6 ***Chimes at Midnight*** (Orson Welles). Spain/ Switzerland, bw. Orson Welles, surmounting unimaginable difficulties with funding and filming, plays Falstaff to the Prince Hal of Keith Baxter in his own adaptation of Shakespeare's *Henry IV* plays. With John Gielgud, Margaret Rutherford, and Jeanne Moreau. Seldom were critics more sharply divided. Some of the film comes close to ideal, some of it is spoiled by inept dubbing and camera work, and never is it quite so good or so bad as both critics and audiences have found it. Alternate title: *Falstaff.*

7 ***Cool Hand Luke*** (Stuart Rosenberg). US, color. Indomitable Luke (Paul Newman), a convict sentenced to two year's hard labor in a chain gang, becomes a legend among the other prisoners. With George Kennedy (AA) and Jo Van Fleet, and with Strother Martin as the sadistic guard whose phrase, "What we have here is a failure to communicate" was used as a slogan by both sides of the sixties generation gap.

8 ***Far From the Madding Crowd*** (John Schlesinger). UK, color. A widescreen adaptation of the Thomas Hardy novel set in windswept Wessex, with Julie Christie as the headstrong Bathsheba Everdene confronting her three men, played by Alan Bates, Terence Stamp, and Peter Finch. We've since become accustomed to seeing this sort of thing on TV's "Masterpiece Theater", but seldom with such luxuriant casting and such skillful photography as is here provided by Nicholas Roeg - where a flock of sheep appears to hang quite literally on a steep hillside.

9 ***Closely Watched Trains*** (Jiri Menzel). Czechoslovakia, bw. The sexual problems, personal failures, and tragic death of a young train dispatcher in a Czech village during World War II. Proof positive, after *The Shop on Main Street*, that Czech filmmakers

had quite a bit to say about human nature and that Czech films had definitely arrived on the world scene. Several more by other directors followed. Oscar for best foreign film.

10 *Ulysses* (Joseph Strick). UK, bw. A brave - some said foolhardy - stab at putting one of the longest, densest, bawdiest, and wordiest novels of the century on film, a stream-of-consciousness challenge that even Eisenstein had balked at. Much of it works as a movie, thanks to Barbara Jefford, Milo O'Shea, and the precedent set by Fellini's pioneering *8½*. Shot on location in Ireland, the film was banned there and elsewhere for its "indecent" language. Strick went on to film Joyce's *Portrait of the Artist as a Young Man*, but wisely never attempted *Finnegans Wake*.

Contending for tenth place was *Guess Who's Coming To Dinner*.

1968

1 *2001: A Space Odyssey* (Stanley Kubrick). UK, color. We watch in awe as, through four million years, man, with the compliance of a mysterious monolith, evolves from ape to human to whatever it is that will be the next evolutionary stage - while an almost omniscient computer named HAL desperately tries to prevent the human journey towards a state of intelligence higher than its own. Kubrick wrote the pioneering script with sci-fi guru Arthur C. Clarke. MGM panicked when it saw the rushes, pop music mavens were confounded when classical music ("The Blue Danube" and "Also Sprach Zarathustra", by two unrelated Strausses) topped the charts, and pot heads went wild over the Jupiter-landing light-show long before consternated critics saw

anything in the picture to admire. (It must be admitted that the dialogue and acting in the early scenes do seem like what John Simon called "unintended stupidity".)   In any case, within a few years all doubts were qualmed. *2001* - mind-bending, eerily beautiful, and vastly influential - was so easily the only great movie of 1968 that the Academy denied it a nomination for best picture.

2 **War and Peace** (Sergei Bondarchuk) USSR, color.   A truly spectacular dramatization of Tolstoy's novel, five years in production and six hours in the viewing (seven in the country of its origin, where it was made in celebration of the fiftieth anniversary of the Soviet Union). The ballroom scene, the battle of Borodino, and Napoleon's retreat through the snow are all impressively done. "Missing," said Richard Schickel, "is Tolstoy's fascinating theory of history, as well as the Christian message he was propagating (neither fits Marxist theory very well), and without this intellectual and moral underpinning the film lacks power and purpose." Director Bondarchuk is inadequate as Pierre, and the ballet dancer who enacts Natasha has little of the lightness of being that Audrey Hepburn radiated in King Vidor's 1956 version. But virtually every movie technique known to man is put to dazzling use here, and even poor dubbing could not keep the picture from winning the best foreign film Oscar.

3 *The Hour of the Wolf* (Ingmar Bergman). Sweden, bw. Dark, difficult, underrated Bergman study of an artist on a lonely island who is terrorized at the hour before dawn by the dreams and memories that have helped him produce his masterpieces. The film owes something to the fantastic tales of E.T.A. Hoffmann, and its brief puppet-theater scene from Mozart's *The Magic Flute* is more mysterious and telling than the whole of Bergman's subsequent

filming of that opera. The names of the artist's wife, Anna, and his mistress, Vogler, are those of the two main characters in the film's predecessor in the Bergman oeuvre, *Persona*, and the two masterpieces gain from being seen in tandem. The photography by Sven Nykvist and the performances by Bergman's repertory company (Max von Sydow, Liv Ullmann, Ingrid Thulin, and Erland Josephson) are predictably fine.

4 ***Rosemary's Baby*** (Roman Polanski). US, color. Riveting cinema version of Ira Levin's novel: a New York actor ambitious for better roles offers his uncomprehending young wife (Mia Farrow) to a coven of influential devil worshippers so that she can bear Satan's baby. Unlike standard horror stuff, this really does draw on primal fears. Polanski's cool approach keeps it all this side of overboard. John Cassavetes, Ruth Gordon, Sidney Blackmer, Ralph Bellamy, and Maurice Evans couldn't be more quietly eerie in their roles, and anyone in the audience who isn't pulling for Miss Farrow must himself be in league with the devil.

5 ***Bullitt*** (Peter Yates). US, color. Taut, stylish cop thriller with deft performances from Steve McQueen, Jacqueline Bisset, and Robert Vaughn. The highlight is a car chase through the steep streets of San Francisco, more thrilling even than the famous chase under the New York elevated railway in *The French Connection*.

6 ***Hot Millions*** (Eric Till). UK, color. The sleeper of the year, with Peter Ustinov as a lovable confidence man and Maggie Smith as a clueless meter maid who can play the flute solo from Gluck's *Orpheus and Eurydice* from memory. Pure pleasure.

7 ***Oliver!*** (Carol Reed). UK, color. The exclamation point hopefully attached (à la *Oklahoma!*) to the London stage musical's

title really means something in the film's title. Who would have thought that a jolly romp through Dickensian misery, overproduced and with only a smattering of good songs, could challenge David Lean's memorably atmospheric *Oliver Twist* of twenty years before? Astonishingly, in his first and only big studio musical, Reed's way with children (cf. *The Fallen Idol*) and his meticulous attention to detail (cf. *The Third Man*) pay off, after years of second-rate work. Joseph Morgenstern, a critic who hadn't yet figured out what *2001* was all about, exclaimed, "*Oliver!* redeems the whole rotten year." The Academy, on the same wavelength, agreed, and gave it the Oscar for best picture.

8 *Yellow Submarine* (George Dunning). UK, color. An insouciant, surprisingly successful, swinging-sixties cartoon in which the Beatles save a Pepperland of love and music from the philistine attacks of the Blue Meanies. Only a few torpedo-puns miss their mark. Lots of familiar ditties. Oodles of op, pop, and other quasi-crazy artistic styles.

9 *Fist in His Pocket* (Marco Bellocchio) Italy, bw. The startling debut film of Bellocchio (preceded in North America by the almost-as-startling *China is Near*). It was thought that a major talent had appeared, but over the years the director's work became so idiosyncratic and overheated that it has had difficulty finding its way around the world. This melodramatic story of a troubled Italian family remains the best of Bellocchio. Terrific performance by Lou Castel as the epileptic son.

10 *The Lion in Winter* (Anthony Harvey). It's Christmas in Chinon, and time (1183) for the king and queen to swap anachronistic Broadway wisecracks. Peter O'Toole and Katherine Hepburn (AA) sink their teeth deep into their roles and bite ham.

Anthony Hopkins, in his film debut, looks understandably glum, and director Harvey seems more interested in his zoom lens than in disciplining his performers. Some critics were appalled, others (in New York!) voted it the best film of the year. Well, *2001* apart, it wasn't much of a year. So *The Lion* loomed large.

Contending for tenth place were *Mouchette*, *Belle de Jour*, *Isadora*, and *Once upon a Time in the west*.

1969

1 *The Wild Bunch* (Sam Peckinpah). US, color. Awesome turn-of-the-century Western that, in Stanley Kaufmann's words, "enlarged the form aesthetically, thematically, demonically." It also set a new high, if that is the word, in slow-motion screen violence: the film begins and ends with bloodbaths indebted to, but going beyond, the carnage in Kurosawa's *Seven Samurai* and the shocking evening news coverage of the then-raging Vietnam War. With William Holden, Robert Ryan, Ernest Borgnine, Ben Johnson, and Edmund O'Brien. Student filmmakers on American campuses loved it. The establishment hated it. No Oscars.

2 *The Bailiff* (Kenji Mizoguchi). Japan, bw. Luminously photographed saga of an eleventh-century Japanese family: the father is exiled, the mother and her two children set out in search of him and are kidnapped, the mother is forced into prostitution, and the boy and girl are enslaved to a cruel bailiff. Some forty years later, you may not remember what happens thereafter in the story, but you do remember being immensely moved. Alternate title: *Sansho the Bailiff.*

3 *Midnight Cowboy* (John Schlesinger AA). US, color. Joe Buck (Jon Voigt), a naïve cowboy unable to make it as a high-priced stud in New York, befriends Ratso Rizzo (Dustin Hoffmann), a tubercular con artist fallen on hard times, and gets him to Florida before he dies. The two actors show unusual skill in enlisting audience sympathy for the unsavory characters they play, and director Schlesinger conveys the rancid atmosphere of Manhattan sex joints and cheap hotels with chilling realism. Somehow all of this is conjured up again whenever Harry Nilsson's "Everybody's Talkin'" gets a spin on the radio. The only X-rated film ever to win the Oscar for best picture.

4 *The Red and the White* (Miklós Jancsó) Hungary, bw. The chaotic clash of revolutionary Reds and Czarist Whites in 1919, filmed almost as a nightmare vision in stunning black and white, using every inch of the big cinemascope screen with stunning virtuosity. Banned for many years in the USSR. Jancsó's fascination with horses and uniforms is also evident in another impressive film released here in 1969, *The Roundup*.

5 *The Wanderer* (Jean-Pierre Albicoco). France, color. Color photography as stunning as Jansco's black and white limns two different worlds in this filming of *Le Grand Meaulnes*, Alain-Fournier's novel about a schoolboy's mystical experiences. The director's father, Quinto Albicoco, used wire mesh and discs to dazzling effect for the phantasmagoric visions, while his real-world pictures (Alain-Fournier's native village was used) glow by night and shimmer like water colors by day. But filming directly from a literary classic left audiences who had not read the book anchorless.

6 ***The Prime of Miss Jean Brodie*** (Ronald Neame). UK, color. The film adaptation of Muriel Spark's wry, perceptive novel about an Edinburgh schoolmistress who plays favorites among, and has devastating effects on the lives of, the girls she teaches. Effective performances by Maggie Smith (AA), Celia Johnson, Robert Stephens, and Gordon Jackson.

7 ***La Femme Infidèle*** (Claude Chabrol). France, color. A firmly controlled psychological thriller from the director who happily acknowledged his indebtedness to Hitchcock but usually went beyond the master emotionally: getting rid of the corpse is the main problem for the cuckolded husband, but for his wife (Stéphane Audran) the concern is that, after the murder, she discovers that her love for her husband has come alive again.

8 ***Z*** (Costa-Gavras). France/Algeria, color. A fast-paced political thriller based on events following an assassination in Greece during the time of the colonels. An international sensation in 1969, it seems now to have lost the excitement it had when it was, as the phrase goes, ripped from the headlines. With Jean-Louis Trintignant, Yves Montand, and Irene Pappas. Oscar for best foreign film.

9 ***Butch Cassidy and the Sundance Kid*** (George Roy Hill). US, color. A box office bonanza that tells much the same story as *The Wild Bunch*, but with coy and sometimes off-putting humor. With the new male-bonding duo, Paul Newman and Robert Redford, as the two legendary outlaws, and a fetching Burt Bacharach tune, "Raindrops Keep Fallin' on my Head."

10 ***Simon of the Desert*** (Luis Buñuel), Mexico, bw. A fifth-century saint who preaches atop a column is approached by a

series of Buñuelesque figures, including the devil in female guise. In a sudden ending (reportedly tacked on when financial problems would not allow Buñuel to complete the film as originally contemplated), the saint is discovered in a Manhattan beatnik den contemplating the incomprehensible chaos around him. For some, Buñuel's forty-minute film as just another surreal attack on Catholicism. Others are not so sure: this is the director who said "Thank God I am still an atheist."

Contending for tenth place were *The Roundup*, *Lola Montes*, *Popi*, and *Easy Rider*.

The 1970s

1970

1 *My Night at Maud's* (Eric Rohmer). France, bw. The third and best of the director's "Six Moral Tales". A high-minded young Catholic (Jean-Louis Trintignant) spends a virginal night talking about life and love with the enchantingly unbelieving Maud (Françoise Fabian) and then woos the girl (Marie-Christine Barrault) he has seen at morning Mass. Something of a demonstration of Pascal's famous wager, this perceptive and highly sophisticated film became an unexpected art-house hit in America. With luminous photography by Nestor Almendros and with a Mozart violin sonata (played by Leonid Kogan) to start the ideas flowing. 1970 was a big year in America for unlikely films from France. See three more entries and one runner-up below. OT: *Ma Nuit Chez Maud.*

2 *Au Hasard Balthazar* (Robert Bresson). France/ Sweden, bw. A stinging, unsettling Christian parable about, *mirabile dictu*, a donkey, filmed by the world's most austere director with a cast of non-professionals. Gentle Balthazar passes from master to master, loved by some, maltreated by others, patiently and humbly enduring, witnessing all manner of human misery, his eyes intimating an understanding humans do not have. Perhaps inspired the donkey episode in Dostoevsky's *The Idiot*, and certainly enhanced by the pervasive use of Schubert's A Minor piano sonata. As always, Bresson's narrative is episodic and elliptical, and his real subject is the human soul. The final scene is unforgettable.

3 **Patton** (Franklin Schaffner AA). US, color. George C. Scott (AA), in a bombs-away overture of a speech before an immense American flag, rivets our attention at the very start of this bio on the most aggressive of World War II American generals (a most unusual subject for the hippie era), and maintains interest for the entire length of the almost three-hour film by convincing us that he *is* that general as much as that general thought he was Hannibal. With Karl Malden as Omar Bradley. Oscar for best picture, six others.

4 *M*A*S*H** (Robert Altman) US, color. Different war, different times. As hip as, in 1970, *Patton* was square:three medical cut-ups and one hopeless misfit at a Mobile Army Surgical Hospital unit in Korea save lives while the war is busy destroying them. The anti-establishment attitudes of Ring Lardner Jr.'s script, heightened by Altman's breezy directorial style, appealed mightily to opponents of the war in Vietnam, and four virtual unknowns - Donald Sutherland, Elliott Gould, Tom Skerritt, and Robert Duvall - jump-started their careers. The long-running TV series, now more familiar than the film itself, soft-pedaled the satire considerably; the film is a black comedy seriously mad at the madness of war. Palme d'Or at Cannes.

5 **The Wild Child** (François Truffaut). France, bw. A French scientist, played by Truffaut himself, takes custody of a boy who has been living wild in the forest and brings him to the brink of speech and moral awareness. Straightforwardly filmed, and dedicated to Jean-Pierre Léaud, who had played the troubled boy in Truffaut's *The 400 Blows*. OT: *L'Enfant Sauvage*.

6 **The Rise of Louis XIV** (Roberto Rossellini). France, color. The Italian neo-realist director made several semi-documentaries

on historical subjects for French television in the seventies, and this, commercially released in America, is the best of them. A psychological study of a man seizing power and maintaining it through ceremony and spectacle, it is also, through its realistically detailed depiction of the period, neo-realism of a kind. OT: *La Prise de Pouvoir par Louis XIV.*

7 **Women In Love** (Ken Russell). UK, color. D.H. Lawrence's novel about two English women having their first sexual experiences is filmed by an erratic director who, just this once, stays under the top and puts his considerable talent for pictorial composition to good use. Glenda Jackson (AA) attracted a good deal of attention, but the most buzz was about the nude wrestling scene between Alan Bates and Oliver Reed. It was reckless Russell out-Lawrencing Lawrence.

8 **Five Easy Pieces** (Bob Rafelson). US, color. 1970's very sixties character study of an alienated dropout who drifts from a California oil rig to his Puget Sound family and eventually turns his back on both. Jack Nicholson lets every raw emotion explode. A half dozen other characters are acutely observed. What the "five easy pieces" are is anybody's guess. The Chopin E-minor prelude is one. The characters sharply played by Karen Black and Susan Anspach might make two more...

9 **I Never Sang For My Father** (Gilbert Cates). US, color. When his mother dies, a middle aged man (Gene Hackman) must decide whether to move away to marry the woman he loves or to take on the responsibility of caring for the father (Melvyn Douglas) who has never loved him. An almost unbearably painful and cleansing experience for many viewers, with two remarkable performances. Adapted by Robert Anderson from his play.

10 ***Fellini Satyricon*** (Federico Fellini). Italy, color. The director of *8½* films the bawdy two-thousand-year-old picaresque novel by Petronius, Nero's arbiter of elegance. It should have been a magical meeting of talents across twenty centuries, and some of it is. But, despite many stunning visual compositions, the suspicion keeps nagging away that Fellini actually disapproves of the lewd classic he has chosen to adapt. What was light and lively in the original - "Trimalchio's Dinner", for example - becomes decadent and distasteful in Fellini's hands. Alberto Moravia told him he had the moral sense of a Catholic schoolboy. (Fellini might have profited from seeing *My Night at Maud's*.)

Contending for tenth place were *This Man Must Die* and *The Private Life of Sherlock Holmes*.

1971

1 ***Death in Venice*** (Luchino Visconti). Italy, color. Thomas Mann's short story about a high-minded German intellectual who finds himself falling in love with a Polish boy on the Lido - and risking the plague to prolong his distanced, aesthetic passion - is filmed very slowly and elaborately in Venice by one of the masters of cinema. Dirk Bogarde is close to perfect as Gustav von Aschenbach, but the decision to change his occupation from writer to composer leads to some confusing flashbacks, and his Tadzio is overage and off-puttingly effeminate. Music by Gustav Mahler, who may well have been Mann's model for the smitten intellectual.

2 *The Conformist* (Bernardo Bertolucci). Italy/France/ West Germany, color. Alberto Moravia's novel about a repressed homosexual in Rome attempting to conform to established Fascism and caught in a strange sequence of events. Bertolucci, thought at the time the man most likely to inherit Visconti's mantle, deals largely in metaphor. Plato is, surprisingly, the main metaphor here. With Jean-Louis Tritingant and Dominque Sanda. OT: *Il Conformista*.

3 *The Sorrow and the Pity* (Marcel Ophuls). Switzerland/ France/West Germany, color. A soul-searching, unbiased, four-and-a-half-hour documentary about France during the Nazi occupation, drawn from interviews with Albert Speer, Anthony Eden, Pierre Mendès-France, and scores of citizens, soldiers, writers, collaborators, resistance fighters, and ordinary townspeople from Clermont-Ferrand. Ophuls, far from being a mere investigative reporter like Claude Lelouche in the later *Shoah*, invites us to ask ourselves what we might have done in the same circumstances. Possibly the most valuable of all screen documentaries.

4 *The French Connection* (William Friedkin AA). US, color. Nice guy Gene Hackman was the seventh choice for the role of "Popeye" Doyle, a brutal New York cop tracking down drug smugglers, and he won a career-changing Oscar for it. Friedkin's on-location shooting is impressive, and the famous car chase is great edge-of-your-seat stuff. The real-life "Popeye" Doyle, Eddie Egan, plays a bit part. With Fernando Rey and Roy Scheider. Oscar for best picture, four others.

5 *Le Boucher* (Claude Chabrol). France, color. In a provincial French town, a butcher haunted by his war experiences meets a schoolteacher hurt by a previous love affair. She is fascinated by

the way this village Cro-Magnon carves a roast. Meanwhile there are three shocking murders... One of the best of Chabrol's subtle psychological thrillers. With Stéphane Audran (from Chabrol's *La Femme Infidele*) and Jean Yanne (from Chabrol's *This Man Must Die*).

6 **Claire's Knee** (Eric Rohmer). France, color. The fifth of Rohmer's "Six Moral Fables", with conversations almost as witty and probing as those in *My Night at Maud's*. Beautifully photographed by Nestor Almendros on Lake Geneva. One of the young men is played by the son of Falconetti, the star of *The Passion of Joan of Arc*.

7 **The Go-Between** (Joseph Losey). UK, color. A twelve-year-old English lad carries love letters between a farmer (Alan Bates) and gentrified girl (Julie Christie). Sophisticated movie-making, with especially inventive use of color and sound, a score by Michel Legrande, and with Margaret Leighton and Michael Redgrave in support. Visconti was incredulous when it beat out his *Death in Venice* to win the Palme d'Or at Cannes.

8 **The Last Picture Show** (Peter Bogdanovich). US, bw. For this end-of-an-era story of a Texas movie house showing its last movie, Bogdanovich, a movie critic turned director, wanted a nostalgic fifties look, and used black-and-white. He gets good performances from Ellen Burstyn and Jeff Bridges, and Oscar-winning ones by Chloris Leachman and veteran Ben Johnson, both in supporting roles. Johnson delivers the movie's signature speech with touching authority, but almost all of the others seem to be taking off their clothes more than is necessary, and there was nothing very fifties, cinematically speaking, about that. The last picture show, by the way, is Howard Hawks' *Red River*.

9 *Sunday, Bloody Sunday* (John Schlesinger). UK, color. A bisexual triangle with both Peter Finch and Glenda Jackson in love with Peter Head. The script, by *New Yorker* critic Penelope Gilliat, is intelligent and compassionate. The problem is that it is impossible to believe that either of the high-powered stars could ever have been interested in any way in the lackluster Mr. Head. But it certainly was easy to believe, from their performances, that he might, like the rest of us, admire them.

10 *The Garden of the Finzi-Continis* (Vittorio de Sica). Italy/West Germany, color. Poignant, unsentimental story of a Jewish family in Rome, living in luxury's lap and inevitably, with the arrival of Fascism, headed for extermination. Unfortunately the plot that supports this is not really equal to the demands put on it. With Dominque Sanda and Helmut Berger.

There were no contenders for tenth place.

1972

1 *The Godfather* (Francis Ford Coppola). US, color. Mario Puzo's compulsively readable best seller about a Mafia patriarch and his sons, brought vividly and violently to the screen by a young director enjoying his first big success (and who co-wrote the script with author Puzo.) The three-hour picture jump-started the careers of Al Pacino and Robert Duvall, was a comeback success for Marlon Brando (AA) and, both critically and at the box office, simply swept everything before it. It was only a matter of months before a *Godfather II* was planned (and a matter of fifteen years before an ill-advised *Godfather III* appeared). With James Caan,

John Cazale and, some distance behind the others, Diane Keaton. Oscar for best picture, two others.

2 *Tokyo Story* (Yasujiro Ozu). Japan, bw. The best loved and most critically praised of the more than fifty films turned out by a director who for the better part of a lifetime produced beautifully observed, quietly moving pictures about life in twentieth-century Japan, often (as in *Late Spring, Early Summer,* and *Late Autumn*) attuned to seasonal changes. Here an old couple travel from the provinces to Tokyo to visit their married children and their son's widow (the radiant Setsuko Hara). The elders find disappointment at almost every turn, accept that quietly as a part of life, and return home to die. Nothing further from *The Godfather* and its family could be imagined. Yet the films are of comparable stature. Made in 1953, it took almost two decades for the subtle, elliptical, and in the end very perceptive *Tokyo Story* to reach these shores.

3 *The Emigrants* (Jan Troell). Sweden, color. The first part of yet another family story - that of 19th-century Swedish emigrants crossing the Atlantic and staking a claim in Minnesota. Epic in scope but lyric in treatment, perhaps overly long at two-and-a-half hours, it was followed next year by *The New Land,* equal in length, more accomplished in its story-telling, and with Max von Sydow and Liv Ullmann surpassing even the fine performances they give here. Nominated by the Academy for best picture - only the third foreign language film to be so honored.

4 *Two English Girls* (François Truffaut). France, color. The French New Wave director casts his alter ego, Jean-Pierre Léaud, in a story by the author of *Jules and Jim*: a young 19th-century novelist meets an English girl in Paris, visits her in Wales, falls in love with her sister there, and a ménage not unlike that in

Jules and Jim results, but with a melancholy rather than a tragic outcome. Superb photography by Nestor Almendros.

5 **Deliverance** (John Boorman). US, color. An apocalyptic parable about four suburbanites (Jon Voigt, Burt Reynolds, Ned Beatty, and Ronny Cox) proving their manhood by canoeing down a rushing river in the frightening backwoods of Georgia. The trip becomes one of unexpected horror and self-discovery. With author James Dickey as a local sheriff. Graced by the bluegrass hit "Dueling Banjoes".

6 **Cabaret** (Bob Fosse AA). US, color. This X-rated film version of the Broadway musical uses the plot of John Van Druten's play *I Am a Camera* to the disadvantage of the original material from Christopher Isherwood's *Goodbye to Berlin*. That means that an American (Liza Minelli AA) can sing and dance her way through the role of the English Sally Bowles, and an Englishman (Michael York) can play the Yank she toys with. Fosse seems impatient with the script but handles the dance numbers with tremendous verve, and preserves almost intact the remarkable stage performance of Joel Grey (AA). The Kander-Ebb songs, including the newly written "The Money Song", are performed not as "book" numbers advancing the plot and detailing character but as stage performances. (It seemed as if we had moved at last beyond Rodgers and Hammerstein.) Eight Oscars, but the best picture award went, after some moments of suspense, to *The Godfather*.

7 **Sounder** (Martin Ritt). US, color. Ground-breaking film about a family of black sharecroppers in 1930s Louisiana surviving when the father is sent to prison for a minor offense. Filmed with immense sympathy by director Ritt, who gets moving performances from Paul Winfield and Cecily Tyson.

8 **The Discreet Charm of the Bourgeoisie** (Luis Buñuel). France/Spain/Italy, color. Amusing, half-surreal parable about six bourgeois socialites forever prevented from enjoying their dinner parties. Buñuel, in the final phase of his career, decided to relax and have a good time behind the camera. With perennials Fernando Rey and Stéphane Audran. Oscar for best foreign film.

9 **The Heartbreak Kid** (Elaine May). US, color. A comedy somewhat less sophisticated than *Discreet Charm*, with director May's daughter, Jeannie Berlin, gamely playing the slovenly Jewish bride that the heartbreak kid (Charles Grodin) abandons on their honeymoon. With Cybill Shepherd as the Waspish beauty he falls for and Eddie Albert as her father. Many found it hilarious; some were offended at its cheerful heartlessness. Scripted by Neil Simon.

10 **Mon Oncle Antoine** (Claude Jutra). Canada, color. Still more about families: a fifteen-year old boy in a Quebec mining town observes his elders at their most loveable and fallible. Gently amusing and, by the end, deeply touching.

Contending for tenth place were *Slaughterhouse Five*, *Frenzy*, and *Sleuth*.

1973

1 **Cries and Whispers** * (Ingmar Bergman). Sweden, color. Bergman's most harrowing and enduring film. See the essay later in this book.

2 ***Andrei Roublev*** (Andrei Tarkovsky). USSR, bw/color. Some marvelously realized, if largely fictional, episodes from the life of a Russian monk, famous for his skill at painting religious icons, who is caught in the swirl of 15th-century political upheaval. The look and feel of an exotic medieval Russia previously known only from paintings is uncannily conveyed from the early scenes of a balloon flight to the closing sequence about the casting of a giant church bell. Long delayed by the Communist regime, and long known only in condensed versions, its 1973 release in complete form created a sensation among critics around the world.

3 ***The New Land*** (Jan Troell). Sweden, color. The two-part saga that began in 1972 with *The Emigrants* finally achieves what Elia Kazan's ambitious *America, America* did not: it depicts one of the great mass migrations of human history in the most human terms. The scene in which the father (Max von Sydow), to save his little son from freezing in a raging snow storm, kills his beloved ox and folds the boy inside the carcass while he goes for help, is one of the most memorable sequences in movie history. Memorable in a quieter way is the scene where the mother (Liv Ullmann) tries on a hat that is utterly unsuited to her natural beauty. Troell not only directed but wrote, photographed, and edited his two-part masterpiece.

4 ***The Sting*** (George Roy Hill AA). US, color. A studioesque and somewhat leisurely period comedy about two Chicago con men, played by Butch Cassidy and the Sundance Kid (all right - by Paul Newman and Robert Redford), with a twisty plot, a good supporting cast, and a dozen or so infectious Scott Joplin rags on the sound track. Audiences went more than slightly crazy over it. Oscar for best picture, six others.

5 ***American Graffiti*** (George Lucas) US, color. A made-on-a-shoestring memoir of director Lucas' youth in 1962 in a hot-rod, rock-and-rolling California town, covering a day in the lives of four youths preparing to leave for college. A surprise money-maker, unexpectedly absorbing and, finally, moving: 1962, it turned out, was really the end of the fifties. With Richard Dreyfuss and (as the future director of *A Beautiful Mind* was then called) Ronny Howard.

6 ***Sleeper*** (Woody Allen). US, color. A Rip Van Winkle update that is almost abnormally funny. One of the earliest and best of the "written, directed by, and starring" comedies of a nebbish filmmaker ready to come into his own. Diana Keaton finally finds her film niche as his side-kick love interest.

7 ***The Spider's Stratagem*** (Bernardo Bertolucci). Italy, color. An earlier effort by the director of 1971's *The Conformist*, made when he was still in his twenties and learning to make metaphor his stock-in-trade. His main metaphor in this story of a son who discovers that his sainted father was actually a traitor is, intriguingly, Verdi, that operatic master of father-son conflicts. With Alida Valli as the strategist and Giulio Grogi as both the son and, in flashbacks, the father.

8 ***Mean Streets*** (Martin Scorsese). US, color. Yet another young director destined for big things remembers his youth. The explosive performances of Harvey Keitel and Robert De Niro - and Scorsese's very cinematic vision of the mean streets of New York's Little Italy —were harbingers of even more impressive work to come. (1973 is the year most often cited by tiresome baby-boomer critics as the magic moment when, spurred on by 1969's *Easy Rider*, a generation of American *auteurs* emerged from

university film courses to save Hollywood from the doldrums; witness the emergence in 1973 of Scorsese and Lucas, with Altman and Coppola fresh on the scene. The revolution, if such it was, soon gave way to the summer blockbuster - most notably Steven Spielberg's *Jaws*, in 1975.)

9 *The Day of the Jackal* (Fred Zinnemann). UK/France, color. Tense, low-keyed film version of the best seller about a professional killer hired by an alienated faction in the French army to assassinate Charles de Gaulle. Zinnemann's meticulous craftsmanship is everywhere in evidence – but the baby-boomer critics (see above) thought the whole thing hopelessly old-fashioned. With Edward Fox, Michel Lonsdale, and Cyril Cusack.

10 *Don't Look Now* (Nicholas Roeg). UK, color. A short story by Daphne du Maurier expanded into an intriguing if pretentious and poorly acted thriller. A British couple (Julie Christie and Donald Sutherland) whose little daughter has drowned meet two women in Venice who claim they can communicate with the dead girl. Then a little figure in a red coat begins to appear along the gray, wintry canals. A number of strange misadventures lead to a violent ending, with many loose strings left deliberately dangling. Pictorial motifs abound: Christie and Sutherland have a love scene in which they seem almost to be twins. Weird.

Competing for tenth place were *Paper Moon*, *The Paper Chase*, *The Way We Were*, and *The Homecoming*.

1974

1 *The Godfather II* (Francis Ford Coppola). US, color. Better than *The Godfather* in almost every way, this complex, beautifully detailed prequel/sequel brought stardom to Robert De Niro (AAS), who played Don Corleone as a young man, speaking Italian. (One of his few English lines was a subliterate variant on the recurrent *Godfather* motif: "I make an offer he don't refuse.") With Al Pacino, Robert Duvall, and others from what now came to be called *Godfather I*. (The two films were subsequently reassembled with all the incidents in chronological sequence, and with additional footage, for a ten-hour television series called *The Godfather Saga*.) Oscar for best picture, five others.

2 *Amarcord* (Federico Fellini). Italy, color. After ten years of doing lesser work, the maestro director returns happily to form with this kaleidoscopic memoir of his youth in a provincial Italian town during the early days of fascism. ("Amarcord" is dialect for "io mi ricordo" – "I remember".) Affectionate, satiric, vulgar, bizarre, whimsical, poignant, heart-stoppingly beautiful - it takes a string of adjectives just to begin to describe *Amarcord*. Oscar for best foreign film.

3 *The Conversation* (Francis Ford Coppola). US, color. An electronic surveillance whiz (Gene Hackman), whose profession is his whole life, suspects that he has overheard a murder plot, attempts to stop it, and becomes a something of a victim himself. Critic Stanley Kauffmann excitedly observed that American films of the seventies were learning rapidly from the most inventive

European films of the sixties. Certainly Coppola had seen *Blow-Up* and other films by Antonioni. Yet everything about *The Conversation* is palpably American. Palme d'Or at Cannes.

4 ***Chinatown*** (Roman Polanski). US, color. A complex view of Los Angeles - how many more were to follow! - in which a private eye (Jack Nicholson) almost loses his nose (to a switchblade-hood played by director Polanski), gets involved with a doomed femme fatale (Faye Dunaway), and exposes widespread corruption, much of it masterminded by a paternalistic monster played by John Huston. Realistically filmed and yet thoroughly bizarre.

5 ***Scenes from a Marriage*** (Ingmar Bergman). Sweden, color. Bergman's surprisingly popular film, in which a marriage painfully disintegrates before our eyes, was edited down from six television episodes - and so is not quite the subtly unified drama we had come to expect from its director. With an expert performance from Liv Ullmann and expectedly good ones from Erland Josephson and Bibi Anderson.

6 ***Murder on the Orient Express*** (Sidney Lumet). UK, color. Albert Finney is a forced, unamusing Hercule Poirot, but everything else about this deluxe Agatha Christie romp is first-rate. Among the upper-class suspects are Lauren Bacall, Wendy Hiller, Vanessa Redgrave, and Sean Connery, but acting honors went to the less glamorous travelers on board - Ingrid Bergman (AAS), John Gielgud, and Anthony Perkins. More new filmings of Miss Christie's mysteries followed this one down the tracks.

7 ***Day For Night*** (François Truffaut). France, color. The French director's movie about movie-making ("day for night" is the term for shooting a scene in daylight with filters to simulate night)

is something of a tribute to Hollywood: its original title was *La Nuit Americaine*. Truffaut plays himself, Graham Greene does a cameo as an insurance representative, and Valentina Cortese has a extraordinary scene as an actress who goes to pieces when, despite repeated attempts, she can't get a scene right. With Jacqueline Bisset, Jean-Pierre Aumont, and, inevitably, Truffaut's protégé Jean-Paul Léaud. Oscar for best foreign film.

8 *Badlands* (Terrence Malick). US, color. A young garbage collector (Martin Sheen), unable to connect with the world around him, picks up an aimless teenager (Sissy Spacek), calmly shoots her father (Warren Oates), sets the house on fire, and embarks with her on a shooting spree across the Dakota badlands. We are not, as we are in would-be Significant Statements like 1977's *Equus*, expected to take these atrocities as revealing anything significant about human nature. Malick, in his directorial debut, observes the action impassively, with the most impressive camera work of the year, carefully placing everything we see in a morally neutral landscape and leaving us to sort out our feelings by ourselves. The film soon attracted a cult, and Malick was poised to make his masterpiece four years on. See 1978.

9 *The Seduction of Mimi* (Lina Wertmuller). Italy, color. Giancarlo Giannini makes a strong bid to inherit Chaplin's comic mantle in this story of a sad-faced Sicilian metalworker ("They call me Mimi") befuddled in Bologna and befriending there a motor-mouthed Marxist maid (Mariangela Melato). Irresistible.

10 *Love and Anarchy* (Lina Wertmuller). Italy, color. More monkeyshines from Giannini, and more mothering from Melato. He wants to assassinate Mussolini; she works in the brothel he uses as his locus operandi. The two of them are priming for next year's

Swept Away, also to be directed by Wertmuller, a tough-minded Swiss feminist with a soft spot for undersized Italian men.

Competing for tenth place were *Lacombe, Lucien* and *Alice Doesn't Live Here Anymore*.

1975

1 **Nashville** (Robert Altman). US, color. Five days in the lives of twenty-four people in the capital of country music. The interlocking stories range from exuberant to sympathetic to satiric to soap-Opry, but the total effect is kaleidoscopically grand. With Lily Tomlin, Ronee Blakley, Keith Carradine, Ned Beatty and twenty more personages, most of them from Altman's repertory stable and all of them speaking in Altman's patented overlapping dialogue. A subtly orchestrated sprawl that, when the camera backs away after almost three hours, has become a mosaic of middle America.

2 **Barry Lyndon** (Stanley Kubrick). US/UK, color. What? Thackery's picaresque novel given picture-book film treatment by Stanley Kubrick? The director's long-time admirers felt betrayed. Actor Ryan O'Neill's fans didn't want to see him in period costume. Critics wanted more matter with less art. And yet with the passage of years *Barry Lyndon* seems to have grown in stature. A scene shot only by the light of hundreds of candles - in what other of the arts could such an effect be achieved? In time, the film's critics relaxed, grateful that Kubrick, in a movie that paid tribute to what only movies can do, was odysseying again.

3 ***Swept Away*** (Lina Wertmuller). Italy, color. The partnership between Wertmuller and her favorite leading man, Giancarlo Giannini, reaches new heights in this uproarious tale of a tiny, sad-eyed communist sailor (Giannini) and a blabbermouthed capitalist termagant (Mariangela Melato) who are swept away, as the film's subtitle has it, "by an unusual destiny in the blue sea of August." Alone on an island, their roles are reversed as he beats and berates her into loving submission. Few found it offensive at the time. But a generation later, audiences were not ready to accept a remake - and not just because Giannini's son had only a fraction of his father's charm, and the pop figure Madonna was only a melted-down Melato.

4 ***The Passenger*** (Michelangelo Antonioni). Italy/ France/Spain, color. The director of *L'Avventura* couldn't get backing for his new picture without the financial guarantee of an American star, and Jack Nicholson obliged. He is the best thing about this existential mystery in which a burnt-out reporter swaps identities with a corpse. Critics are still finding Antonionian meaning in a seven-minute shot wherein the camera moves through the bars of the passenger's North African hotel window, pans around the square and returns to the room - a record-shattering, virtuoso piece of filming.

5 ***One Flew Over the Cuckoo's Nest*** (Milos Forman AA). US, color. No studio wanted to waste money on a movie version of Ken Kesey's cult novel about a free spirit rebelling against restrictions in a state mental hospital – till, once again, Jack Nicholson came to the rescue. This time he landed an Oscar. In fact, for the first time since *It Happened One Night* in 1934, one film won all four major Academy Awards - picture, director, actor, and actress (Louise Fletcher). The picture's appeal, in the Vietnam War

era, was largely due to its anti-establishment stance, but it has riveting moments that still shock and elate. Produced by Michael Douglas, whose father Kirk had acted the Nicholson role on the stage fourteen years earlier and wanted to make the film then but – surprise! - couldn't get financing.

6 *The Enigma of Kaspar Hauser* (Werner Herzog). West Germany, color. Similar in subject to Truffaut's *The Wild Child*, and also based on a true story: Kaspar is found in the town square of 19th-century Nuremberg, having lived through his first sixteen years deprived of all human contact. The film is an affecting, oddly paced, artfully composed portrait of a vulnerable, innocent man (played here by a real-life schizophrenic) who is eventually killed by, presumably, the one who had kept him imprisoned. With music by Pachelbel, Albinoni, and, enigmatically at the end, Mozart. Alternate title: *Every Man For Himself and God Against All*.

7 *Dog Day Afternoon* (Sidney Lumet), US, color. Offbeat comedy-drama about a Brooklyn bisexual (Al Pacino) who robs a bank to get money for a sex-change operation for his boyfriend (Chris Sarandon). Lumet's street-smart style enables him to make acute observations about a variety of big-city psychoses. Based on an actual incident. With John Cazale and Charles Durning.

8 *The Story of Adele H.* (François Truffaut). France, color. Victor Hugo's neglected daughter (Isabelle Adjani) follows a soldier to Halifax. A true story, nowhere as touching on film as Truffaut's fans had hoped it would be, but the camera loved Adjani and so did both critics and public.

9 ***Lancelot du Lac*** (Robert Bresson). France, color. Bresson's fastidiously unromantic minimalist view of   Arthurian chivalry in its death-throes. As with *A Man Escaped*, sounds are more important than words. As with *Au Hasard, Balthazar*, austerity is all. The film's acting style has been called anti-theatrical, and the total effect alienated some while it elated others. Certainly this *Lancelot* is an antidote for John Boorman's comic-book *Excalibur* and Joshua Logan's soggy screen version of Lerner and Loewe's lovely *Camelot*. But it is definitely not for every filmgoer.

10 ***Jaws*** (Steven Spielberg). US, color. A midsummer release that set a Hollywood distribution pattern for the next forty years, this heavily promoted potboiler about a man-eating shark had some fairly frightening sequences but hardly anything to "suggest what Eisenstein might have done if he hadn't intellectualized himself out of reach" (Pauline Kael). Millions lined up at the box office, and there were shark-sightings on virtually every beach in America. The summer blockbuster era was to last in Hollywood until the breakthrough of independent films in the new millennium. With Robert Shaw, Roy Scheider, and Richard Dreyfuss.

Contending for tenth place were *Three Days of the Condor* and *The Man Who Would Be King*.

1976

1 ***Seven Beauties*** (Lina Wertmuller). Italy, color. The high point in the Wertmuller-Giancarlo Giannini series, rapturously received as a "milestone" and an "instant classic" on its release. But, however accomplished the Chaplinesque performance of

Giannini, however dazzling the directorial flair of Wertmuller, this story of an Italian's survival in a concentration camp seemed to some unsettlingly reminiscent of the real-life experiences of author Primo Levi. Poised to claim four major Oscars, the film was attacked in *The New Yorker* by Bruno Bettleheim, and support for and interest in it quickly evaporated. Director and star found their international careers virtually ended. No Oscars.

2 *The Memory of Justice* (Marcel Ophuls). France/West Germany/US/UK, bw/color. Another four-and-a-half-hour documentary from the son of veteran director Max Ophuls, this patient and painstaking film examines the Nuremberg war trials, the Nazi death camps, the offenses committed by the Allies, the French experience in Algeria, and the American involvement in Vietnam in an all-out plea for moral accountability in warfare.

3 *Network* (Sidney Lumet). US, color. A sensational vision of what television news coverage might become and - even though Walter Cronkite thought it unlikely to happen - almost *has* become since the picture's release. Scripted by Paddy Chayefsky, who insisted he was writing real stuff, not satire. So cannily overacted by Peter Finch (AA), Faye Dunaway (AA), Ned Beatty, and Robert Duvall that the quieter performances of William Holden and Beatrice Straight (AA) were thrown into vivid relief. Finch, who played Howard Beale, the "mad prophet of the airwaves", dropped dead of a heart attack as he waited to plug the film on *Good Morning, America*. Today Fox News and CNN might be advised to take a close look at this far-from-dated melodrama.

4 *All the President's Men* (Alan Pakula). US, color. Deft, determinedly authentic account of the investigation of the Watergate break-in by two young *Washington Post* reporters

(played by Robert Redford and Dustin Hoffman). Something of the tension of the times, as well as the thrill of discovery, is swiftly and surely conveyed. With Jason Robarts, Jr. (AAS), Martin Balsam, Hal Holbrook, and Jane Alexander. (It's amazing what those two dudes were able to do without cell phones!)

5 *Taxi Driver* (Martin Scorsese). US, color. Director Scorsese called this sordid but unforgettable film "a continuation of *Mean Streets*... dealing with religious anxiety, guilt, and one man's attitudes towards women - attitudes that were arrested at age thirteen." Scorsese's Catholic understanding was often interestingly at odds with the Protestant rigor of scriptwriter Paul Schraeder. Robert De Niro is the desperate Vietnam War veteran Travis Bickle, and Jody Foster plays a prepubescent prostitute. Some viewers called it hell on earth. With the last musical score by Hitchcock's favorite composer, Bernard Herrmann. Palme d'Or at Cannes.

6 *Face to Face* (Ingmar Bergman). Sweden, color. Liv Ullmann plays a psychiatrist who has a severe nervous breakdown and must use other resources to heal herself when her own science fails her. Like *Scenes from a Marriage*, this is a condensed version of a series Bergman made for television rather than a meticulously realized concept. But it has Ullmann in her most harrowing performance.

7 *Obsession* (Brian de Palma). US, color. 1975's *hommage* to the master of suspense, more Hitchcockian that most Hitchcock *hommages*. Cliff Robertson plays a man who meets a woman (Geveviève Bujold) identical with his dead wife. Sound familiar? Bernard Herrmann's score almost makes you believe this is the real Hitchcock thing. It almost is.

8 ***The Marquise of O...*** (Eric Rohmer). France, color. A quietly observant film version of the 19th-century novella by Heinrich von Kleist about an Italian noblewoman (Edith Clever) rescued by, and then compromised by, a man (Bruno Ganz) she thinks of almost as an angel. More serious and ambivalent than its German source - as one might expect from the perceptive Frenchman directing it.

9 ***Robin and Marian*** (Richard Lester). US, color. Robin Hood (Sean Connery) and Maid Marian (Audrey Hepburn) grow old together and meet their deaths with humor and resignation in an England that has lost its storybook glory. With Robert Shaw, Richard Harris, Ian Holm and several other British veterans. Too revisionist for some, it has essential career performances by the two lovers.

10 ***All Screwed Up*** (Lina Wertmuller). Italy, color. We might as well wrap up the year with another seriocomic Wertmuller jamboree, released in America for the first time in the wake of her later successes. The tale of lower class Italian workers is not bad, but it could have benefited from the acting skills of - you guessed it - Giancarlo Gianinni.

Contending for tenth place was *The Pink Panther Strikes Again*. The Oscar went to *Rocky*.

1977

1 ***Star Wars*** (George Lucas). US, color. Luke Skywalker, Princess Leia, Han Solo, R2-D2, C-3PO, Chewbacca, Obi-Wan Kenobe, and Darth Vader enter the pantheon of childhood heroes in this

interplanetary original dreamed up by young director-writer Lucas. Not since *Snow White* were audiences of children held so enthralled. But much of the rest of a six-part *Star Wars* yielded, in subsequent years, increasingly disappointing dividends, despite advances in computer technology. It now appears that this exuberant 1977 fantasy set Hollywood movie-making on what the prophetic Pauline Kael called "a retrograde course, where it's now joining forces with video-games manufacturers". All the same, this first installment gave Harrison Ford his breakthrough role, and featured the widest-seen performance by Alec Guinness. Seven Oscars, though the best picture award went to *Annie Hall*.

2 ***Annie Hall*** (Woody Allen). US, color. New York neuroses and California crassness, one-liners and live lobsters, crazy clothes, vivid vignettes, intellectual attitudinizing (Marshall McLuhan defends himself in person), and Allen and Diane Keaton all but playing themselves at the end of their relationship - it sounds like *Star Wars* for grown-ups, and in some ways it is. Oscar for best picture, three others.

3 ***La Grande Bourgeoise*** (Mauro Bolognini). France/ Italy, color. In 19th-century Bologna, a rich upper middle class family with liberal views is prosecuted by a Catholic conservative faction after the son (Giancarlo Giannini) murders the detested husband of the daughter (Catherine Deneuve). Almost forgotten today, but fondly remembered by those few who went to see Giannini in a serious role and became utterly absorbed in the drama. Also known as *The Murri Affair*.

4 ***Julia*** (Fred Zinnemann). US, color. Skillful dramatization of a largely fictional story from Lillian Hellman's memoir, *Pentimento*, with Jane Fonda as Hellman, Jason Robarts (AAS) as Dashiell

Hammet and Vanessa Redgrave (AAS) suitably cast as Julia, a standard bearer of unpopular causes. (In her pro-Palestinian Oscar acceptance speech, Redgrave criticized "a small bunch of Zionist hoodlums whose behavior is an insult to the stature of Jews all over the world.")

5 *The Turning Point* (Herbert Ross). US, color. The often-filmed story of career vs. motherhood, set this time in the backstage (and occasionally onstage) world of ballet, with Mikhail Baryshnikov in his acting debut, and with a famous cat fight between the former ballerina (Anne Bancroft) and the housewife who gave up her career when a baby was on the way (Shirley McLean). Ten nominations, no Oscars. Tears on-screen and off.

6 **Padre Padrone** (Paolo and Vittorio Taviani). Italy, color. Vivid filming of the autobiography of a professor of classics who grew up as an illiterate Sardinian shepherd brutalized by his father (Omero Antonutti). The powerful film that introduced the talented brother-directors to the wide world. Palme d'Or at Cannes.

7 **3 Women** (Robert Altman). US, color. A timorous drifter (Sissy Spacek), a self-deluded worker in a rehab center (Shelley Duvall), and a painter of enigmatic murals (Janice Rule) bond together in this moody, intriguing study derived from a dream that director Altman couldn't get out of his head. All the Altman devices are at work, and Duvall gives her best performance.

8 **The Goodbye Girl** (Herbert Ross). US, color. A Neil Simon original, with his wife Marsha Mason playing a single mom who unwillingly opens her apartment to an insecure actor with a highly original approach to *Richard III* (Richard Dreyfuss AA). Mason's

ten-year-old daughter, Quinn Cummings, holds her own amid the one-liners, mayhem, laughter, and occasional tears.

9 *That Obscure Object of Desire* (Luis Buñuel). France/Spain, color. A middle-aged man (Fernando Rey) is put upon by his mistress, who is played by two different actresses. Buñuel's last film, in the relaxed and playful mood of his old age, but not without the expected surrealist tricks. Very loosely based on a novel, *La Femme et le Pantin*, once considered as a subject by Puccini, and filmed previously by Joseph von Sternberg, with Marlene Dietrich, as *The Devil is a Woman*.

10 *Close Encounters of the Third Kind* (Steven Spielberg). US, color. A very popular big-budget UFO fantasy with a wisp of a plot blown up to ridiculous length. Re-released two years later in a corrected version that was not much of an improvement. But the ending, in which we non-believers are allowed at last to see creatures from outer space, is truly magical. With a spaced-out Richard Dreyfuss and (what on earth is he doing in this picture?) François Truffaut.

Contending for tenth place were *1900* and *Derzu Uzala*.

1978

1 *Days of Heaven** (Terrence Malick). US, color. A wonderfully innovative American imagination at work. See the essay later in this book.

2 ***Autumn Sonata*** (Ingmar Bergman). Sweden, Germany, UK, color. Ingmar finally meets Ingrid Bergman, and directs her farewell to the screen. All of the picture, about a concert pianist revisiting her estranged daughter after seven years, is riveting, but the scene where Ingrid demonstrates to her daughter (Liv Ulmann) how Chopin's A minor Prelude should be played - done in a close-up frame of the two faces, one proudly confident, the other filled with suppressed rage - is the emotional equal of anything in the director's output. The autumn colors are caught beautifully by Sven Nykvist's camera.

3 ***Bread and Chocolate*** (Franco Brusati). Italy, color. A working man leaves his native Italy (bread) to make his fortune in Switzerland (chocolate) and gets into a lot of trouble. A Chaplinesque performance by Nino Manfredi and a perceptive analysis of two quite distinct European cultures. The surreal bits are, however, a miscalculation.

4 ***The Deer Hunter*** (Michael Cimino AA). US, color. The stars were all in the right places for young Cimino when he made this terribly long, confused, penitentially patriotic film about three Pennsylvania steelworkers scarred by their experiences in Vietnam. The stars in place were Robert De Niro, John Cazale, John Savage, Christopher Walken (AA), and Meryl Streep. The picture alienated as many people as it impressed: at the Berlin festival an Eastern bloc walked out in protest over the notorious scene where the Vietcong force American prisoners to play Russian roulette, while at the Academy Award ceremony the film was picketed by Vietnam veterans. It nonetheless won the Oscar for best picture, and four others. Cimino has done nothing of substance since.

5 ***Death on the Nile*** (John Guillermin). UK, color. Peter Ustinov as Hercule Poirrot in one of Agatha Christie's more exotic mysteries. Jack Cardiff's camera captures the Nile scenery nicely, and Anthony Schaffer's script allows us to see several contradictory versions of what the suspects might have been up to when the murder took place. Angela Lansbury is the standout among the suspects, outdoing even Bette Davis and Maggie Smith. Enough said?

6 ***The Duellists*** (Ridley Scott). UK, color. Stunningly beautiful color, ironic Joseph Conrad story, good supporting cast (Albert Finney, Edward Fox, Robert Stephens), and two duellists (Keith Carradine and Harvey Keitel) who, sadly, are utterly unconvincing as Hussar officers, betrayed as they are by their American accents.

7 ***Perceval*** (Eric Rohmer). France, color. The unfinished medieval epic by Chrétien de Troyes (one of the sources of Wagner's *Parsifal*), piously filmed by the great purist among contemporary filmmakers, with real actors and horses moving among doll-house castles and stylized trees photographed by *Days of Heaven*'s Nestor Almendros. If you think that sounds arty, you're right. Not for everyone. A work of art for some.

8 ***An Unmarried Woman*** (Paul Mazursky). US, color. Seventies woman's lib in full throttle: an intelligent New York housewife (Jill Clayburg) is deserted by her husband (Michael Murphy), fights with her daughter, gets psychiatric help, and tentatively starts a new life with a lover (Alan Bates). It seemed to be every woman's story at the time. Now it infuriates Generation X-ers. Clayburg's performance, however, is a tour de force.

9 ***Coming Home*** (Hal Ashby). US, color. Hardly the Vietnam War's *Best Years of Our Lives*, which in its day it was confidently said to be, this award-winner was seventies-predictable and, in a surprising number of scenes, stagily unconvincing. At Oscar time, the picture's star, Jane Fonda (AA), campaigned against *The Deer Hunter*, though she hadn't seen it. At the ceremony, her co-star Jon Voigt (AA) tearfully deferred to Laurence Olivier's acting prowess as greater than his own. Extended use of period rock songs. Number nine in a very lean year.

10 ***Superman*** (Richard Donner). US, color. This megabuck extravaganza didn't exactly move with the speed of a flying bullet, but it did provide those of us who are not fans of the man of steel with the mythic details we needed to understand why kids who read comic books aren't bored. With Christopher Reeve as Clark Kent and his muscled alter ego, and with Gene Hackman as villain Lex Luthor. (One notorious expenditure: Marlon Brando got three million dollars and a share of the gross – for ten minutes on screen.)

There were no contenders for tenth place. A year that brought only two memorable movies.

1979

1 ***The Tree of Wooden Clogs*** (Ermanno Olmi). Italy, color. A three-hour memoir of nineteenth-century peasant life in the Po valley, lovingly fashioned by Olmi from stories his grandmother told him, and acted by a cast of non-professionals speaking Bergomesque. Partly an indictment of a cruel and outmoded

feudalism, the film, which flows along as majestically as the Po itself, is also a Virgilian affirmation of man's oneness with a natural world that, like the God he worships, sends him both blessings and sorrows in due measure. This is Olmi's finest film, winner of the 1978 Palme d'Or at Cannes. Critic Andrew Sarris said, "To see it is to be stirred to the depths of one's soul."

2 *Manhattan* (Woody Allen). US, bw. Allen's rhapsodic love song to his isle of dreams, and perhaps his best film. With Diane Keaton, Mariel Hemingway, and Meryl Streep as the New York women in his life, with superb black and white photography by Gordon Willis (curiously unnominated by the Academy), and a dozen richly orchestrated Gershwin pieces on the sound track.

3 *The Black Stallion* (Caroll Ballard). US, color. The first hour of this affectionate filming of a favorite children's book - the death of the boy's father in a shipwreck and the friendship that develops on the coast of North Africa between the boy (Kelly Reno) and the other survivor, a magnificent stallion - is a wonder to watch. The rest, with the boy returned to his mother and befriended by a racing pro (Mickey Rooney) is merely watchable. Superb color photography (curiously unnominated by the Academy) by Caleb Deschanel.

4 *Apocalypse Now* (Francis Ford Coppola). US, color. Joseph Conrad's *Heart of Darkness* reset in Vietnam during the war, magnificently cinematographed by Vittorio Storaro, with a cannily over-the-top performance by Robert Duvall as a war-mad general and an outrageously self-indulgent one by Marlon Brando as Vietnam's own Mr. Kurtz. The story of its filming, with eight famous actors ultimately unable to go on with the lead role and Martin Sheen undertaking it only to suffer a heart attack at age

thirty-seven, made a remarkable documentary, *Hearts of Darkness*. And yet the film stands, a mesmerizing commentary on the whole Vietnam disaster. Re-released with restored footage in 2001. Co-winner, with *The Tin Drum*, of the 1979 Palme d'Or at Cannes.

5 ***Kramer vs. Kramer*** (Robert Benton AA) US, color. An affecting little picture in which an advertising executive (Dustin Hoffman AA) and the wife who divorced him (Meryl Streep AAS) battle it out for their seven-year-old son (Justin Henry). The Academy, disinclined to honor *Apocalypse Now* except for its photography, showered *Kramer vs. Kramer* with five awards, including the Oscar for best picture.

6 ***Alien*** (Ridley Scott). US, color. Astronauts returning from space are killed off one-by-one by a monstrous Thing they pick up on a moribund planet. Tingling fun for all. The cinematically literate may remark that each character seems to meet his/her end as punishment for a performance he/she has given in the past - Ian Holm for *A Severed Head*, Veronica Cartwright for *Invasion of the Body Snatchers*, Yaphet Kotto for *Live and Let Die*, Tom Skeritt for *Maneaters Are Loose*, and John Hurt for his disemboweling Caligula in *I, Claudius*. Only Sigourney Weaver, who had never made a film before, escapes from the alien Thing, who clearly is some sort of movie critic.

7 ***Breaking Away*** (Peter Yates). US, color. An English director uses the annual bicycle race in Bloomington, Indiana - between the university's preppies and the "townies" from the local limestone quarries - as a way of examining class distinctions in the United States. Dennis Christopher plays a townie fascinated by all things Italian (ironically, most of his enthusiasms are not Italian at all),

and Dennis Quaid plays his coming-of-age buddy. Everything works for Yates in this small, unpredictable, engaging film.

8 *The China Syndrome* (James Bridges). US, color. Expertly told story of the attempted cover-up of an accident at a nuclear power plant and the efforts of television reporters to get at the truth. Energy companies were enraged by the film, but two weeks after its premiere an accident similar to the one in the movie occurred at the nuclear plant at Three Mile Island. With Jane Fonda, Jack Lemmon, and Michael Douglas, who co-produced.

9 *Norma Rae* (Martin Ritt). US, color. A poor Southern textile worker (Sally Field) becomes a union organizer. Another heart-in-the right-place statement from director Ritt and a big, generous performance by Sally Field (AA) that turned her career around.

10 *All That Jazz* (Bob Fosse). US, color. A Broadway psychobiography siphoned off from Fellini's *8½*, self-indulgent and exhausting, with song and dance numbers intercut with graphic footage of open-heart surgery. Roy Scheider plays Fosse (aka Joe Gideon) trying to whip a show into shape while on the brink of a coronary. Many thought it brilliant in 1979; today it hasn't even much of a cult following. With Jessica Lange and Ann Reinking.

Contending for tenth place was *The Europeans*.

The 1980s

Pre-1840s

1 *The Empire Strikes Back* (George Lucas). US, color. The next installment of the *Star Wars* saga (the second to be made, the fifth in the overall design), is more assured and technically accomplished than its predecessor, with new battalions (most notably the legions that lumber like giant giraffes), new characters (most notably Yoda, a diminutive Merlin figure who educates Luke Skywalker), and a new interest in the hero-myth as outlined by Carl Jung and Joseph Campbell. (Every little boy in the audience began to wonder, "Who is Luke Skywalker's father?")

2 *Raging Bull* (Martin Scorsese). US, bw. Often cited as the best film of the eighties, this scorching black-and-white bio of boxer Jake La Motta firmly established Scorsese as a pantheon director. Famous for its meticulously edited close-ups of punishingly bloody fights in which the roar of the crowd, the hiss of exploding flashbulbs, and the amplified thud of blows to the head are suddenly stilled, the visuals of spattered blood and sweat go slow motion, and luxuriant Mascagni melodies quietly flood the sound track - one of the many cinematic ways in which Scorsese acknowledges both the savagery and the beauty his own heritage and asks us to understand a man who cannot understand himself. Robert De Niro (AA) attacked his role with total dedication: production was shut down for several months while he put on sixty pounds to play the washed-up boxer at his most brutish. With Joe Pesci as La Motta's brother, manager, and sparring partner, and Cathy Moriarity as his wife, so beautiful she

drives him mad with unfounded suspicions. When La Motta saw the film he said, "I kinda look bad in it."

3 ***The Stunt Man*** (Richard Rush). US, color. A brilliant study in cinema deception. A Vietnam veteran on the run accidentally kills the stunt man on a movie set and hides out by taking his place in a picture directed by a weirdo named Eli Cross who thinks he is God. (Peter O'Toole claimed he was just imitating David Lean.) No studio would touch the script, and when Rush produced the movie independently no studio would release it. But audiences who got to see it after a two-year wait found that they hadn't been so deliciously baffled, so wrong in their guesses, and so exhilarated in a long, long time. Pauline Kael, exhilarated, said "You joyride through this picture."

4 ***Kagemusha*** (Akira Kurosawa). Japan, color. During the clan wars in medieval Japan, a condemned thief who resembles a chieftain is pardoned so that when the chieftain dies he can take his place in battle. (The look-alikes are played by the same actor.) The "shadow warrior" begins to think he *is* the man he is impersonating, but his horse knows the difference, and eventually that makes all the difference. Some prints run close to three hours, but stunning color and spectacle make every minute count. Produced by Francis Ford Coppola and George Lucas in gratitude to and in respect for the great Kurosawa, who hadn't been able to finance a film in ten years. Palme d'Or at Cannes.

5 ***Eboli*** (Francesco Rosi). Italy, color. Carlo Levi, a liberal Italian writer (Gian Maria Volonte) is sent by the Fascist regime south to the town of Eboli, which is as far the railroad extends, and from there he is exiled to a God-forsaken mountain village at his country's extremity. This is director Rosi's masterpiece, and

seeing it, either in its two- or its three-and-a-half-hour version, is a cathartic experience, with unforgettable moments. From Levi's autobiographical novel *Christ Stopped at Eboli.*

6 *The Tin Drum* (Volker Schlöndorff). West Germany/ France, color. A boy, unhappy with the world he has known since his embryonic days, decides to remain a child forever. A startling, disturbing, often explicitly sexual film made from the satirical novel Günther Grass wrote both for and about the Germany that spawned the Nazis. Not for everyone: Roger Ebert devoted a chapter to it in his book *I Hated, Hated, Hated This Movie.* All the same, it shared the 1979 Palme d'Or at Cannes with *Apocalypse Now* and won the 1980 Oscar for best foreign film.

7 *The Great Santini* (Lewis John Carlino). US, color. A cocky but frighteningly insecure Marine fighter pilot takes out his frustrations, in the years when there is no war to fight, by bullying his family, especially his adolescent son. A terrific performance by Robert Duvall, with heart-in-throat scenes involving Blythe Danner as the wife and Michael O'Keefe as the son. Unfortunately, a subplot with David Keith as a local redneck almost seems part of another movie; director Carlino ought to have had some help adapting Pat Conway's novel. The film flopped in all of its tryout towns and was sold to cable TV and the airlines before it opened in New York to raves and sold-out houses. (Shades of *The Stunt Man.*)

8 *Ordinary People* (Robert Redford AA). US, color. It's the mother who is the problem in this family, which is striving to deal with the death, by drowning, of the eldest son. The film is tighter and more professionally done than *The Great Santini* but not as searingly painful. With Mary Tyler Moore as the mother

(tragically, her real-life son took his own life a month after the film's release), Donald Sutherland as the father, Timothy Hutton (AAS) as the son, and Judd Hirsch as the psychiatrist. Redford copped the director's award his first time out, and the Academy also awarded his film the Oscar for best picture. Fans of *Raging Bull* are still raging about that.

9 ***Breaker Morant*** (Bruce Beresford). Australia, color. Three Aussie officers are court-martialed on trumped up charges during the Boer War to save the honor of the British Empire. Fact-based and fascinating, it won several awards down under and was a command-performance event for Queen Elizabeth.

10 ***Mon Oncle d'Amerique*** (Alain Resnais). France, color. That rarity, an entertaining film made to illustrate the theories of an established scientist – in this case, the theories of the psychologist Henri Laborit, who is on hand to explain why Gérard Depardieu can survive the crises of existence as long as two, or even one, of his fellow human beings is worse off than he.

Contending for tenth place were *The Last Metro* and *The Elephant Man*.

1981

1 ***Chariots of Fire*** (Hugh Hudson). UK, color. Two fleet-of-foot young Britons, one defiantly Jewish and one devoutly Christian, compete in the 1924 Olympics in Paris. Each runs to prove a point - Harold Abrahams (Ben Cross) to prove his Englishness in the face of English anti-Semitism and snobbery,

and Eric Liddle (Ian Charleson) to give glory to the God he can feel empowering him when he runs. Perhaps the finest film ever made about sport, partly because it is also about so much else. Audiences responded emotionally to the film's lyrical heroics without quite being able to say why. But surely one reason was the deliberately elliptical, beautifully written script, and another was the unusual musical score by Vangelis, sometimes sharply modern in deliberate contrast to the carefully sustained period visuals, inviting us to see the film's events metaphorically. *Chariots of Fire* launched a new effort to make British films competitive in the world market, and soon became the highest-grossing film from any foreign country ever to reach American shores. With Alice Krige, Nicholas Farrell, John Gielgud, Lindsay Anderson, and, in a small but real triumph of characterization, Ian Holm. Oscar for best picture, three others.

2 *Man of Marble/Man of Iron* (Andrjez Wajda). Poland, color. A timely and absorbing diptych from a veteran Polish director. In *Man of Marble*, a student filmmaker uncovers, *Citizen Kane*-style, the story of a labor leader discredited and killed in the seventies. In *Man of Iron*, set in the eighties, a journalist is enlisted by the secret police to discredit the son of the same labor leader and the entire Solidarity movement. Footage from the 1980 strikes at Gdansk is worked into the narrative, and Lech Walesa appears as himself. *Man of Iron* was nominated by the Academy as best foreign film, over protests from the (then Communist) Polish government, and it won the Palme d'Or at Cannes.

3 *Body Heat* (Lawrence Kasdan). US, color. Torridly erotic, shrewdly updated version of *Double Indemnity*, relocated in Florida and almost as good as the original. With William Hurt as the infatuated chump and Kathleen Turner as the *femme fatale*

who dupes him into killing her rich husband so she can get the money. The steamy forties feel of *Double Indemnity* is preserved in the cool eighties by setting the story in the midst of a tropical heat wave. (Actually,it was filmed on location during an unexpected cold snap.) Critics in 1981 weren't too impressed by the debuts of director Kasdan and star Turner, but the picture has a big following today.

4 ***Prince of the City*** (Sidney Lumet). US, color. Fact-based, powerful story of a young New York cop (Treat Williams) who is recruited by the U.S. Justice Department to inform on his corrupt fellow officers - at considerable cost to himself. The sort of thing director Lumet does very well. With Jerry Orbach, Bob Balaban, and James Tolkan.

5 ***Raiders of the Lost Ark*** (Steven Spielberg). US, color. A collaboration between the two young geniuses who were bucking each other at the box office in the eighties - George Lucas, who conceived the idea of an archaeologist named Indiana Jones going on adventures like those in the serials he had himself seen in movie houses as a boy, and Steven Spielberg, to whom Lucas turned the project over when he already had his hands full with *Star Wars*. The picture starts off with so much excitement - Harrison Ford as Jones running for his life with an immense and improbably rounded boulder in pursuit - that even Spielberg must have wondered how he could keep up the pace. (He does.)

6 ***Gallipoli*** (Peter Weir). Australia, color. A moving, relatively small-scaled film about two Aussies - one a phenomenal runner (Mark Lee), one a likeable underachiever (Mel Gibson) - who meet ironic deaths under British leadership in the disastrous 1915

battle of Gallipoli. If only the runner had not suggested that the underachiever do the running through the trenches...

7 ***Pixote*** (Hector Babenco). Brazil, color. Devastating story of a ten-year-old boy maltreated in a São Paolo reformatory who faces even worse horrors when he escapes and tries to survive - pimping, mugging, and even murdering - on the streets. Babenco actually used abandoned children as his actors to add point and pathos to his plea for reform.

8 ***Reds*** (Warren Beatty AA). US, color. The experiences, in America and in revolutionary Russia, of John Reed, author of *Ten Days That Shook the World*. Too long at three-and-a-quarter hours, but carefully detailed, with several good quarter-hours. With director Beatty as John Reed, Diane Keaton as his mistress, Jack Nicholson as Eugene O'Neill, Maureen Stapleton (AA) as Emma Goldman, author Jerzy Kosinski, and a mess of quasi-documentary interviews with the unlikely likes of Henry Miller and Will Durant.

9 ***True Confessions*** (Ulu Grosbard). US, color. Robert Duvall plays a hardened Los Angeles police detective, homicide division, and Robert De Niro plays his brother, the ambitious monsignor who is chancellor of the archdiocese. In 1981 they were the two most impressive actors in American films, and here they give beautifully detailed performances. With Charles Durning and Burgess Meredith. Adapted by John Gregory Dunne from his novel, and co-scripted by his wife, Joan Didion.

10 ***The French Lieutenant's Woman*** (Karel Reisz). UK, color. In John Fowles' novel, the Englishwoman who stands hooded and haunted, looking out to sea, tells an aristocratic man two

different stories of her relationship with a French lieutenant. In Reisz's film, Meryl Streep is the woman and Jeremy Irons the man; they are also the actress and actor playing the roles in a movie made from the book. It was the only way script-writer Harold Pinter thought they could make the novel's two points of view work on the screen. (Six other directors of note had given up on the project.) The result: the 19th-century couple are fascinating, the contemporary twosome are at best uninteresting.

Contending for tenth place was *Atlantic City*.

1982

1 **E.T.** (Steven Spielberg). US, color. A sad little extra-terrestrial, left behind when his space ship takes off, is befriended by a lonely boy in California (Henry Thomas). Spielberg said that of all his films this was "closest to my own fantasies, my own heart". Audiences responded in the millions world-wide. Its effect on directors was still potent two decades later, in Jim Sheridan's poignant *In America*.

2 **Sophie's Choice** (Alan Pakula). US, color. An overly literal adaptation of William Styron's novel, turned into something transcendent by the performance of Meryl Streep as a Holocaust survivor whose life in 1947 Brooklyn is haunted by the choice she had to make years before at Auschwitz. Sophie is still the finest of more than a dozen fine screen portraits by the phenomenally skillful actress. With Kevin Kline and Peter MacNicol.

3 ***Three Brothers*** (Francesco Rosi). Italy/France, color. Three disaffected brothers - a judge threatened by terrorists (Philippe Noiret), a teacher in a boys' correctional institution (Vittorio Mezzogiorno), and a rebellious factory worker (Michele Placido) - return to rural southern Italy for their mother's funeral. Together they represent the social problems of Italy in the eighties, but the film, with its leisurely pacing and superb camera work, is anything but didactic. The finest performance is that of veteran Charles Vanel (of *The Wages of Fear*) as the father who has lived his whole life in close contact with nature, unaware of the conflicts his sons have had to face.

4 ***Veronika Voss*** (Rainer Werner Fassbinder). West Germany, bw. The prolific, erratic Fassbinder's best (and penultimate) film is at least three things: a noirish mystery à la *Sunset Boulevard;* an *hommage* to the chiaroscuro movie-making of Berlin's old UFA studios; and a metaphorical account (as the middle part of a trilogy that includes *The Marriage of Maria Braun* and *Lola*) of an ambivalent Germany struggling to survive in the forties, fifties, and sixties. Indelible performances by stage actors Rosel Zech and Hilmar Thate and stunningly original black-and-white cinematography by Xaver Schwarzenberger. The director appears next to his star in the opening scene.

5 ***Das Boot*** (Wolfgang Petersen). West Germany, color. A carefully detailed account of German heroism aboard a U-boat during World War II, with Jürgen Prochnow as the captain. All of it is compelling, and the final scene is devastating. Re-released in the nineties in a more-than-three-hour director's cut.

6 ***The Long Good Friday*** (John Mackenzie). UK, color. In one desperate day the empire of a London mobster comes

crashing down on his head. A hugely enjoyable surprise-a-minute *Godfather*-violent whodunit with sizzling performances by Bob Hoskins and Helen Mirren and with a cameo role for Europe's favorite American on-screen gangster, Eddie Constantine.

7 **Tootsie** (Sydney Pollack). US, color. An unpromising subject - an unemployed actor dresses as a woman to get a role on a television soap opera - is turned by skillful handling into a near-classic comedy. With Dustin Hoffmann in a virtuoso performance, and with good performances by Jessica Lange (AA), Charles Durning, Teri Garr, Dabney Coleman, Bill Murray, and director Pollack himself.

8 **The Verdict** (Sidney Lumet). US, color. A burnt-out Boston lawyer handles a case of medical malpractice and finds himself up against the medical profession and the archdiocese. The seriousness of it all is emphasized by gray and brown settings, and the performances of Paul Newman and James Mason are perhaps the most powerful of their careers. Scripted by David Mamet.

9 **Fitzcarraldo** (Werner Herzog). West Germany, color. A fictionalized account of the attempts of an Irishman named Fitzgerald to build an opera house in the Amazonian jungle. The filming of the mad sequence in which director Herzog has "Fitzcarraldo" and his extras haul a riverboat over a Peruvian mountain made an unusual documentary, *Burden of Dreams*. (The real-life Fitzgerald dismantled his boat and had it transported overland in sections.) With Klaus Kinski and Claudia Cardinale.

10 **Mephisto** (Istvan Szabo). Hungary/West Germany, color. An actor famed for playing the devil in Goethe's *Faust* sells his soul to the Nazis and is destroyed by them. Overlong, overly portentous,

and unnecessarily lurid, but with a remarkable performance by Klaus Maria Brandauer. Oscar for best foreign film.

Contending for tenth place were *Diva* and *Gandhi*, which won the Oscar for best picture.

1983

1 ***Fanny and Alexander*** (Ingmar Bergman). Sweden, color. Bergman's last film, made for television but commercially released, is a three-hour celebration of a the joys and sorrows of an exuberant turn-of-the-century family that, perhaps, he would have liked to have had for his own (Alexander is a figure for his young self). Bergmanites looked in vain for the enigmatic quality of the director's earlier work but, as critic Pauline Kael proclaimed, "It's a cornucopia of a movie". Few foreign films have been so honored by the Academy: there were Oscars for best foreign film, art direction, costumes, and cinematography (by Sven Nykvisk, as always).

2 ***Zelig*** (Woody Allen). US, bw. Crazy quasi-documentary detailing the early twentieth-century experiences of one Leonard Zelig (Allen, of course), a "human chameleon" with no personality of his own who turns into facsimiles of other people when he is with them - and can be spotted in newsreel footage with the likes of Babe Ruth, Adolf Hitler, and Pius XI. (That is to say, he is a figure for millions of celebrity-mad wannabes today.) With Mia Farrow as his psychiatrist and with Saul Bellow, Susan Sontag, and Bruno Bettleheim as themselves, straight-facedly testifying to the profound influence Zelig has had on popular culture. Such

technological trickery you never saw! What *will* they think of next?

3 ***The Night of the Shooting Stars*** (Paolo and Vittorio Taviani). Italy, color. A woman remembers the tragic and comic events she lived through waiting for the American armies to liberate her Tuscan village in 1944. At the end we discover why the memories - lyrical, touching, life-affirming, and true - have taken on the feeling of a fairy tale. With Omero Antonutti. OT: *La Notte di San Lorenzo*.

4 ***Tender Mercies*** (Bruce Beresford). US, color. An alcoholic country singer (Robert Duvall AA, singing his own songs) quietly finds a new life in the love of a Texas widow (Tess Harper) whose husband was killed in Vietnam. Written for Duvall by his friend Horton Foote, and made for a pittance in little more than a month, it contained the best performance of the year, Duvall's, and a very good one from Ellen Barkin as well. Jaded critics were amazed when audiences loved it.

5 ***The Draughtsman's Contract*** (Peter Greenaway). UK, color. A stylized and heartlessly ironic mystery set on a queasy 17th-century English estate teeming with intrigue, sexual activity, and sheer nastiness. Writer-director Greenaway subsequently went over the edge, cinematically speaking, with this kind of material, but here his special talent for the enigmatic and the grotesque is under control and uniquely impressive.

6 ***The Return of Martin Guerre*** (Daniel Vigne). France, color. Another intriguing period enigma, but based on fact and more straightforwardly filmed than *The Draughtsman's Contract*: a stranger returns to his 16th-century French village and the

townsfolk are not sure he is the man he claims they should remember. With Gérard Depardieu and Nathalie Baye.

7 *Terms of Endearment* (James Brooks AA). US, color. A glossy laughter-and-tears sitcom kept on course by the verve and versatility of its stars - Shirley MacLaine (AA) as a feisty Houston mother, Deborah Winger as her headstrong daughter, and Jack Nicholson (AAS) as the randy astronaut who lives next door. With John Lithgow and Jeff Daniels. Oscar for best picture, four others.

8 *The King of Comedy* (Martin Scorsese). US, color. A talentless bore named Rupert Pupkin (Robert De Niro), abetted by his dragon of a girl friend (Sandra Bernhard) kidnaps television's best known comedian (Jerry Lewis) in an attempt to bribe his own way to comic stardom. Frightening and funny, with remarkable acting all around. It took quite a while for this audaciously cast black comedy to find its audience.

9 *Betrayal* (David Jones). UK, color. We begin at the end of the affair between a literary agent (Jeremy Irons) and his lover (Patricia Hodge), and then move backwards, scene by scene, to the beginning. The episodes between the end and the beginning are dominated by the woman's silently menacing husband (Ben Kingsley). Harold Pinter adapted his own ingenious and perceptive play for the screen.

10 *Trading Places* (John Landis). US, color. Two Wall Street millionaires (Don Ameche and Ralph Bellamy), in an argument over heredity vs. environment, secretly arrange for a down-and-out street hustler (Eddie Murphy) to take the place of an upper-crust stockbroker and for the stockbroker (Dan Aykroyd) to take

to the streets. A picture that would have worked in the 1930s worked beautifully, given the talent, in the 1980s. Too bad it goes overboard in the last reel.

Contending for tenth place were *Local Hero*, *The Dresser*, and *Berlin Alexanderplatz*.

1984

1 ***And the Ship Sails On*** (Federico Fellini). Italy, color. It seems as if we're on the luxury liner that all the townsfolk in Fellini's 1974 *Amarcord* rushed to see from the shore. But what we find on board, along with a lovesick rhinoceros in the hold, is a Europe sailing towards the disaster of World War I. Another return to form by the irrepressible Fellini, who lets his operatic imagination run riot here as never before - too much so for some of his critics. OT: *E la Nave Va*.

2 ***Places in the Heart*** (Robert Benton) US, color. Writer/ director Benton's memories of his childhood, filmed in the Texas town where he grew up. With Sally Field (AA) as the widowed mother of family struggling to survive, John Malkovich as the blind boarder she takes in, Danny Glover as a migrant worker, and Ed Harris, Lindsay Crouse, and Amy Madigan as townsfolk. All of it is beautifully done (the cinematography is by Nestor Almendros), but the almost surreal ending, in which a communion cup is passed from hand to hand and those who have been hurt are reconciled with those who hurt them, is more than merely beautiful.

3 ***The Ballad of Narayama*** (Shohei Imamura). Japan, color. The Cannes Palme d'Or winner for 1983, this folkloric depiction of a Japanese community where for economic reasons those who reach the age of seventy are abandoned to die on a mountain top overwhelmingly conveys horror, pathos, even humor, and above all a sense of individual worth and the importance of self-sacrifice. An earlier version, filmed in 1958, was also much admired.

4 ***A Passage to India*** (David Lean). UK, color. Lean's characteristically meticulous filming of E.M. Forster's novel about cultural clashes under the Raj was his first directorial effort in more than twelve years, and something of a triumph after the relative failure of his *Ryan's Daughter*. The New York critics who had denounced him in person in 1970 made amends, after a fashion, by voting him the best director, and *A Passage to India* the best film, of 1984. Careful viewers will spot virtual quotations from most of Lean's earlier work. With Peggy Ashcroft (AAS), Judy Davis, Victor Bannerjee, James Fox and, inevitably, Alec Guinness. Lean never made another film; *Passage* was to be his *envoi*.

5 ***All of Me*** (Carl Reiner). US, color. Steve Martin brilliantly plays a lawyer who, thanks to a careless guru, must share half of his brain - and sometimes half of his body - with a vindictive millionairess (Lily Tomlin) who has passed away. Was there ever a comedy more screwball?

6 ***Le Crabe-Tambour*** (Pierre Schoendoerffer) France, color. A philosophical sea story in which aging and embittered officers swap stories about the "drummer crab", a brave young Alsatian whom they betrayed during the collapse of France's colonial empire in Indochina and Algeria, and who is now an almost mythic "flying

Dutchman" sailing beyond the heart of darkness. The film, with its multiple flashbacks, is perhaps too hesitant to reveal its ironic secrets, but it has an epic sweep, and Raoul Coutard's photography of jungles, deserts, and especially of the wintry North Atlantic is awesome. Originally released in 1977.

7 *The Killing Fields* (Roland Joffé). UK, color. A tense and sometimes frightening reenactment of the experiences of an American war correspondent and his Cambodian interpreter during and after the fall of Phnom Penh. With Sam Waterston, John Malkovich, and Haing S. Ngor (AAS), who was himself a Cambodian refugee who had been tortured by, and lost his family at the hands of, the Khmer Rouge.

8 *A Soldier's Story* (Norman Jewison). US, color. Riveting film version of a Pulitzer-Prize-winning play about a murder in an all-black army base during World War II, with several actors from the off-Broadway production repeating their roles, and with Howard E. Rollins, Adolf Caesar, and Denzel Washington.

9 *Beverly Hills Cop* (Martin Brest). US, color. Originally conceived as a violent vehicle for the humorless Sylvester Stallone (who turned it down), the story was revamped, largely by its new star, the hip Eddie Murphy, and played uproariously for comedy. It grossed over $200 million (and Murphy moved into Stallone's bungalow at Paramount).

10 *Once Upon a Time in America* (Sergio Leone). US, color. The director of several Italian "spaghetti Westerns" based on the samurai epics of Akira Kurosawa (and of 1968's long, hallucinatory *Once Upon a Time in the West*) tries his hand at a Martin Scorsese gangster film with Robert De Niro and James Woods. Filmed

with impressive technical skill by a largely Italian crew, this was hopelessly confusing at 139 minutes in the first American release, but better – and certainly longer - in the 227-minute re-release. (Italian prints are longer still.) For some, a great tragic statement. For others, overly violent when it isn't being painfully slow and self-indulgent.

Contending for tenth place were *L'Argent*, *Amadeus* (AA), and *Romancing the Stone*.

1985

1 **Prizzi's Honor** (John Huston). US, color. A delectable black comedy about the Mafia in which most of the actors are Irish-Americans and which in the end seems not to be about the Mafia at all but about Hollywood. With Jack Nicholson and Kathleen Turner as a hit man and his hit-lady wife, William Hickey as the godfather, and Huston's daughter Anjelica (AAS) as the Brooklyn girl who misbehaves and is banished by her family to Manhattan.

2 **Ran** (Akira Kurosawa). Japan, color. The 75-year-old master's adaptation of *King Lear*, set in his familiar medieval Japan, with elements of Noh in the acting, a strain of Buddhist redemption in the narrative, several massive battle scenes blazing with color, and an imposing performance by Tatsuya Nakadai as the Lear-like warlord who is betrayed, in this version, by two of his three *sons*. The scene where he descends the steps of his flaming castle is truly awesome. Hollywood took notice, nominating Kurosawa for best director and his picture for art direction and cinematography

- and awarding an Oscar for the fifteen hundred hand-woven, specially dyed costumes.

3 *The Kiss of the Spider Woman* (Hector Babenco). US/Brazil, color/bw. A political anarchist (Raul Julia) and a homosexual with fond memories of Hollywood movies (William Hurt AA) share a prison cell in an unidentified Latin American country. The movie is not so much about how they come to accept each other as about how each meets his fate armed with something of the other's values. Hurt's performance has always been controversial; Julia's is solidly professional.

4 *Out of Africa* (Sidney Pollack). US, color. A long but lushly romantic and consistently interesting drama about Danish writer Isak Dinesen (Meryl Streep), her weak-willed husband (Klaus Maria Brandauer), and her idealistic lover (Robert Redford). Streep's accent (not your average Danish-English but the peculiar inflection Dinesen actually spoke) is so good that Redford prudently doesn't try to affect an English one to suit his role. Wonderful feeling for landscape and period. Oscar for best picture, four others.

5 *The Color Purple* (Steven Spielberg). US, color. The most commercially successful director in Hollywood tries his hand at something more ambitious than sci-fi: filming forty years of a black family's experience in the rural South as related by Alice Walker in her Pulitzer-Prize-winning novel. Audiences were certainly moved by the story, but Spielberg's luxuriant production values tended to overwhelm the good performances of Whoopi Goldberg, Oprah Winfrey, Margaret Avery, and Danny Glover, and the picture was dogged with bad luck - protests from the NAACP, pickets from the Coalition Against Black Exploitation,

and, conversely, cries of "racism at the Oscars" when it won no awards despite eleven nominations.

6 ***Home and the World*** (Satyajit Ray). India, color. One of the last films of the master of Indian cinema, this is the story of a rich Bengali, educated in England, who encourages his wife to break with the purdah tradition of female seclusion, only to have her fall in love with his best friend. Based on a novel by Tagore, preserving too much of the novel's dialogue and told with too little of the visual poetry we expect from Ray, but with a suggestion of despair that is touching and unique in the director's work.

7 ***The Official Story*** (Luis Puenzo). Argentina, color. A politically unaware teacher (Norma Aleandro) finds that her adopted daughter is the child of parents murdered by the regime under which, unthinkingly, she has been content to live. The scene in which Aleandro begins to suspect this is a riveting piece of realistic acting, and the film makes a powerful statement while telling a good story. Oscar for best foreign film.

8 ***The Shooting Party*** (Alan Bridges). UK, color. Guests spend a weekend at an English country estate, and events foretell the coming of the First World War and the end of an era. A modest film with a superb cast: John Gielgud, Edward Fox, Gordon Jackson, Dorothy Tutin, and James Mason - who, in the film, helps a dying man to pray while, in real-life, he was suffering from his own last illness.

9 ***Witness*** (Peter Weir). US, color. A Philadelphia detective (Harrison Ford) lives among the Amish to protect a young boy who has witnessed a murder. A nicely crafted melodrama, not without

clichés but with good detail and a refreshingly uncondescending view of Amish life. With Kelly McGillis and Danny Glover.

10 ***When Father Was Away on Business*** (Emir Kusturica). Yugoslavia, color. The charming story, told through the eyes of a very imaginative boy, of a family that must survive when the father is sent to a labor camp for a minor indiscretion. Winner of the Palme d'Or at Cannes because, reportedly, it was the only film in contention that had nobody didn't like.

Contending for tenth place were *Colonel Redl* and *Shoah*.

1986

1 ***Kaos*** (Paolo and Vittorio Taviani). Italy, color. The masterpiece of the Taviani brothers tells four Sicilian stories by Pirandello: "The Other Son", about a mother's inability to love the only one of her sons who has not left for America; "Moonstruck", about a woman whose husband who has epileptic seizures when the full moon rises; "The Jar", about a potter who unwittingly encloses himself in the jar he is repairing; and "Requiem", about a feudal lord outsmarted by his serfs. In an epilogue, Pirandello (Omero Antonutti) returns to his childhood home, and his deceased mother appears to him to tell him a tale of her own childhood. The brothers' respect for nature's rugged beauty and for the poorest of the poor is everywhere in evidence.

2 ***Platoon*** (Oliver Stone AA). US, color. A tense, visceral, psychologically venturesome film based on Stone's own experiences as a soldier in Vietnam, with Willem Dafoe, Tom Berenger,

Forest Whitaker, Emilio Estevez, and (as Stone's narrator and stand-in self) Estevez's brother Charlie Sheen. Treated with some indifference by critics who thought the war an exhausted subject, it was the Vietnam picture the public had been waiting to see, and a groundswell of interest eventually landed it the Oscar for best picture and three other awards.

3 *A Room With a View* (James Ivory). UK, color. The Merchant-Ivory-Jhabvala team, often condescended to as genteel purveyors of art-house costume dramas, silenced their critics with this beautifully realized screen version of E.M. Forster's novel about (no marks for guessing) a repressed English girl who awakens to passion – this time amid the splendors of Florence. With Maggie Smith, Simon Callow, Denholm Eliot, Rupert Graves, and Judi Dench (too briefly) as proper Edwardians, and with the almost improperly proper Daniel Day-Lewis stealing every scene he is in. Only Helena Bonham Carter, as the girl, disappoints.

4 *The Sacrifice* (Andrei Tarkovsky). Sweden, color. As a nuclear explosion spreads over the earth, an eminent writer (Erland Josephson) offers - to the God he has never believed in - himself, his home, and the gift of speech as a sacrifice if his little son, his loved ones, and the world can be restored as they once were. The opening scene where he plants a withered tree with his son, beautifully filmed by Bergman's cinematographer Sven Nikvyst and set to the "Forgive Me" aria from Bach's St. Matthew Passion, is unforgettable, but the meanings of many other symbols –– Christian, pagan, Nietzschean, and personal images familiar from Tarkovsky's earlier films - remain obscure (to many viewers off-puttingly obscure). What *is* clear is that Tarkovsky, with only a few months left to live, was calling for a spiritual awakening,

and the extremely slow-moving film is his last will and testament, dedicated to his surviving son.

5 *Hannah and Her Sisters* (Woody Allen). US, color. A bounteous family saga, beginning and ending at Thanksgiving dinners, with Mia Farrow, her real-life mother Maureen O'Sullivan, Diane Wiest (AAS), Michael Caine (AAS), Max von Sydow (what unexpected actors turn up in Allen's films!), and Allen himself - all of them at various stages of neurosis. As the Oscar campaign started up, Woody puckishly told *Variety*, "My favorite picture of this year is *Blue Velvet*."

6 *Blue Velvet* (David Lynch). US, color. An audacious "original" that begins with a grisly tribute to Luis Buñuel and proceeds to ferret out all sorts of bizarrerie in a seemingly normal American town. Career-peak opportunities for former has-beens Dean Stockwell and Dennis Hopper, sporadic critical raves, and many cult followings. Popular critic Leonard Maltin called it "terminally weird". Lynch's defense was, simply,"It's not a normal picture."

7 *Thérèse* (Alain Cavalier). France, color. A curiously moving screen biography of the quietly joyous Carmelite nun who died at twenty four and was almost immediately sainted. Filmed austerely in medium shots against white backgrounds, often suggesting Dreyer's *Passion of Joan of Arc* but with welcome touches of humor. A clueless London critic straightfacedly remarked that it might be of some interest in Catholic countries, but "there seems little point in bringing it here".

8 *Mona Lisa* (Neil Jordan). UK, color. A naive ex-con (Bob Hoskins) is hired by a mob boss (Michael Caine) to chauffeur an expensive call-girl (Cathy Tyson) around London, and begins

to understand something about racism, the sleaziness of the sex industry, and the importance of human relationships. The first of writer/director Jordan's moral tales to attract international attention, this is grimly realistic at times, but the immensely likeable Hoskins makes it work. With Nat King Cole singing the vintage title song on the sound track.

9 *My Beautiful Laundrette* (Stephen Frears). UK, color. A wry, incisive examination of race relations, social problems, and homosexual relationships in post-imperial Britain, scripted by Pakistani Hanif Kureish and starring the versatile Daniel Day-Lewis. The first of several films to make its way successfully from the BBC's channel 4 to the wider screen.

10 *Salvador* (Oliver Stone). US, color. Stone's first directorial effort, a failure in its first release but a success on cable TV and at the video stores once the public had seen his *Platoon*, liked it, and wanted more. Based on the experiences of photo-journalist Richard Boyle in strife-torn Central America, with James Woods, James Belushi, and John Savage.

Contending for tenth place was *The Angry Harvest.*

1987

1 *The Dead* (John Huston). UK, color. Huston's last film stays faithful to James Joyce's short story about a Christmas dinner party given by two Dublin spinsters for their friends and relations, but also interpolates, half-way through, an affectionate tribute to Irish dramatist Lady Gregory. The story is surely one of the greatest ever

written, and the movie is a beautiful valedictory from a director, working with a small budget and under considerable physical difficulties, who made his first film, *The Maltese Falcon*, forty-five years earlier. Huston's son Tony served as scriptwriter, and his daughter Anjelica plays the wife who admits to her husband that her dead lover still haunts her memory. The only disappointment is that, doubtless due to budget restrictions, we never see the vast snowfall that, at the end of the story, covers all Ireland, indeed all the world.

2 *Jean de Florette/ Manon of the Spring* (Claude Berri). France, color. A Provençal landowner and his nephew (Yves Montand and Daniel Auteuil) covet the property of a hunchback (Gérard Depardieu), cheat him of the water he needs, and indirectly cause his death. A generation later, the hunchback's wild daughter wreaks vengeance on the culprits. The story is engrossing, the scenery is astonishing, and the three actors give the performances of their careers. Adapted from a novel by Marcel Pagnol which was itself adapted from the an earlier screen version (1952), also by Pagnol. American audiences were bowled over by the first feature and lined up in droves for the second, which was released in the U.S. the next year.

3 *Moonstruck* (Norman Jewison). US, color. John Patrick Shanley's script is the real star of this marvelous comedy about an Italian-American family in Brooklyn - although Cher (AA), Olivia Dukakis (AAS), Nicolas Cage, and Vincent Gardenia all give remarkably effective and in the end quite touching performances in roles that are far from the usual stereotypes. *La Bohème* has sold out at the Met ever since *Moonstruck* took audiences there to see it (in a production actually filmed in Toronto).

4 ***The Last Emperor*** (Bernardo Bertolucci). Italy/UK/ Japan, color. Lavish account of the life of Pu Yi, the last emperor of China: crowned at age three and kept virtually imprisoned and powerless in the Forbidden City, he was deposed by the Revolution at age eighteen, set up as puppet ruler in Manchuria by the Japanese during the Second World War, captured by the Russians when hostilities ended, sent back to Communist China as a prisoner of war, and, after a "re-education" process, was eventually allowed to fend for himself as a private citizen. The picture is oddly structured and, despite its almost three-hour length (almost four hours in the director's cut), it leaves much unexplained for Western viewers. But Bertolucci filmed several scenes in the Forbidden City itself and, with superb photography throughout by Vittorio Storaro, managed easily to win a world-wide audience and the Academy's Oscar for best picture, plus eight other golden statuettes.

5 ***The Assault*** (Fons Rademakers). Holland, color. A twelve-year-old Dutch boy grows up haunted by the memory of the time when his family was liquidated by the Nazis in reprisal for a crime they did not commit, and discovers, forty years later, why things happened as they did. The answers raise new questions about guilt, responsibility, injustice, and heroism. Oscar for best foreign film.

6 ***Radio Days*** (Woody Allen). US, color. A kaleidoscopically comic series of vignettes from Jewish family life in Rockaway as the Depression gave way to World War II. Woody narrates while his repertory company cavorts. A delight for anyone who remembers when radio was every American home's lifeline to the wide world. (Even those unlucky enough to be boomers or Generation Xers have been known to like this genial comedy.) Dozens of nostalgic ballads and instrumentals.

7 ***Fatal Attraction*** (Adrian Lynne). US, color. A cautionary tale about the dangers of one-night-standing. One wag said it was "enough to scare the pants back on you". Director Lynne's first ending had audiences booing, and the second (more Hitchcockian) ending had them cheering - though the picture was promptly labeled woman-hating by about one-half of the population.

8 ***Broadcast News*** (James L. Brooks). US, color. Writer-director-producer Brooks' timely comedy about television newscasting, with William Hurt as a smooth but unintelligent anchor man, Albert Brooks as an intelligent but decidedly unsmooth alternative, and Holly Hunter, in her much admired film debut, as torn between the two of them.

9 ***No Way Out*** (Roger Donaldson). US, color. They don't get much twistier than this taut tale of murder, cover-up, and counter-cover-up in Washington high places - actually a trendy eightyish remake of 1947's *The Big Clock*. With Kevin Costner as the good guy, Gene Hackman as the baddie, and Will Patton as the goodie-goodie. Now did I get that right? Isn't Costner the baddie? Let me know, when you've got half-way through the picture, what *you* think.

10 ***House of Games*** (David Mamet). US, color. More twists, and very enjoyable ones, this time from a Broadway playwright making his debut as writer/director with his wife (Lindsay Crouse) as the star. She plays an expert on compulsive behavior who finds herself compulsively drawn into a confidence game, trying to match wits with a card shark (Joe Mantegna) and his buddies.

Contending for tenth place were *84 Charing Cross Road*, *Full Metal Jacket*, *Hope and Glory*, and *Wall Street*.

1988

1 **Wings of Desire** (Wim Wenders). West Germany, bw/color. A wondrously photographed, more-than-whimsical tale about angels hovering in the skies over divided Berlin, watching over humans, listening to their secret thoughts, offering comfort, and occasionally longing to be human themselves. Children half-sense their presence, and, just possibly, world-weary people may feel their gentle influence in subways, libraries, and hovels. The conceit, developed by Wenders with novelist Peter Handke, owes something to Homer, something to Rilke, and for most of its considerable length the film appears to be a masterpiece. With Bruno Ganz as the angel who becomes a man, and Peter Falk, playing himself, as a man who remembers once being an angel.

2 **Babette's Feast** (Gabriel Axel). Dermark, color. A practical demonstration, by a sophisticated Frenchwoman who comes unexpectedly to a primitive Jutland village, that sensual delight can be reconciled with Christian righteousness. Skillfully adapted from a story by Isak Dinesen, this modest film works on a number of levels, and is deliciously suspenseful, funny, compassionate and, in the end, touching. It is also a feast of understated acting, with Stéphane Audran (of *La Femme Infidèle*), Birgitte Federspiel (of *Ordet*), Bibi Anderson (of many Bergman films) and, in one of the few effective performances on film by an established opera singer, Jean-Philippe Lafont. Surprise winner of the Oscar for best foreign film. Transcendent.

3 ***The Last Temptation of Christ*** (Martin Scorsese). US, color. Homer's Achilles was given a choice between a short, unhappy life of deathless glory and a long, unheroic life of domestic happiness, and chose the former. Nikos Kazantsakis, in his 1955 novel, gave the same choice - or temptation - to Christ on the cross. Scorsese, risking failure as never before, filmed the novel with devotion and considerable skill: in no Biblical film is Christ so terrified and his crucifixion so terrifying. Though neither Willem Dafoe (Christ) nor Harvey Keitel (Judas) nor Barbara Hershey (Mary Magdalene) nor Paul Schrader's dialogue is much more than adequate, the film is hardly the blasphemy fundamentalists who didn't see it insisted it was. (Presumably they wanted a Christ who was God but not man.)

4 ***Au Revoir Les Enfants*** (Louis Malle). France, color. Fourteen years after his *Lacombe, Lucien* - the story of a French peasant boy who, rejected by the Resistance, begins to collaborate with the German occupational forces - Malle remembers his own childhood in a Catholic boarding school and his inadvertent betrayal of a rival classmate who had become his friend - a Jewish boy being hidden from the Nazis. Slightly fictionalized and deliberately understated for most of its length, the film ends with a scene of shattering impact. Winner of the Golden Lion at Venice.

5 ***Red Sorghum*** (Zhang Yimou). China, color. A sensationally vivid memory of violent events in early 20th-century rural China, climaxing in the Japanese invasion. Cinematographer Yimou's directorial debut, the breakthrough film for Chinese cinema in the West, and the first of many remarkable films by Yimou and his star, Gong Li.

6 *Salaam Bombay!* (Mira Nair) India/UK, color. A homeless boy survives among the beggars, drug pushers, street hustlers, pimps, and prostitutes of a teeming city. Unlike Satyajit Ray's films about India, there is some manipulation of audience sympathy here, but this is nonetheless a remarkably confident first film - from a Harvard-trained woman who explored her subject in four documentaries before attempting, with non-professional actors, to film it as a story.

7 *Rain Man* (Barry Levinson AA)). US, color. A glib, self-centered salesman (Tom Cruise) discovers that he has an autistic older brother (Dustin Hoffman AA) who is able to function in severely methodical ways and has the extraordinary mental powers of an idiot savant. Hoffman, who was amusingly one-dimensional in *The Graduate*, proves here that he can do anything demanded of a screen actor. Oscar for best picture, three others.

8 *Die Hard* (John McTiernan). US, color. That rarity – a blockbuster action film that is not only high-tech and hi-fi explosive but genuinely tense, ingenious, and fun. The breakthrough undershirt film for Bruce Willis, with Alan Rickman as a creepy German villain and Reginald Veljohnson as the cuddliest cop in all New York.

9 *Big* (Penny Marshall). US, color. A runty twelve-year-old boy makes a carnival wish ("I want to be big"), wakes up the next morning as a thirty-year-old Tom Hanks, and is soon celebrated in New York as a business genius who seems instinctively to know what kids want in toys. The scene of Hanks footing "Chop Sticks" with Robert Loggia on an giant F.A.O Schwarz piano keyboard is sheer joy. So is most of this unexpectedly charming piece of whimsy.

10 ***Big Business*** (Jim Abrahams). US, color. Less charming than *Big*, but laugh-out-loud funny. In a modern variant of a plot as old as Plautus and improved on by Shakespeare, two sets of identical twins are accidentally mismatched at birth. Lily Tomlin and Bette Midler get to play both the hayseed and the harpy type, but never at a time when it will make sense to suitors, businessmen, and Plaza Hotel bellhops. Thanks to the comic skills of the ladies, this glitzy farce almost reaches the level of the screwball comedies of the thirties.

Contending for tenth place were *Dangerous Liaisons*, *A World Apart*, and *Pelle the Conqueror*.

1989

1 ***Field of Dreams*** (Phil Alden Robinson). US, color. A tender-hearted (but not simple-minded) ghost story about baseball, J.D. Salinger, choices made in life, and coming to terms with the father you never really knew. Adapted by Robinson from the novel "Shoeless Joe" by W.P. Kinsella, about the eight members of the Chicago White Sox who threw the World Series in 1919. Source of the now familiar sayings, "If you build it, he will come," "Ease his pain", and "Go the distance", and widely known as the picture that makes strong men weep. "Bogus!" cried some. "Brave and beautiful!", others said, rightly. With Kevin Costner, Ray Liotta as Shoeless Joe Jackson (unfortunately depicted here as an street-smart right-handed hitter), and James Earl Jones as Salinger (for obvious reasons metamorphed here into a reclusive writer called Terrence Mann). Burt Lancaster appears at two pivotal points in his last, unforgettable, big-screen appearance. The *New York Times* called *Field of Dreams* "a work so smartly written, so beautifully

filmed, so perfectly acted, that it does the almost impossible trick of turning sentimentality into true emotion."

2 *Glory* (Edward Zwick) US, color. A moving, large-scale depiction of an almost forgotten incident of the American Civil War - the storming of a coastal Confederate fort by the first black regiment in US history. Led by an inexperienced twenty-six year old white colonel, the attack was all but suicidal, the bravery overwhelming. Closer in spirit to the patriotic war films of the forties than to the embittered post-Vietnam variety, *Glory* nonetheless shows in detail the prejudice and injustice the 19th-century recruits had to face. Memorable performances by Matthew Broderick, Morgan Freeman, Andre Braugher, and Denzel Washington (AAS).

3 *Henry V* (Kenneth Branagh). UK, color. Half as good as Olivier's version, and that means very good indeed. Branagh expects us to know Olivier's work: scene after scene is a deliberate variant of the earlier film. Olivier's Globe Theater becomes a movie sound stage. Olivier's gently stylized, Book-of-Hours French lesson becomes an earthy study of suppressed passion. Olivier's stirring patriotism is replaced by bitter anti-heroics. Olivier's textual excisions are dutifully restored while other cuts are made. Branagh even got his wife, Emma Thompson, for the final wooing scene (Olivier couldn't get *his* wife, Vivien Leigh, away from her commitment to David O. Selznick.) Brangah in fact has a better crew of actors than Olivier, in wartime, had at his disposal: Derek Jacoby, Ian Holm, Paul Scofield, Alec McCowen, Judy Dench and her husband, Michael Williams (whose passion fiercely lifts the campfire scene to a level beyond that reached in Olivier's wistful reverie). We're fortunate to have both films.

4 ***My Left Foot*** (Jim Sheridan). UK, color. Moving account of the life of Irish poet, novelist, and artist Christy Brown, born into a large, loving family in a working-class Dublin neighborhood and afflicted from birth with cerebral palsy. This is not an "inspirational" picture: Christy, whose left foot is the only limb that functions, is testy, demanding, and by necessity a schemer. An extremely skillful performance by Daniel Day-Lewis (AA), a magnificently sympathetic one by Brenda Fricker (AAS), and a breakthrough for director Sheridan.

5 ***Do the Right Thing*** (Spike Lee). US, color. On his third time out as writer-director, Lee does some right and some wrong things. On a long hot summer day in a black/Puerto Rican/Korean Brooklyn neighborhood life centers, amicably enough at first, around a pizza parlor bedecked with pictures of Italian celebrities. The day's heated atmosphere is palpable, the characters (played by veterans Ossie Davis and Ruby Dee, by newcomers Samuel L. Jackson and Rosie Perez, and by Lee himself, not to mention Danny Aiello and John Turturro as the pizza makers) are vividly realized, and the movie-making is buoyant - until Lee throws in a violent, incomprehensible ending that alienated audiences of all races and prompted a lot of unproductive controversy. But for most of its length, *Do the Right Thing* is, as the *New York Times* said, "one terrific movie."

6 ***Crimes and Misdemeanors*** (Woody Allen). US, color. Allen's most serious film, and also one of his funniest. In two interlocking stories, a wealthy and respected Jewish ophthalmologist (Martin Landau) is driven to commit a crime, and a myopic nebbish (Allen, of course) proves himself incapable even of a misdemeanor. The criminal eventually goes unpunished and prospers, the innocent is left loveless and unrewarded. Conflicting views expressed by wives,

lovers, relatives, a family patriarch, a rabbi, and a philosopher-guru suggest ultimately that there is no purpose to human existence, no moral order to see that justice is done, no evidence for a God who cares or even sees. Compulsively watchable, with Anjelica Huston, Alan Alda, Sam Waterston, Mia Farrow, and Claire Bloom ready to take small parts for small pay to help Allen realize his ambitions.

7 **Driving Miss Daisy** (Bruce Beresford). US, color. Remarkably successful "opening up" for the screen of Alfred Uhry's small-scaled Pulitzer-Prize-winning play, with performances of remarkable range and depth from Jessica Tandy (AA) as a crotchety Southern widow and Morgan Freeman as her unflappable black chauffeur. Both of them are social outsiders (Miss Daisy is Jewish), and through a quarter-century of change a touching bond develops between them. With Dan Aykroyd and Patti Lupone in support. Oscar for best picture, three others.

8 **Under the Sun of Satan** (Maurice Pialat). France, color. Another Georges Bernanos story of a saintly French country priest (Gerard Depardieu) ready to wrestle with Satan for the soul of a sinner (Sandrine Bonnaire). Austere and demanding, it won the Palme d'Or at Cannes - not without a riot in which drector Pialat (who also plays the priest's superior in the film) expressed his disdain for his disdainful critics.

9 **Story of Women** (Claude Chabrol). France, color. The prolific founder of the *nouvelle vague* finds the perfect subject for his cool, ironic, opaque approach to human problems: the execution of a female abortionist (Isabel Huppert) in Vichy France. Chabrol, always more interested in depicting the descent of men and women into criminal activity than in probing their motives for

doing so, recreates the facts of the case without taking sides. We are left to decide for ourselves the morality of what we see.

10 ***Enemies: A Love Story*** (Paul Mazursky). US, color. Isaac Bashevis Singer's novel, about a Holocaust survivor and the three women who claim him in post-war New York, dared to make the funny/sad point that even Holocaust survivors survive with all their faults intact. The film version - witty, ribald, and poignant in turn - is nicely acted by Ron Silver, Anjelica Huston, and Lina Olin.

There were no contenders for tenth place.

The 1990s

The 1990s

1990

1 *The Decalogue* (Krzyztof Kieslowski). Poland, color. Though two parts of this bleak and beautiful ten-part series were issued earlier in North America (as "A Short Film on Killing" and "A Short Film about Love"), the complete work, made for Polish television, first arrived here in 1990. The ten stories are parables subtly derived from the ten commandments (in the Catholic numbering). They are not literal, didactic "thou shalt nots" but open-ended meditations on life, death, love, survival, despair, and hope. The ten parts are tantalizingly connected by recurrent motifs - the almost faceless apartment complex in Warsaw where many of the stories reach their moments of crisis; the silent man who, like the angels in *Wings of Desire*, appears and reappears without explanation; the main characters in some stories who are peripheral in others; the importance, to most of the parables, of children. The new decade produced nothing comparable in stature to this series of haunting tales of ethical challenges and moral - that is to say, searchingly human - choices. OT: *Dekalog*.

2 *Cinema Paradiso* (Giuseppe Tornatore). Italy/France, color. A successful film director remembers his boyhood collusion with the avuncular projectionist of a tiny Sicilian cinema. Charming and perceptive throughout, with an unexpected, unforgettable ending that is a tribute to the movies that the man and the boy watched together. With Philippe Noiret. Oscar for best foreign film.

3 **GoodFellas** (Martin Scorsese). US, color. A whole lot tougher than Coppola's Corleone family pictures, a whole lot uglier than Huston's ironically detached *Prizzi's Honor*, this vivid demonstration of the banality of mafia evil is likely to be remembered longest for Scorsese's confident film making, for the bravura camera work (e.g., the long tracking shot through the kitchen and, following a "special" table carried aloft, into the dining area of a crowded restaurant), and the explosively brutal performances of mobsters Paul Sorvino, Robert de Niro, Joe Pesci (AA), and their corrupted half-Irish recruit Ray Liotta.

4 **The Grifters** (Stephen Frears). US, color. Frears makes a splashy American debut in this generous slice of pulp fiction about three heartless L.A. con artists who finally get theirs. John Cusack and Annette Bening are perversely good, masking their maliciousness behind baby faces, and Anjelica Huston, tough as her sharpened finger nails, cold as the color of her hair styling, is nothing short of terrific. Even that nice Pat Hingle turns out to be a sadistic bounder. Martin Scorsese (this is clearly his Hollywood year) co-produced, bowed out of directing in favor of Frears, and instead spoke the two lines of introductory narration.

5 **Pretty Woman** (Gary Marshall). US, color. What? A modern Cinderella story with no irony, no gloomy let-down, no well-what-did-she-expect conclusion? You mean, in this day and age, they're actually going to let this Cinderella get her prince? You'll want to stand up and cheer as Richard Gere returns, practically on a white horse, to rescue plucky Julia Roberts from her unmaidenly, distressful past. Why, in the pessimism of these times, did it take so long for fairy tales to come stylishly true in the movies?

232

6 ***Reversal of Fortune*** (Barbet Schroeder). US, color. The sensational case of Claus von Bulow (Jeremy Irons AA, in his subtlest and wittiest screen performance), narrated by the brain-dead wife (Glenn Close) he may or may not have tried to murder. Vastly entertaining, though the scenes with Ron Silver as defense lawyer Alan Dershowitz, on whose best seller Schroeder based his script, are hardly up to the glittering rest.

7 ***Alice*** (Woody Allen). US, color. A slender but charming picture in which a pampered and unfulfilled Manhattan wife (Mia Farrow) finds liberation in the herbal remedies of a Chinatown healer and self-discovery after a visit to (Woody always surprises!) Mother Teresa of Calcutta. With William Hurt, Joe Mantegna, and Alec Baldwin.

8 ***Dances With Wolves*** (Kevin Costner AA). US, color. Overlong, overly solemn, but heart-in-the-right place tale of a cavalry officer (Costner) adopted by the Sioux. Impressively filmed in South Dakota, with a battle sequence and a Buffalo stampede that are near-classic set pieces. Costner's directorial debut. Good question: how did it manage to win the Oscar for best picture, along with six others?

9 ***Presumed Innocent*** (Alan J. Pakula). US, color. Intense, involving filmization of Scott Turow's popular criminal-investigation page-turner. While a gloomy Harrison Ford is the nominal star, it's the supporting cast - Brian Dennehy, Raul Julia, and Paul Winfield - who really make the picture sizzle. Good question: how is it that the audience can tell who done it a half hour before the final fade out? It wasn't that way with the book.

10 *The Godfather III* (Francis Ford Coppola). US, color. Michael Corleone attempts unsuccessfully to buy his redemption and go straight. When this solemn, self-conscious sequel to his two-part *Godfather* epic appeared shortly after *GoodFellas*, Coppola finally yielded supremacy in the mafia genre to Scorsese. Paradoxically, the relative failure of Coppola's part III increased respect for the achievements of his parts I and II. Al Pacino and Talia Shire, the only commanding figures left from the earlier films, give strong performances. Coppola's daughter Sofia gives a disastrous one. (She was eventually to prove herself a successful director.)

Contending for tenth place were *The Field* and *Misery*.

1991

1 *My Father's Glory/ My Mother's Castle* (Yves Robert). France, color. A two-part filming of the coming-of-age memoirs of Marcel Pagnol, author of the *Marius/César/Fanny* plays (see 1948) and the two *Jean de Florette* novels (see 1987). Beautifully photographed in Provençe. The emphasis is on innocent nostalgia, and the film is sheer bliss for any lover of French cinema.

2 *Boyz N The Hood* (John Singleton) US, color. An often violent, occasionally funny, and genuinely moving coming-of-age study of three young blacks from a Los Angeles ghetto, with something of the on-the-spot realism, desperation, and loving father/son bonding of *The Bicycle Thief.* The breakthrough film for Ice Cube and Cuba Gooding, Jr., with Angela Bassett and Larry Fishburne as parents. The twenty-three-year old Singleton propels his own script to a shattering conclusion.

3 ***The Silence of the Lambs*** (Jonathan Demme, AA). US, color. The first Hollywood shocker since *Rosemary's Baby* to draw on primal fears. The terrifying, witty performance of Anthony Hopkins (AA) as the imprisoned cannibal Hannibal Lecter has passed into legend. The matching performance of Jodie Foster (AA) as the FBI trainee is a study in steely resistance to intimidation. The movie remains undimmed by the inadequate sequels it spawned. Oscar for best picture, four others – and only the third picture to win all four top statuettes.

4 ***The Vanishing*** (George Sluizer). Holland/France, color. Perhaps the first European shocker since the silent era to draw, as *The Silence of the Lambs* did, on primal fears. A vacationer obsessively searches for his girl friend, who has suddenly disappeared, is finally contacted by her abductor, and comes to a horrific (but bloodless) discovery. Unfortunately Sluizer remade the film in America a few years later, with truly terrible results.

5 ***The Miracle*** (Neil Jordan). UK, color. Jordan tops all of his previous efforts with the year's third coming-of-age study: a teen-aged boy and girl who amuse themselves making up stories about people they watch in an Irish seaside resort are fascinated by a mysterious new arrival in town (Beverly D'Angelo). By the time God manifests his presence in their lives through the eye of a circus elephant, it has become clear that this is one of the rare English-speaking films that demand, and reward, an audience's feeling for fantasy and metaphor.

6 ***Life Is Sweet*** (Mike Leigh). UK, color. Leigh tops all of *his* previous efforts with this funny/sad story of a dysfunctional British working-class family. As usual with this filmmaker, none of the actors knew much about what the others had been told to say and

do, and as a result the performances by Leigh's repertory company - Alison Steadman, Jim Broadbent, Timothy Spall, Stephen Rea, David Thewlis, Claire Skinner, and above all Jane Horrocks - are small wonders of improvisation.

7 *Ju Dou* (Zhang Yimou). China, color. This gorgeously filmed folk tale - about a dyer who abuses his beautiful wife (Gong Li) and finally destroys her and her lover - was banned in its land of origin. Presumably government officials suspected that it was a parable about their own oppressiveness. But how could they really determine the intent of a film in which dyed fabrics are used to externalize inner states? Be forewarned: the young son of Ju Dou is likely to re-appear in your nightmares.

8 *Europa Europa* (Agnieszka Holland). Germany/France, color. True story of a Jewish boy who, passing for Aryan, survives a number of World War II experiences in Poland, Russia, and Germany (where he is actually initiated into the Hitlerjugend). Harrowing, humorous (the boy's circumcised state is no asset to him) and humane.

9 *Thelma and Louise* (Ridley Scott). US, color. A feminist road movie, with Susan Sarandon and Geena Davis fleeing their men and, finally, the law. There hasn't been such a watchable pair on the run since the handcuffed couple in *The 39 Steps*. The story proceeds by leaps and - literally at the close - bounds. Brad Pitt exudes star power in a small role.

10 *Beauty and the Beast* (Walt Disney studios). US, color. Hardly on a level with what the studio did fifty years before under Uncle Walt, this feminist updating of the familiar fairy tale plays like a Broadway musical, which is what it eventually

became. Angela Lansbury provides the voice of a tea pot and sings the super-sweet title song without a trace of irony. The cups and spoons do a Busby Berkeley production number. This is so far the only animated film to be nominated for the best picture Oscar.

There were no contenders for tenth place.

1992

1 ***Howards End*** (James Ivory). UK, color. This adaptation of E.M. Forster's novel about Edwardian England in decay is the finest achievement of the charmed team of director Ivory, producer Ismail Merchant, and writer Ruth Prawer Jhabvala. With superbly nuanced performances by Emma Thompson, Anthony Hopkins, and Vanessa Redgrave, and a not-too-sulky one by Helena Bonham-Carter. (One of the smaller treasures of the year was another Forster novel on film, *Where Angels Fear To Tread* - not by the Merchant-Ivory team.)

2 ***The Crying Game*** (Neil Jordan). UK, color. An IRA thriller turned, by one of the most famous surprises in recent movie history, into a telling examination of human nature. (There will be no spoilers in what follows here.) Director Jordan wrote the stunningly original script. With Stephen Rea, Forest Whitaker, Jaye Davidson, Miranda Richardson, and, all too briefly, Jim Broadbent.

3 ***Unforgiven*** (Clint Eastwood, AA). US, color. A dark, brutal Western parable with a moral edge. Four actors of stature -Clint Eastwood, Gene Hackman (AAS), Morgan Freeman, and Richard

Harris, each at the peak of his form - enact four ambivalent and carefully differentiated characters. Eastwood's direction is stunning. Oscar for best picture, three others.

4 *The Best Intentions* (Bille August). Sweden, color. Ingmar Bergman's account of the troubled married life of his parents, straightforwardly filmed by director August. Essential viewing for Bergmanites. Winner of the Palme d'Or at Cannes.

5 *Hear My Song* (Peter Chelsom). US/UK, color. An Irish impresario, down on his luck in London, brings the legendary tenor Josef Locke over to sing for his fellow countrymen, who are trying to beat the blahs in Britain. A tiny comedy of great charm, irresistible when it crosses the sea to the Emerald Isle. Chelsom's debut as writer-director. Ned Beatty is astonishingly good as the tenor.

6 *Enchanted April* (Mike Newell). UK, color. Four English women (Josie Lawrence, Miranda Richardson, Joan Plowright, and Polly Walker), all in desperate need of getting away, share an Italian villa for a month and find so much rapture amid the flowers and lizards that we dread the inevitable appearances of two husbands (Alfred Molina and Jim Broadbent). Four fetchingly feminine performances. Pure pleasure.

7 *Glengarry Glen Ross* (James Foley). US, color. Terrific ensemble acting (Al Pacino, Jack Lemon, Ed Harris, Alan Arkin, Kevin Spacey, Alec Baldwin) make the macho, all-male David Mamet play about foul-mouthed and near-despairing real estate salesmen even more riveting on film than it was on the stage.

8 *Like Water for Chocolate* (Alfonso Arau). Mexico, color. In a border-town hacienda, the youngest daughter of the family, not allowed to marry, turns to cooking to keep her emotions below the boiling point - like water for making chocolate. A sensual, flavorsome fable from south of the border that became an unexpected success world-wide.

9 *Belle Epoque* (Fernando Trueba). Spain, color. A deserter from the Republican army is taught lessons in love by four sisters during the "beautiful era" before Spain was plunged into civil war. A lightweight and likeable celebration of sex and innocence. Oscar for best foreign film.

10 *White Men Can't Jump* (Ron Shelton). US, color. Wesley Snipes is the black man who can jump, Woody Harrelson is the white man who can dribble and pass, and Rosie Perez is the girl-friend who goes on "Jeopardy" to make money to support the two guys, who just want to play basketball. Director Shelton proves he knows as much about slam dunks as he knew about sinkers and sliders in his earlier *Bull Durham*.

Contending for tenth place were *Raise the Red Lantern*, *The Last of the Mohicans*, *My Cousin Vinny*, *A Few Good Men*, and *Where Angels Fear to Tread*.

1993

1 *Schindler's List* (Steven Spielberg AA). US, bw. A moving three-hour film account of the factually true rescue of more than a thousand Polish Jews from Auschwitz, filmed mainly on location

and told with surprising control and restraint by the world's most commercially successful filmmaker. With Liam Neeson as the war-profiteer Oskar Schindler, Ben Kingsley as the Jew who serves as his conscience, and Ralph Fiennes as an unhinged Nazi camp commander. A disappointingly static penultimate scene is redeemed by an overwhelming ending. Oscar for best film, six others.

2 *The Remains of the Day* (James Ivory). UK, color. Another winner from the Merchant-Ivory-Jhabvala team, this eloquent filming of a novel (by Kazuo Ishiguro) that was so interiorized it was thought unfilmable contains what is arguably Anthony Hopkins' finest performance: as an emotionally repressed butler who finds that his unquestioning loyalty to his master was tragically misplaced, he quietly conveys a thousand subtleties with his face, shoulders, gait, speech, and whole demeanor. With Emma Thompson, who matches him scene for scene, and with James Fox and Christopher Reeve in support.

3 *The Piano* (Jane Campion). New Zealand, color. A Gothic feminist romance in which a grand piano plays the monster. A mute Scottish woman (Holly Hunter) arrives with her piano and a prepubescent daughter (Anna Paquin AAS) on the coast of New Zealand. She has been married by arrangement to a reticent landowner (Sam Neill), but soon she yields, in the oddest seduction scene in movie history, to the uncouth English settler (Harvey Keitel) who buys her piano. The most unthinkable things ensue, including the unexpected emergence of New Zealand as a presence on the international film scene. Though the piano theme music is hopelessly inadequate to the part it is expected to play in the proceedings, the virtuoso, highly original film was co-winner of the Palme d'Or at Cannes (see the next entry).

4 ***Farewell My Concubine*** (Chen Kaige). China, color. A spectacular, fast-paced epic that follows the careers, across several decades of turbulent history, of two boys who become stars - one playing male, the other female roles - at the Peking Opera. Also a parable about art imitating life, of art surviving historic upheavals, and - when the male singer finds a lover (Gong Li) to upset the relationship between the men - of art as a solace for human misery. Co-winner, with *The Piano*, of the Palme d'Or at Cannes. Oscar for best foreign film.

5 ***Short Cuts*** (Robert Altman). US, color. Nine short stories of Raymond Carver linked together, in ways that Carver never intended, to make a kind of Southern California *Nashville*. Some of Carver's fans objected, but much of the picture is first-rate Altman, and it clearly influenced Paul Thomas Anderson's later *Magnolia* and several other films of the decade. Enduring their tortured lives under the helicopters spraying LA medflies are Lily Tomlin, Julianne Moore, Francis McDormand, Anne Archer, Tim Robbins, and Robert Downey, Jr.

6 ***In the Name of the Father*** (Jim Sheridan). UK, color. This powerful indictment, based on fact, of the corruption of English rule in Northern Ireland is also the moving story of a father (Pete Postlethwaite) reconciled with his IRA son (Daniel Day-Lewis). With the ubiquitous and always welcome Emma Thompson. The British magazine *Sight and Sound* indignantly called the picture "unashamed Irish myth-making". The world beyond Britain believed it.

7 ***Philadelphia*** (Jonathan Demme). US, color. When a promising young lawyer (Tom Hanks AA) contracts AIDS and is fired by his firm, he sues his firm and is defended by an ambulance-chasing

homophobe (Denzel Washington) - who comes to respect and understand his client when he hears his passionate defense of Maria Callas' recording of "La Mamma Morta". A timely, necessary film that, disappointingly, turns over-earnest and preachy. With Jason Robarts, Antonio Banderas, Mary Steenburgen, and (briefly) Joanne Woodward.

8 *In the Line of Fire* (Wolfgang Petersen). US, color. An unusual thriller in which an aging Secret Service agent (Clint Eastwood), haunted by his failure to protect President Kennedy from assassination, is hounded by a crazed killer (John Malkovich) intent on assassinating the current president. One of Eastwood's best performances. Malkovich may give you nightmares.

9 *The Age of Innocence* (Martin Scorsese). US, color. The Edith Wharton novel about 1870s upper-crust New York was an unusual choice for Scorsese, whose New York is usually the mean streets of his boyhood. But, as in the later *Gangs of New York*, in which he also chose to document the city's more remote past, he shows a surprising attention to period detail and fills his picture with memorable set pieces. Daniel-Day Lewis and Michele Pfeiffer give good performances in a cast of, it must be admitted, rather varying effectiveness.

10 *Mrs. Doubtfire* (Chris Columbus). US, color. Robin Williams gives the performance of his career as a resourceful but undependable husband who, divorced by his wife (Sally Field), dresses as an English nanny to be with his three children. A box-office blockbuster too sentimental by half, but with enough hilarity to keep the sentiment from getting out of hand.

Contending for tenth place were *The Scent of Green Papaya*, *Groundhog Day*, and *The Fugitive*.

1994

1 ***Pulp Fiction*** (Quentin Tarantino). US, color. This first mainstream American postmodernist film tells three stories with an insouciant disregard for Aristotle's "beginning, middle, and end". The ingredients of pulp - sex, murder, and everything in between - are devilishly mixed for maximum shock, surprise, and entertainment value. With John Travolta and Samuel L. Jackson as hit men who criticize hegemonic social structures as they talk about hamburgers, and with Bruce Willis, Harvey Keitel, and Uma Thuman in other go-for-broke roles. Non-linear storytelling at its headiest. Palme d'Or at Cannes.

2 ***Forrest Gump*** (Robert Zemeckis AA). US, color. An immensely popular, sentimental, often hilarious original, with an astonishing new use of digital wizardry and with Tom Hanks (AA) in a career-peak role as a slow-witted participant in most of the major events of the past three decades in America. The picture falters only when the likeable Gump goes trendily hippy in the last half hour. Janet Maslin grumped in *The New York Times* that Zemeckis's hero was "the embodiment of absolutely nothing" and that the film "dumbed down" its audiences. Audiences wildly disagreed. With Gary Sinise and Sally Field. Oscar for best picture, five others.

3 ***Tricolor: Blue, White, Red*** (Krzystof Kieslowski). France, color. Three films cryptically based on the three colors of the French flag. In *Blue* (Liberté), a Parisian woman (Juliette Binoche) tries

to deal with her husband's death. In *White* (Egalité), a sexually incompetent down-and-outer smuggles himself out of Paris to his native Poland in a suitcase. In *Red* (Fraternité), a young woman in Geneva forms an unusual friendship with a retired judge (Jean-Louis Trintignant) who wiretaps on his neighbors. The main characters in each story meet by coincidence at the end of the last. Each of the three films - the tragic, the comic, and the romantic - is dominated by its own color, is shot through with motifs that are never quite symbolic, and leads us on with an ever-increasing sense of wondering where we are going. Yes, it's a thinkpiece, but a very satisfying one. *Blue* won the Golden Lion at Venice.

4 *The Shawshank Redemption* (Frank Darabont). US, color. An innocent man imprisoned for life (Tim Robbins) is befriended in a brutal prison by a "fixer" (Morgan Freeman) and eventually makes his escape. The sleeper of the year, packing an huge emotional wallop, it was largely dismissed by critics as overlong and predictable but taken up enthusiastically by audiences once word-of-mouth had spread. Many people, almost all of them men, now cite it as their all-time favorite movie.

5 *The Last Seduction* (John Dahl). US, color. In 1994 Dahl seemed hell-bent on reinventing the forties' *film noir* in garish colors, and his brazen, man-hating heroine (Linda Fiorentino) was equally hell-bent on helping him out. The result: a small, riveting, erotic, fast-paced film worthy of mentioning in the same breath with *Double Indemnity*.

6 *Red Rock West* (John Dahl). US, color. Dahl in another small, compact *noir* sleeper, made for cable television but, after the success of *The Last Seduction*, quickly caught up for major

release. With a plot full of surprises and with terrific performances by Nicolas Cage, Dennis Hopper, and J.T. Walsh.

7 *Raining Stones* (Kenneth Loach). UK, color. It was a good year for small films. Loach tells the ironic, bittersweet story of an unemployed Manchester working-class Catholic who falls into the hands of a loan shark when he needs money for his daughter's First Communion dress. (Critics were equally impressed with Loach's *Ladybird, Ladybird*, also released in 1994.)

8 *The Madness of King George* (Nicholas Hytner). UK, color. A historical recreation of the reign of George III - the king who ruled England for sixty years, lost the American colonies because of excessive taxation, and periodically succumbed to madness. Based on the play by Alan Bennett, but brilliantly "opened up" by director Hytner, making his screen debut. With Nigel Hawthorne, Helen Mirren, and Ian Holm.

9 *Eat Drink Man Woman* (Ang Lee). Taiwan, color. In interlocking stories that are all at least partly concerned with eating, a Taiwanese master chef who has lost his sense of taste almost loses his three daughters. The acting is consistently good, and director Lee shows much of the sense and sensibility he was to demonstrate in his filming of Jane Austen in the year to come.

10 *Hoop Dreams* (Steve James) US, color. A long, ambitiously detailed documentary on basketball, the sport in which many African-American boys have some hope of lifting themselves up out of the ghetto. *New York* magazine rightly observed that it was "tragic in its implications", that "America is interested in making these boys into stars but not into men."

Contending for tenth place were *Ladybird, Ladybird, Bullets Over Broadway*, and *To Live*.

1995

1 *The Usual Suspects* (Brian Singer). US, color. A labyrinthine thriller in which a gimpy con man (Kevin Spacey AAS) is interrogated by a US customs agent (Chazz Palminteri) about his four accomplices, all of them killed setting fire to a Hungarian ship they thought was filled with cocaine. Now a cult classic (and every cult member is sure he knows who the mysterious "Keyser Söse" is), it seemed at first, even to so astute a critic as Stanley Kauffmann, a prime example of how not to make a thriller. But it repays repeated viewings so well that it may in time become a classic beyond its cult. (Two viewings may not be enough to sort things out.) With Gabriel Byrne, Benicio Del Toro, and Pete Postlethwaite.

2 *Sense and Sensibility* (Ang Lee). UK, color. The hugely talented Emma Thomson does her own adaptation of Jane Austen's novel about two sisters and their suitors, and, under a Taiwanese director, everything, including the novel's exposé of a society that is cruel to its women, goes astonishingly right. With Kate Winslet, Alan Rickman, Hugh Grant, and Elisabeth Spriggs. (Jane Austen had quite a year, with a somber *Persuasion* filmed for BBC television and released commercially, and with a delicious *Emma* peopled with young Silicon Valley ladies and gentlemen and retitled *Clueless*.)

3 ***Dead Man Walking*** (Tim Robbins). US, color The now-familiar true story of a Louisiana nun, Sister Helen Prejean (Susan Sarandon AA), who counsels a murderer on death row (Sean Penn). An eloquent and, with its recurrent flashbacks of the murder, painful plea for the abolition of the death penalty. The film at once acknowledges the heinousness of the crime, sympathizes with the bereaved parents of the murdered children, and asks for understanding.

4 ***Il Postino*** (Michael Radford). Italy, color. The exiled Chilean poet Pablo Neruda (Philippe Noiret) is befriended on the isle of Capri by the humble man who delivers his mail (Massimo Troisi), and the poet teaches the postman the romantic potency of words. A world-wide audience was not surprised, after seeing Troisi's poignant performance, to hear that he was dying as he made the film, and survived only one day after the shooting was completed. The film is not as factual as it could be (the political Neruda was actually *persona non grata* in Italy), and it is further marred by a heavy-handed ending that seems unconnected with what went before. But for most of its length it rings touchingly true.

5 ***Smoke*** (Wayne Wang). US, color. A gently perceptive and unsentimental examination of human failings and human goodness as witnessed by the proprietor of a Brooklyn cigar shop (Harvey Keitel in a nicely nuanced performance). With William Hurt, Forest Whitaker, Stockard Channing, and Ashley Judd. Beautifully written and acted. (Avoid the quasi-sequel *Blue in the Face*, apparently concocted from outtakes and discarded ideas from the original film.)

6 ***Apollo 13*** (Ron Howard). US, color. A straightforward but stirring film account of the 1970 moon mission that, after the

successful landing in 1969, everyone was blasé about until things started to go wrong. Typical of the proficient middle-brow product that former child star Howard was to turn out for the next decade. With Tom Hanks, Kevin Bacon, and Ed Harris.

7 ***Lamerica*** (Gianni Amelio). Italy, color. In post-communist Albania, two Italian con artists take advantage of the natives who hope to escape to a better life in Italy. A series of unpredictable and heart-breaking events ensues. Amelio pulls a Hitchcock surprise when the man we thought was to be the lead character, played by veteran Michele Placido, drops out of the picture early on. The eighty-year-old Carmelo di Mazzarelli, who had never acted before, gives a remarkable performance as a man who thinks that the escape ship is taking him to America.

8 ***Braveheart*** (Mel Gibson AA). US, color. A three-hour blockbuster retelling of the tale of Scots hero William Wallace. After any number of bloody battle scenes, Gibson as Wallace undergoes the torments of the damned before he dies - a preparation for his project of writing and directing his brutally realistic 2004 movie on Jesus. *Braveheart* is undoubtedly powerful and technically accomplished, yet some moviegoers preferred the subtler *Rob Roy*, the tale of another Scotsman released the same year - especially for the swaggeringly malicious sword-wielding of Tim Roth. All the same, it was patriot Gibson's epic labor of love that won the Oscar for best picture, and four others.

9 ***Before the Rain*** (Milcho Manchevski). Macedonia/England/France, color. Manchevski's first feature film, this story of strife between Macedonian Christians and Albanian Muslims in the former Yugoslavia and, later, in London is earnest, overplotted,

and logy with symbols, but undeniably watchable and still timely. Golden Lion at the Venice film festival.

10 *Losing Isaiah* (Stephen Gyllenhall). US, color. An African-American mother (Halle Berry), crazed by crack, leaves her baby in a trash bin, and discovers, when she tries desperately to reclaim him, that he has been adopted by a dedicated social worker (Jessica Lange) and her husband. No character in this wrenching story is unflawed, but everyone reaches some point of understanding. With Cuba Gooding, Jr. and Samuel L. Jackson.

Contending for tenth place were *Persuasion*, *Clueless*, and *Once Were Warriors*.

1996

1 *Secrets and Lies* (Mike Leigh). UK, color. Leigh and his repertory actors (who as usual are only partially told in advance how they are supposed to interact with each other, or even what the picture they will make is really about) bring off their most astonishing film. The meeting, after more than twenty years, of the mother (Brenda Blethyn) and the daughter she gave away immediately after childbirth (Marianne Jean-Baptiste) leaves both actresses and audience slack-jawed. The scene is not a stunt, but the centerpiece of a long, emotionally charged, and often funny view of life in working-class London. With Timothy Spall. Winner of the Palm d'Or at Cannes.

2 *Fargo* (Joel Coen). US, color. A deliberately two-dimensional, perversely snowy black comedy out of which one character, the

pregnant police chief played by Frances McDormand (AA), emerges unpredictably as not only three-dimensional but right up there with the cherishable characters we remember from the screwball comedies of the thirties - though this commonsense woman with the awful Minnesota drawl is decidedly not a screwball. There is also a funny-pathetic performance, the first of many more to come, by William H. Macy. Ingenious script by director Joel and producer Ethan Coen.

3 ***The English Patient*** (Anthony Minghella). UK, color. Picturesque locales, big passions, painstaking filming in the David Lean tradition - but Minghella had to turn Michael Ondaatje's torturous novel inside out to get a workable script. Ralph Fiennes is the hideously burned World War II flyer, Juliette Binoche (AAS) is the Canadian nurse who tends him and, in flashbacks, Kristin Scott Thomas is the love of his life. Oscar for best picture, eight others.

4 ***Breaking the Waves*** (Lars von Trier). Denmark, color. Emily Watson, in her screen debut, plays a half-witted Scottish girl who has mystical experiences and believes that by taking lovers she can cure her husband of his paralysis. This has some of the strange power of Carl Dreyer's Scandinavian miracle plays from a half-century earlier. The use of a hand-held camera enhances the decidedly unsettling mood. Von Trier's subsequent career was even more decidedly unsettling.

5 ***Jerry Maguire*** (Cameron Crowe). US, color. In the 1996 Oscar race, this was only best picture nominee to come from a major Hollywood studio. Fortunately it was a terrific movie: a disgraced sports agent (Tom Cruise) and the sole client who stays with him (Cuba Gooding, Jr. AAS) learn valuable lessons from

each other, while winsome Renée Zellweger watches in wonder and quietly helps. The picture starts slowly, gains momentum, and ends with the movie audience on its feet cheering.

6 *La Cérémonie* (Claude Chabrol). France, color. Another of Chabrol's depictions of criminal behavior left largely unexplained - and all the more chilling for that. (The title refers to the ritual that once took place before a victim was guillotined.) With Isabelle Huppert, Sandrine Bonnaire, and Jacqueline Bisset.

7 *Sling Blade* (Billy Bob Thornton). US, color. Touching portrait of a mentally deficient murderer who is released from prison after twenty years and helped by a boy to find his way back into an often incomprehensible world. Thornton wrote, directed and, with startling vividness, acted the lead role. Equally effective are Lucas Black as the boy and John Ritter as a sensitive homosexual.

8 *Lone Star* (John Sayles). US, color. A lawman in a Texas border town deals with the memory of his hated father (the former sheriff), while the townsfolk - Latinos, Seminoles, African-Americans and whites - remember their divisive pasts and try to create a future together. (Sayles, who always works as an independent, has done similarly complex examinations of life in Florida, West Virginia, and other parts of the US.) With Kris Kristofferson, Chris Cooper, and Frances McDormand.

9 *Kolya* (Jan Sverák). Czech Republic, color. Laughter and tears as a womanizing Prague cellist suddenly finds himself in charge of a five-year-old boy from Russia on the eve of Czechoslovakia's winning its independence from the USSR. People of a certain age

may have seen it sixty years earlier *mutatis mutandis* with Shirley Temple. Oscar for best foreign film.

10 **Hamlet** (Kenneth Branagh). UK/US, color. Branagh challenges Olivier again, with less success this time. But once again we are expected to know the earlier version and mark the differences. Olivier cut the text mercilessly, Branagh gives us every word (at four hours!). Olivier opted for German expressionism, Branagh aims at nineteenth-century romanticism. Oliver shot in gloomy black-and-white, Branagh chooses glitzy color. Olivier used little-known actors with stage experience, Branagh gives us a roster of international stars, mainly movie stars, who give extremely variable performances. Yet through it all Branagh's Shakespeare holds our interest.

Contending for tenth place were *Courage Under Fire, Emma, Michael Collins*, and *The Horseman on the Roof.*

1997

1 **L.A. Confidential** (Curtis Hanson). US, color. Russell Crowe, Guy Pearce and Kevin Spacey play three very different L.A. cops in this sensational adaptation of James Ellroy's complex novel about tabloid journalism and police corruption in the city of the angels. With Kim Basinger (AAS) as a Veronica Lake look-alike, Danny DeVito, and James Cromwell. Blink and you might miss something - this is a movie that really moves. Everyone involved is brilliant.

2 *As Good As It Gets* (James L. Brooks). US, color. The title says it exactly. Jack Nicholson (AA) is outrageously good as an obsessive-compulsive jerk, and Helen Hunt (AA) is absolutely wonderful as the womanly waitress who tames him. This is also a picture brave enough to show gay men as sensitive yet sensible (Greg Kinnear), macho yet artistic (Cuba Gooding Jr.) and brutally destructive (Skeet Urich and his awful crew).

3 *Good Will Hunting* (Gus Van Sant). US, color. A blue-collar problem kid who also happens to be a mathematical genius (Matt Damon) fights it out with a teacher/psychologist (Robin Williams, AAS). Written by Damon and his buddy in the film and in real life, Ben Affleck, when each of them realized that the best way to get a good role in the movies was to write one for yourself.

4 *Amistad* (Steven Spielberg). US, color. A cargo of chained Africans, led by a giant of a man named Cinqué, take over the Spanish slave ship Amistad, kill most of the crew, and are diverted to America where they are tried for murder, defended by American abolitionists, and saved by the oratory of John Quincy Adams (Anthony Hopkins). The powerful, historically based but not always historically accurate film was grossly underrated by critics put off by what they thought Spielberg's uppity high-mindedness. With Djimon Hounsou as Cinqué and Morgan Freeman as a fictional black abolitionist.

5 *My Best Friend's Wedding* (P.J. Hogan). US, color. A super-smart New York writer (Julia Roberts) sets out for Chicago to sabotage the wedding of her former lover (Dermot Mulroney) and a little rich girl (Cameron Diaz), while her gay editor (Rupert Everett) provides sage counsel from the wings. An exhilarating neo-screwball comedy whose every unpredictable plot turn (devised by

writer Ronald Bass) is a delight. Both ladies are splendid. Everett's work promised much more than he has delivered since.

6 **Shall We Dance?** (Masayuki Suo). Japan, color. A married accountant sneaks off to a dancing school, finds several other shy stumblers there, and falls in love with one of the teachers. Touching, funny, and a surprise hit in North America. (Predictably, there was an unfortunate American remake.) The title comes not from the Astaire-Rogers film but from the polka Yul Brynner danced with Deborah Kerr, famously, in *The King and I*.

7 **Kundun** (Martin Scorsese). US, color. Auteurists have had a difficult time reconciling this stunningly beautiful film with the rest of the Scorsese oeuvre. An account of the boyhood and young manhood of the fourteenth Dalai Lama, it seems - in style, pacing, and subject matter - utterly different from the rest of the director's output - including his quasi-religious life of Christ. Some audiences were puzzled, some alienated. The *New York Times* called it "as much a prayer as a movie".

8 **The Sweet Hereafter** (Atom Egoyan). Canada, color. A lawyer (Ian Holm) comes to a snowy Canadian town after fourteen children have been killed in a school bus accident, and we see, mostly in flashbacks, not just the accident itself but the splintered secrets of both the lawyer and the townsfolk. A relentless search for moral truth, produced and scripted by director Agoyan, with Canadian actors Bruce Greenwood and Sarah Polly.

9 **La Promesse** (Jean-Pierre and Luc Dardenne). Belgium, color. There's still more relentless searching for moral truth in this cinema-verité story of a father who runs an illegal immigrant racket and his conscienceless son who moves towards compassion

and a sense of personal responsibility when he makes a promise to one of the victimized "clients". A gritty and uncompromising film, with no musical score and no emotional let up.

10 *Titanic* (James Cameron). US, color. OK, so the prologue is execrably acted, the ship's crew doesn't see the iceberg coming because they're watching Leo DiCaprio and Kate Winslet make love, and the stupendous scenes of the great vessel going under lose much of their effect as we cut away constantly to the lovers wading through watery corridors. It's still one of the most awesome and technologically accomplished of all movie spectacles. Every penny of the two hundred million dollars spent on it is right up there on the screen. And Cameron and crew deserve respect for carrying on when it looked like, financially, the movie was going to go down with the ship. Oscar for best picture, ten others, a record it shared with *Ben-Hur* and would share, in six years' time, with *Lord of the Rings: The Return of the King*.

Contending for tenth place was *The Apostle*.

1998

1 *Saving Private Ryan* (Steven Spielberg AA). US, color. The gut-wrenchingly realistic twenty-minute opening sequence at Omaha Beach on D-Day instantly qualified as one of the great passages in the history of cinema, and the extended combat scene near the end is almost as impressive. The central story, about an infantry captain (Tom Hanks) searching for a young private whose three brothers have been killed in battle, is not on that level,

though thousands of World War II veterans wept while watching it. With Tom Sizemore, Jeremy Davies, and Matt Damon.

2 *The Thin Red Line* (Terrence Malick). US, color. A close contender, with *Saving Private Ryan*, for the all-time best American film about war. Malick, on Guadalcanal, takes a wholly different approach from Spielberg - introspective, grimly poetic, pacifist, and unsentimental - but his combat scenes are surprisingly powerful. Among the many actors eager to work with Malick, (who hadn't made a movie since his twenty-year-old classic *Days of Heaven*) are such virtual unknowns (at the time) as Adrien Brody, Jim Caviezel, and, most notably, Elias Koteas as a captain who refuses to send his men to certain death. Among the more familiar faces are Sean Penn, Nick Nolte, John Cusack, John Travolta, and George Clooney.

3 *Shakespeare in Love* (John Madden). US/UK, color. How did the young Shakespeare come to write *Romeo and Juliet*, and why did he move from that success to write *Twelfth Night*? Marc Norman and Tom Stoppard have come up with a set of answers - implausible, even impossible answers that are also exhilarating, ingenious, and often laugh-out-loud hilarious. Gwyneth Paltrow (AA) engagingly plays a nubile lady in love with poetry who poses as a boy to get on the Elizabethan stage and is upstaged only when Elizabeth herself (Judi Dench, AAS) puts in an all-too-brief appearance. The picture boasts a wonderful recreation of Shakespeare's London and delicious performances by Joseph Fiennes, Colin Firth, Geoffrey Rush, and Simon Callow. Oscar for best picture, six others - after a relentless campaign by its pushy independent production company, Miramax.

4 *Central Station* (Walter Salles). Brazil/France, color. Fernanda Montenegro, the Bette Davis of Brazil, travels across her vast country with a small boy in search of his father. Many scenes are permeated with a human feeling reminiscent of *The Bicycle Thief*, which is high praise indeed.

5 *Life is Beautiful* (Roberto Benigni). Italy, color. What? A feel-good comedy about the Holocaust? Not everyone was receptive, but a vocal majority, charmed by Benigni's exuberant boldness - writing, directing, and (AA) starring - wanted to cloak him in Chaplin's mantle. A touchingly ironic appearance by an aged Horst Buchholz. Oscar for best foreign film.

6 *Affliction* (Paul Schrader). US, color. The powerful, career-peak performances by Nick Nolte as a man on the edge and James Coburn as his savagely abusive father almost lift this stark drama to the level of tragedy. With Sissy Spacek and Mary Beth Hurt.

7 *The Truman Show* (Peter Weiss). US, color. A sci-fi parable in which a young man unwittingly lives his whole life before a television audience of millions. Jim Stewart would have made a more sympathetic common man than Jim Carrey, but Laura Linney as Carrey's wife (how long can she hold out on the secret?) and Ed Harris as the sinister Prospero who masterminds the whole venture are letter-perfect.

8 *A Simple Plan* (Sam Raimi). US, color. A psychological thriller in which the color spectrum is artfully reduced to black and white, almost as in Breugel's winter scenes. Under horror-film grad Raimi's direction, Bill Paxton and Billy Bob Thornton play brothers whose ill-advised "plan" inexorably leads them to crime upon crime. Audiences were unnerved, but even those who

hated the film were compelled to watch it through to its snowy denouement.

9 *The Spanish Prisoner* (David Mamet). US, color. This year's Mamet con game, with Steve Martin and (in a performance that divided critics and audiences) Mrs. Mamet, aka Rebecca Pidgeon. Good twisty Hitchcockian fun.

10 *Out of Sight* (Steven Soderbergh). US, color. There is more twisty fun in this smart screen version of Elmore Leonard's crime novel. Critics raved, but even the presence of heart-throb George Clooney and the beautiful Jennifer Lopez couldn't help it at the box office. Maybe Samuel L. Jackson should have been credited for his deft cameo. Or maybe the whole thing just *too* twisty.

Contending for tenth place were *A Taste of Cherry* and *Elizabeth*.

1999

1 *Magnolia* (Paul Thomas Anderson). US, color. A kaleidoscopic overview - by turns poignant, ironic, puzzling, and funny - of desperate lives and tortured relationships along Magnolia Avenue in the San Fernando Valley. With standout performances by Jason Robarts, Julianne Moore, Philip Seymour Hoffmann, William Macey, and especially by Tom Cruise in a small but brave, career-risking turn as a violently sexist TV guru and by John C. Reilly as an innocent, not to say angelic, Irish cop. The climactic biblical plague, an extraordinary risk for young writer/director Anderson, divided critics and audiences more widely than any other sequence in the 1990s. Obviously I liked it.

2 *Topsy-Turvy* (Mike Leigh). UK, color. Leigh, the chronicler of contemporary middle-class British life, weighs in unexpectedly with a period piece, detailing at three hours' length why Gilbert and Sullivan succeeded with *The Mikado* after they had failed with *Princess Ida*. The usual Mike Leigh players - Jim Broadbent and Timothy Spall among them – give us at once a bittersweet tribute to the famous composer-librettist team and a celebration of actors who, like themselves, play in repertory.

3 *The Insider* (Michael Mann). US, color. Russell Crowe, the big-gorilla cop in *L.A. Confidential*, is scarcely recognizable here, in an astonishing performance as the mousy, plumpish Jeffrey Wigand who blew the whistle on the tobacco industry on "60 Minutes". Director Mann turns a sensational news story into a taut, intelligent thriller. With Michael Gambon as a tobacco executive, Al Pacino as the producer of "60 Minutes", and Christopher Plummer as its star reporter, Mike Wallace. CBS was not pleased. Critics were. Audiences, sadly, were indifferent.

4 *Being John Malkovich* (Spike Jonez). US, color. A wildly original comedy about a puppeteer (John Cusak) who discovers a portal through which he, and others, can enter the head of actor John Malkovich. It sounds like the makings of a TV skit, but Jonez spins it out to feature length with no end of inventiveness. With Catherine Keener, a scarcely recognizable Cameron Diaz, and (playing himself) John Malkovich.

5 *Three Kings* (David O. Russell). US, color. A highly original view of Operation Desert Storm as, almost simultaneously, a CNN adventure story, a comedy, a heist flick, and an ironic pacifist statement remarkably prescient of the issues and attitudes that were to prevail during the second war with Iraq. With

George Clooney, Ice Cube, Mark Wahlberg, and (see *Being John Malkovich*) Spike Jonez.

6 *The Talented Mr. Ripley* (Anthony Minghella). US, color. An amoral Patricia Highsmith cult novel, filmed in 1960 by René Clement as *Purple Noon*, gets the deluxe treatment in this remake. Audiences who expected Hitchcock thrills and *English Patient* gloss were confounded by the picture's quirky Highsmith heartlessness. Matt Damon is out of his depth as the curiously sexless schemer constantly reinventing himself, but Gwyneth Paltrow, Cate Blanchett, Jude Law, and especially Philip Seymour Hoffman are all excellent in supporting roles.

7 *The End of the Affair* (Neil Jordan). UK, color. This second filming of Graham Greene's quasi-autobiographical novel makes some substantial changes in the material, but I think Greene would have approved of its scrupulous avoidance of romanticizing and its obsessive insistence on the reality of the workings of divine grace in human lives. Jo Stafford's recording of "Haunted Heart" is subtly used on the sound track. With Ralph Fiennes, Stephen Rea, Julianne Moore (in one of the five remarkable performances she gave in 1999), and lots of rain – Greene's all-pervasive symbol for grace.

8 *All About My Mother* (Pedro Almodóvar). Spain, color. An *hommage*, not just to *All About Eve*, but to all the Hollywood "women's pictures" of the 1950s. Set in contemporary Spain and filtered through a gay sensibility, this is the most accessible of Almadóvar's films - complex and compassionate, with a luminous performance by Cecilia Roth as the mother.

9 *Run Lola Run* (Tom Tykwer). Germany, color. Flaming-haired Lola (Franka Potente) has had her mo-ped stolen and must run across Berlin with only twenty minutes to find the hundred thousand DMs needed to save her boyfriend's life - and we get three different scenarios of how she might have done it. A short (80 minutes) and visually inventive thinkpiece, and a refreshing antidote to 1999's plethora of tired examinations of the Suburban American Wasteland (see the next entry for one example).

10 *American Beauty* (Sam Mendes AA). US, color. Stage director Mendes makes a terrific movie debut, turning a sow's ear of a story (a sardonic, smarmy view of contemporary suburbia) into something of a silk purse. The astonishing cinematography by Conrad L. Hall is the last word in 1999 technical accomplishment. With Kevin Spacey (AA), Chris Cooper, Wes Bentley, and Annette Bening, and with - some critics insisted - powerful Jungian subcurrents. Oscar for best picture, four others.

Contending for tenth place were *Children of Heaven*, *Earth*, *Cookie's Fortune*, *The Sixth Sense*, and *The Green Mile*.

The 2000s

The 2000s

2000

1 ***Crouching Tiger, Hidden Dragon*** (Ang Lee). US/China, color. An instant classic. As in the *Iliad* heroes fight with superhuman qualities when their gods are with them, so here warriors of both sexes can rise in the air at heightened moments of heroism to do battle. This martial arts picture, (faulted by the martial arts crowd for being deficient in action) actually has as its aim to tell, in luminous visuals, a story two romances in a past age of inspired warriors. The aerial duels, filmed by Yuen Wo-Ping, had the audience cheering at the Cannes premiere.

2 ***Yi-Yi*** (Edward Yang). Taiwan, color. A family wedding leads to an examination of a dozen interacting lives, and characters who at first appear uninteresting and even unsympathetic become, under Yang's probing direction, figures for us who watch. A small boy takes pictures of the backs of people's heads, where they can't see themselves. So, in its way, does the whole three-hour movie.

3 ***The Color of Paradise*** (Majid Majidi). Iran, color. A blind Iranian boy is farmed out by his father who fears the boy will be a hindrance to him as he looks for a new wife. This is the best of the recent Iranian movies that have, against all odds, begun to dominate film festivals and move audiences with their haunting, poignant stories, mainly about children.

4 ***A Time for Drunken Horses*** (Bahman Ghobadi). Iran, color. Four children involved in smuggling operations in the mountains of Iranian Kurdistan sacrifice their own interests to provide life-

saving surgery for their pathetically dwarfed older brother. The children are all non-professionals, and the movie, immensely touching, bears comparison with the *Pather Panchali* and *The Bicycle Thief.* Winner of a runner-up prize, the Camera d'Or, at Cannes.

5 ***Gladiator*** (Ridley Scott). US, color. The spear-and-sandal genre returns to the screen in some of its old glory, thanks to electronic wizardry that makes the Roman Coliseum look twice its actual size at relatively little cost, and thanks even more to the resourceful Russell Crowe (AA), fighting Germans in their forests and, in a historic upset in the arena, winning the Punic Wars for Carthage! With Joaquin Phoenix, Richard Harris, Derek Jacobi, and Oliver Reed (who died during production). Oscar for best picture, four others.

6 ***You Can Count On Me*** (Kenneth Lonergan). US, color. A young working mother (Laura Linney) tries to help her scapegrace brother (Mark Ruffalo) restart his life and finds that she has to deal with half-understood impulses within herself. A quiet, perceptive examination of human needs, with two remarkable performances. Director Lonergan also wrote the script.

7 ***O Brother, Where Art Thou?*** (The Coen Brothers). US, color. A hayseed *Odyssey* joyously set in a Mississippi awash in practically non-stop country music. Based on Homer (who appears early on as a blind seer on a railway handcar), with slap-happy performances by George Clooney, John Turturro, and Tim Blake Nelson. Note for the cinematically literate: the title is taken from Preston Sturges' *Sullivan's Travels* (see under 1941), and one of this film's best moments clearly evokes the pivotal scene from that earlier classic.

8 *Traffic* (Steven Soderbergh AA). US, color. Why the US "war on drugs" cannot be won by law enforcement. A highly charged, compulsively watchable drama with three interlocking stories – each with its predominant color scheme - set along the Mexican border, in California, and in Ohio. With Michael Douglas, Catherine Zeta-Jones, Benicio Del Toro (AAS), Don Cheadle, Luiz Guzman, and Dennis Quaid. Adapted from a British mini-series about illegal drugs making their way from Turkey across Europe.

9 *Erin Brokovitch* (Steven Soderbergh). US, color. The second half of Soderbergh's 2000 double header (see above), with Julia Roberts (AA) energetically playing a divorced mother who uses her brains, instincts, and exuberant sexuality to take on a powerful California industrial company and win her case. With Albert Finney (who had a cameo in *Traffic*) and with the real Erin B. playing a bit part as a waitress.

10 *Cast Away* (Robert Zemeckis) US, color. A plump Tom Hanks, as a FedEx worker surviving a (scarily realistic) plane crash over the Pacific, has an island - and the screen - all to himself for an hour or more, and is fifty pounds lighter when at last he is rescued. Helen Hunt is the girl who assumes he is dead and marries another. It's predictable, but it certainly has its moments.

Contending for tenth place was *Pollock*.

2001

1 ***Mulholland Drive*** (David Lynch). US, color. A surreal mystery about an ambitious young actress (Naomi Watts) who almost remembers coming to Hollywood and becoming involved with drugs and crime. You watch with growing fascination and bewilderment as Lynch's quasi-symbolic images crowd in on your consciousness. Like several other films released in 2001, this demands two or more viewings, and you won't mind. You'll have the exotic pleasure of trying to figure it out.

2 ***Gosford Park*** (Robert Altman). UK, color. A precisely observed upstairs-downstairs mystery with more complex relationships and sophisticated dialogue than - here we go again! - the eye and ear can take in with one viewing. (Altman wanted people to see it four times.) A superb cast - Maggie Smith, Kristin Scott Thomas, Helen Mirren, Emily Watson, Eileen Atkins, Michael Gambon, Alan Bates, and Derek Jacobi - seems to be re-enacting Renoir's *The Rules of the Game* in an England that has lost its moorings. Bob Balaban plays the lone, intimidated American and Jeremy Northam gives a suave impersonation of Ivor Novello. Unqualified rapture.

3 ***Memento*** (Christopher Nolan). US, color. Writer-director Nolan's retro-structured parable about an insurance investigator (Guy Pearce) searching for the rapist-murderer of his wife while suffering from a memory disorder that allows him to retain information subsequent to the atrocity for only a few minutes at a time. Riveting right up to the ambiguous end - and that's when

you have the pleasure of rethinking it forwards and (here we go again!) seeing it a second time. There are web sites to help you with your problem. Yes, the parable suggests, you, like anyone else, have a selective memory, and all of us suffer from short-term memory loss as we age. No wonder *Memento* developed a cult following among the middle aged!

4 *A Beautiful Mind* (Ron Howard, AA). US, color. With the aid of an ingenious script and a meticulously detailed performance by Russell Crowe, director Howard almost gets us into the mind of Nobel Prize winner John Nash, a Princeton professor of mathematics who suffered from schizophrenic fantasies. (Yes, it's another mind-bender, but this one you won't have to sit through twice to figure out.) With Jennifer Connelly (AA), Christopher Plummer, and Ed Harris. Oscar for best picture, three others.

5 *Black Hawk Down* (Ridley Scott) US, color. The 1993 Somalia disaster, filmed with amazing realism. We in the audience are given an airborne view of the action a good deal of the time, so we come to know the layout and even the logistics as never before in a war film. There are no gung-ho heroics or patriotic speeches, only appalling devastation. In the large cast are Tom Sizemore, Sam Shepard, Eric Bana, and Orlando Bloom.

6 *In the Bedroom* (Todd Field). US, color. A distraught woman drives her husband to murder the killer of their son. The plot is less important than the nuanced characters, who reveal the complexity of their feelings only gradually. With Sissy Spacek, Tom Wilkinson, and Marisa Tomei. Based on a story by Andre Dubus.

7 ***The Deep End*** (Scott McGhee and David Siegel). US, color. A mother (Tilda Swinton) concerned about her oldest son's awakening homosexuality finds herself involved in one suspenseful crisis after another, and is helped by a stranger (Goran Visnjic) with criminal instincts. Hitchcockian, but with the sympathetic insight into character that Hitchcock deliberately avoided.

8 ***The Pledge*** (Sean Penn). US, color. Jack Nicholson, without a single leer or raised eyebrow, plays a policeman who, on the day of his retirement, makes a pledge to find the murderer of a small girl and is eventually faced with moral decisions he has never faced before. As with *In the Bedroom*, the plot is of less interest than the character study. Based on a play by Friedrich Dürrenmatt. With Robin Wright Penn and Sam Shepard.

9 ***Sexy Beast*** (Jonathan Glazer). UK, color. When a boulder comes bounding down a hill plop into his luxurious Spanish swimming pool, a retired English safecracker (Ray Winstone) suspects that trouble is on the way, and sure enough a former colleague, a frightfully intimidating bald sociopath (Ben Kingsley), shows up with an offer he'd better not refuse. The most unusual heist movie since *Topkapi* – though the heist itself is not half as entertaining as the build-up.

10 ***The Lord of the Rings: The Fellowship of the Ring*** (Peter Jackson). UK, color. This first installment of the nine-hour epic released over three years is imaginative at the start, then slips noisily into one-damn-battle-after-another boredom. Based on the trilogy by J.R.R. Tolkien, with jaw-dropping graphics and a cast headed by Ian McKellen and Ian Holm.

Contending for tenth place were *Amores Perros* and *Monster's Ball*.

2002

1 ***Adaptation*** (Spike Jonze). US, color. Now hear this: Nicolas Cage plays on screen the film's actual scriptwriter, Charlie Kaufman, as well as Charlie's fictional twin brother Donald. Charlie has been hired to do the screenplay for a film adaptation of a *New Yorker* short-story-turned-novel about an orchid thief, but he develops writer's block, and is miffed because Donald can turn out successful junk screenplays a mile a minute. Then, as in Fellini's *8½* but with an audacious twist, the attempt to write the movie *becomes* the movie. The most original and exhilarating comedy in years, with Meryl Streep and Tilda Swinton, and with Chris Cooper (AAS) as the orchid thief. In an unusual show of wit (or perhaps from lack of it), the usually rule-ridden Academy allowed the nomination of both Kaufman and his fictional twin brother - for best adaptation, of course.

2 ***The Pianist*** (Roman Polanski AA) Germany/France/Poland, color. One man's story of survival in the Warsaw ghetto. At once a tribute to the power of music and an anguished cry at the sheer randomness of why some live and some die in the cataclysms of history. Polanski's best picture by far, with long stretches of eloquent Chopin and a moving performance by Adrien Brody (AA). Palme d'Or at Cannes.

3 ***The Hours*** (Stephen Daldry). US, color. The intercut stories of three tormented women whose lives are linked by elective

affinities: one is writing, one reading, and one unwittingly re-enacting Virginia Woolf's novel *Mrs. Dalloway*. Nicole Kidman (AA) plays Woolf before her suicide, Julianne Moore plays a suburban American housewife ten years later, and Meryl Streep plays a New York City bohemian a half-century later still. Their remarkable performances are supported by good work from Ed Harris, Miranda Richardson, Alison Janney, and John C. Reilly. A minimalist score by Philip Glass helps establish continuity. Based on the Pulitzer-Prize-winning novel by Michael Cunningham. Riveting.

4 *Russian Ark* (Alexander Sokurov). Russia, color. In his 1926 *Ten Days that Shook the World*, Eisenstein staged the storming of St. Petersburg's Winter Palace in a virtuoso montage of hundreds of shots. Sokurov, with even more mastery, takes us through the same historic palace in a single uninterrupted 86-minute shot. We follow a quizzical French marquis in conversation with an off-camera Russian (voiced by Sokurov) past the famous paintings, through cast-of-thousands recreations of the Czarist period, and straight into the midst of a sumptuous imperial ball. The film is certainly a tour de force. It is also a celebration of and an elegy for two vanished pre-Soviet centuries in Russia. The title is explained (by Sokurov's voice) only in the last of the 86 minutes.

5 *Road To Perdition* (Sam Mendes). US, color. The facile ironies of Mendes' examination of contemporary suburban life, *American Beauty*, were received rapturously in 1999, thanks largely to the photography of Conrad L Hall. But in 2002 the times were not right for Mendes' *Road to Perdition*, a grim story of four father-son relationships set in and around Chicago in the thirties, also cinematographed by Hall, and superior to *American Beauty* in every way. This time Hall turned a Depression-era story into what

The New York Times called "a truly majestic visual tone poem". But most critics were hostile, despite powerful performances by Tom Hanks and Paul Newman, and an unusual one by Jude Law.

6 **Gangs of New York** (Martin Scorsese). US, color. A saga of nativist New Yorkers clashing violently with Irish immigrants at the time of the Civil War, meant to illustrate the agonized emergence of a new American sensibility out of ethnic diversity. Hardly satisfactory as history, and sometimes grotesquely overstated, it is nonetheless imaginatively produced on immense sets built in Rome, with a spectacularly villainous performance by Daniel Day-Lewis - and notably poor ones from some others in the cast. (You have to look quick to see a good one by John C. Reilly, who had quite a year.)

7 **Far From Heaven** (Todd Haynes). US, color. Why would anyone in 2002 recreate, in the most extravagant way, a Douglas Sirk weepie from the fifties? Only a few years back, any attempt to do so might have been an opportunity to indulge in easy irony or (worse) to make a hilarious camp classic for sophisticates. But as Haynes' picture unfolds without a trace of irony or parody, with a magnificent performance by Julianne Moore as a housewife facing problems (racism and her husband's homosexuality) that fifties suburbia opted to ignore, we feel that in the last few years the cultural ground beneath our feet has shifted, that all the isms we lived through since the fifties have provided no real answers to our social and personal problems. The hommage to Sirk becomes deeply unsettling.

8 **Eight Women** (François Ozon). France, color. This is for you only if you have (1) a taste for Agatha Christie whodunits that take place in big country houses where access to the outside world

is temporarily suspended; (2) an affection for deliberately artificial MGM technicolor musicals of the forties; and (3) a high regard for the best French actresses of the last three decades. If you have been so blessed, prepared to be delighted. With those surprise singer/dancers Danielle Darrieux, Catherine Deneuve, Isabelle Huppert and five others who might have had a reason to murder the only man in the picture. (We glimpse him briefly but never see his face.)

9 *My Big Fat Greek Wedding* (Mia Vardalos). US, color. The sleeper of the year, and the biggest grossing independent film ever. Developed from a one-woman play written by and starring its director. Millions couldn't help loving and laughing along with the Cinderella story even though they may have seen it in different ethnic guises many times before. The best joke, pulled on the bridegroom who can't speak Greek, is as old as Aristophanes.

10 *Chicago* (Rob Marshall). US, color. It's good to have a full-scale musical back on the American screen, even if this is mostly post-feminist "flim flam flummox", hectically edited to give the impression that its stars can really sing and dance. (Ironically they didn't let a star who could do both, Ginger Rogers, do either in her version of the story, *Roxie Hart*, back in 1942). And if the editing manages to rip the 1975 Kander and Ebb songs to shreds, at least nothing in *Chicago* is so desperate as virtually everything in last year's over-the-top "musical", *Moulin Rouge*. With Renée Zellweger, Richard Gere, Catherine Zeta Jones (AAS), Queen Latifah, and the ubiquitous John C. Reilly. Oscar for best picture, five others.

Contending for tenth place were *Bloody Sunday*, *About Schmidt*, *Heaven*, *Atanarjuat: The Fast Runner*, and *The Lord of the Rings: The Two Towers*.

2003

1 ***Mystic River*** (Clint Eastwood). US, color. The 1940s Warner Brothers logo – the familiar black-and-white shield - promises from the start a hard-hitting, fast-moving police drama, but nothing Warners did in their greatest era has anything like the searing humanity, the compassion, and the haunting spiritual quality of this detective story set in blue-collar Boston, with Sean Penn (AA) and Tim Robbins (AAS) giving career peak performances, and with Kevin Bacon, Marcia Gay Harden, Laura Linney, and Lawrence Fishburn in solid support. With each riveting plot turn, the characters pivot in prismatic relationships each with the other. Clint Eastwood directs with astonishing control; he also wrote the haunting four-note motif that that recurs like a benediction and gives the tragic story its sign-of-the-cross significance.

2 ***In America*** (Jim Sheridan). US, color. Two small Irish girls (Sarah and Emma Bolger) move to New York with their father (Paddy Considine) and mother (Samantha Morton) and find their ghastly Hell's Kitchen tenement a place of enchantment – even the glowering, muscular black man (Djimon Hounsou) who screams with rage downstairs. Alternately harrowing and hilarious, the film is a semi-autobiographical labor of love from director Sheridan, who brought his family to New York in the early eighties and co-scripted his picture with his two daughters. Just how personal it is to Mr. Sheridan becomes clear when we

read the dedication at the film's end, for the film is not so much about the vicissitudes of life in a new country as about coming to terms with personal loss. The five performances are beyond praise.

3 *21 Grams* (Alejandro Gonzales Iñárritu). US, color. A stunner from the director of 2001's *Amores Perros*, first conceived as a Mexican film, but shot in the US when Sean Penn showed interest. *21 Grams* ("the weight of the human soul") is a horrific vision of three lives, at first viewed separately and in small segments, that begin to interact before our eyes: the details of the lives come at us completely out of chronological sequence, so that sometimes the characters know more than we do, sometimes we know more than they. Roger Ebert, in a notice less enthusiastic than this one, said of the performances of Penn, Naomi Watts, and Benicio Del Toro, "Acting doesn't get much better than this" but found the "fractured technique" unnecessary and unsatisfying. Other critics agreed. But – come on, guys! – after *Memento* and *The Hours*, we should be ready for a virtuoso exercise like this one.

4 *House of Sand and Fog* (Vadim Perelman). US, color. An almost Sophoclean drama of two tragically flawed people – an unstable young woman (Jennifer Connelly) and an exiled Iranian colonel (Ben Kingsley) - laying rival claims to a house on the foggy California coastline. The tragic course of events follows inexorably from their characters and holds the viewer spellbound till the shattering, commendably non-judgmental ending. There is a remarkable, almost silent, performance by Shohreh Aghdashloo as the Iranian wife. Adapted from a novel by Andre Dubus III, the son of the Andre Dubus who wrote the story on which 2001's *In the Bedroom* was based.

5 **Winged Migration** (Jacques Perrin). France, color. An astonishing, strangely humbling pictorial record of the annual flights of various species of birds, painstakingly filmed across a period of more than three years over every continent, and over virtually every sea, on the face of the earth. There is not a trace here of Disney cuteness, informational overkill, or pseudo-poetic commentary. The poetry of the film is the poetry of our awesome planet and the dauntless creatures that wing above it every winter for thousands of miles. (DVD viewers will have access to information about the process of "imprinting" that enabled the film crews to do their work; but they should view the picture first, and wonder.)

6 **Finding Nemo** (Andrew Stanton). US, color. A treasureable cartoon feature from Pixar Animation Studios, released by Disney, markedly superior to Pixar's *Toy Story* movies and blessedly free of the crassness that has marred every Disney animated picture since the forties – always excepting the joyously imaginative "Under the Sea" sequence from *The Little Mermaid*. Here we're under the sea again, at the Great Barrier Reef, where a little clown fish named Nemo has been netted by a scuba diver and is desperately trying to find his way back to his father. Wit, wonder, and imagination are all abundantly present. Everyone will have his favorite moments; mine is watching the giant sea turtles all but floating atop the East Australian Current. Perhaps we should be grateful, these days, that there are no songs. Albert Brooks, Willem Dafoe, Ellen DeGeneres, and Australians Barry Humphries and Geoffrey Rush provide skillful voice-overs.

7 **Master and Commander: The Far Side of the World** (Peter Weir). UK, color. The portmanteau title is not a obeisance to the Tolkien trilogy (see below) but an indication that Weir's movie is

drawn from two separate installments of Patrick O'Brian's (by last count) twenty-volume saga of heroism in the British navy during the Napoleonic Wars. The film's battle scenes are as wonderfully detailed as they are exciting, and the rest is surprisingly and gratifyingly subdued. With Russell Crowe as Captain Jack Aubrey and Paul Bettany as Dr. Maturin.

8 ***Whale Rider*** (Niki Caro) New Zealand, color. We're on land looking out to sea in this modest, off-beat film that combines the best elements of documentary (life in a Maori village) and the coming-of-age drama (in this case the almost mythic story of a fourteen-year-old girl radiantly played by Keisha Castle-Hughes). Audiences around the world were moved to tears and, as the credits rolled, cheers. Much of the film is artless but, as The New York Times put it, "It has the inspiring resonance of found art."

9 ***Girl With a Pearl Earring*** (Peter Webber) UK, color. A few years back, *Shakespeare in Love* purported to tell us, with exhilarating tongue-in-cheek, how the Bard came to write *Romeo and Juliet*. This luminous film sets out to tell us, slowly and with welcome understatement, how Vermeer came to paint one of his subtlest masterpieces. And in telling its somewhat lurid story it magically recreates the seventeenth-century town of Delft and a dozen more of the Dutchman's works. Scarlett Johansson, Colin Firth, Tom Wilkinson, Judy Parfitt, and Essie Davis live and breathe their roles.

10 ***The Lord of the Rings: The Return of the King*** (Peter Jackson AA). UK, color. This massive third installment of the Tolkien trilogy, so relentlessly stupendous as to risk risibility, galumphs along like an oliphaunt and stumbles into overtime with a series of lugubrious curtain calls. But it has amazing

technical proficiency and visual imagination, and the face of Frodo Baggins (Elijah Wood), as he stands poised to drop the eponymous ring into a fiery abyss, looks strikingly like the face of Benvenuto Cellini's Perseus. Unfortunately, in the year of the disastrous U.S. liberation of Bagdad, *TLOTR: TROTK* had more Rumsfeldian "shock and awe" than genuine adventure about it. For real adventure see the Bagdad Alexander Korda brought to the screen in 1940. Jackson's saga won an Oscar for best picture and ten others – a record previously achieved only by *Ben-Hur* (1959) and *Titanic* (2003).

Contending for tenth place were *Monster* and *Cold Mountain*.

2004

1 ***Hero*** (Zhang Yimou). China, color. A jaw-droppingly gorgeous and almost impossibly stylized costume spectacle, à la Ang Lee's *Crouching Tiger*, with a *Rashomon*-like structure, a Fritz Lang taste for massing humanity in proto-fascist fashion, and a substantial musical score by Tan Dun. Only in the movies are such fantasies possible. North American distributors thought *Hero* had no box office potential, and it took Quentin Tarantino's efforts to bring it triumphantly, two years after its Asian release, to these shores.

2 ***House of Flying Daggers*** (Zhang Yimou), China, color. Another demonstration of Asian supremacy at the movies. Yimou's second martial-arts spectacle (new in 2004) is almost on an aesthetic par with *Hero*, and in some scenes – the "Echo Dance" and the battle in a misty bamboo forest – its palette of colors is even more dazzling. But the heavily plotted story - a

romance that pivots on Tang dynasty espionage - is not always well-served by the stylization.

3 **Sideways** (Alexander Payne). US, color. A slow-starting but ultimately perceptive and often hilarious depiction of human nature at its most beguilingly fallible, with Paul Giamatti and Thomas Haden Church as a pair of California losers on a wine-tasting trip, and, as the girls they pick up, Sandra Oh and - giving the most touching and womanly performance since Helen Hunt's in *As Good As It Gets* — Virginia Madsen.

4 **Million Dollar Baby** (Clint Eastwood AA). US, color. Once again, as with last year's powerful *Mystic River*, Eastwood takes an old Warner Brother's genre (this time it's the boxing film) and darkens and deepens it with compassion and an almost spiritual insight. Morgan Freeman (AAS) narrates the story of the ringside trainer (Eastwood) and the hillbilly girl he reluctantly takes on (Hilary Swank AA). The plot, based on "Rope Burns" by veteran fight manager Jerry Boyd (under the pseudonym F.X. Toole) takes unexpected turns before it reaches its shattering and controversial conclusion. Oscar for best picture, three others.

5 **The Aviator** (Martin Scorsese). US, color. Scorsese, long overlooked at Oscar time, makes an all-out bid for Academy recognition with a long, elaborate bio, à la *Citizen-Kane*, of Howard Hughes. Leonardo Di Caprio works hard (he's in every scene but the first), but is overparted. Cate Blanchett (AAS) is a stunning Katharine Hepburn – giving an interpretation rather than an impersonation. Alan Alda, Alec Baldwin, and Willem Dafoe are good as the baddies. The aviation sequences are marvelous, but Scorsese's brisk story-telling falters in the last hour (of three), and

it was no surprise when at the Oscars the big awards went to Clint.

6 *Vera Drake* (Mike Leigh). UK, color. Imelda Staunton gives the performance of the year playing a kind-hearted cleaning lady in post-World War II London who "helps" young women deal with unwanted pregnancies. The issues are dramatized poignantly and with no special pleading, and, as with other hyper-realistic dramas from director Leigh (see *Secrets and Lies* in 1996), there are fine performances all around – remarkably fine in the case of Phil Davis, who plays Mr. Drake.

7 *Hotel Rwanda* (Terry George). US/UK?, color. A true story extracted from the terrible events in Rwanda in 1994, with Don Cheadle as Paul Rusesabagina, the African Oskar Schindler who sheltered hundreds of Tutsis from the murderous Hutus. The picture, perhaps too reticent in its depiction of violence, nonetheless forced Western audiences to face the fact that, had their countries intervened, the genocide might not have happened.

8 *Osama* (Siddig Barmak). Afghanistan, color. Astonishingly, this fact-based story of a twelve-year-old girl who survives the horrors of Taliban tyranny disguised as a boy named Osama was made in Afghanistan shortly after the regime's overthrow. The picture is wrenching, not least because, despite the U.S. military action, conditions in the country are still deplorable.

9 *Collateral* (Michael Mann). US, color. A terrific if at times implausible thriller which is also a duologue between a philosophizing hit man (Tom Cruise) and the decent if unduly ingenuous taxi driver (Jamie Foxx) he commandeers for a night's

work. Mann's direction is wonderfully taut, and L.A. has never looked so lurid.

10 *The Merchant of Venice* (Michael Radford). US/UK/ Italy, color. An unsubtle and almost unrelievedly dark but richly detailed and consistently engaging screen version of Shakespeare's most problematic play. Much of the Bard's poetry, and some of his comedy, are missing, but three remarkable performances – Al Pacino (Shylock), Jeremy Irons (Antonio), and Lynne Collins (Portia) - save the day, and the trial scene is riveting.

Contending for tenth place were *Troy* and *I'm Not Scared*.

2005

1 *Crash* (Paul Haggis). US, color. A heavily ironic, movingly compassionate view of contemporary Los Angeles that, with its dozen intersecting stories, may owe something to Altman's *Short Cuts* and Anderson's *Magnolia*. But, in its emphasis on the irrationality of racism, it cuts deeper and rises to more searing climaxes than they. Don Cheadle, Matt Dillon, Sandra Bulloch, Thandie Newton, and Terrence Howard are the best- known members of the multi-ethnic cast, but every performance in this gripping low-budget film is a standout. (Definitely not to be confused with a dreadful 1996 Cannes contender with the same name.) Fledgling director Haggis won an Oscar for his script and saw his film go on to a surprise Academy Award win for best picture.

2 ***The New World*** (Terrence Malick). US, color. Writer/director Malick uses his patented techniques — voiceover soliloquies from otherwise virtually silent characters, lovingly photographed fauna and flora, languid pacing with sudden explosions of violence, unpredictable yet surprisingly right use of music (here, Wagner and Mozart) - to tell the familiar story of Captain John Smith and Pocahontas as if it were happening for the first time. Audiences expecting a cinema epic or a schoolbook romance were indignant. But what the Los Angeles Times called "in every sense a masterpiece" is at least half as good as Malick's 1978 *Days of Heaven*, and that is very good indeed. With Colin Farrell and the striking fourteen-year-old Q'Orianka Kilcher.

3 ***Capote*** (Bennett Miller). US, color. Not so much a biography of the gifted author of *In Cold Blood* as a cold-blooded, clinical detailing of the price he had to pay – wheedling, lying, eventually closing off all human feeling – to bring his masterpiece to conclusion. The rather free-wheeling script, a cautionary tale for anyone tempted to write autobiographical fiction, is by Dan Futterman. Philip Seymour Hoffman (AA) gives an altogether astonishing performance as Capote, and Catherine Keener is fine as his novelist friend Harper Lee.

4 ***Munich*** (Steven Spielberg). US, color. A riveting if largely fictional account of the 1972 massacre of the Israeli athletes at the Munich Olympics, the vengeance wreaked on the Palestinians who planned it, and the crises that that vengeance wreaked in turn on the consciences of the Israelis. Though its director scrupulously avoided partisan stereotypes, and called his film "a prayer for peace", it was harshly criticized by both Jews and Arabs. In other words, it is a movie that matters. With Eric Bana, Daniel Craig, and Michel Lonsdale.

5 ***March of the Penguins*** (Luc Jacquet). France/US, color. The frozen Antarctic that, Morgan Freeman tells us in voiceover, once teemed with all kinds of life, teaches us who live in more temperate climes touching and achingly beautiful lessons in solidarity and survival – through the one species that stayed on to endure continental drift. Jacquet and his intrepid team of documentarians provide equal amounts of astonishment and awe, both for what they have accomplished and for what this planet gives and does not give to its inhabitants. (We only came to known the details of this miracle of evolution in the last century.) Oscar for best documentary.

6 ***Syriana*** (Stephen Gaghan). US, color. A deliciously complicated thriller that deals seriously with serious issues – American oil interests and insurgent terrorism in the Middle East. Gaghan, who wrote 2000's multi-layered *Traffic*, takes over the director's reins as well this time. Weaving in and out of the story are George Clooney (AAS), Matt Damon, and Christopher Plummer. Father-son relationships provide a psychological context that enhances the intrigue.

7 ***Caché*** (Michael Haneke). France, color. A taut, brilliantly executed psychological thriller that reached the screen just as comfortable Paris awoke to find marginalized Algerians rioting in the slums – something all but predicted in the film. A clue to resolving the most enigmatic ending since Antonioni's *Blow-Up* (see 1966) is given early on: "Please stay seated until the credits have rolled". With Juliette Binoche and, as a man who has kept his past hidden from himself, Daniel Auteuil. Alternate title: *Hidden*.

8 *Cinderella Man* (Ron Howard). US, color. The saga of Depression-era boxer Jim Braddock makes an inspiring film, lovingly directed, edited (the scenes in the ring set new standards), and photographed (the period has seldom been so convincingly captured). There are also memorable performances by Russell Crowe, Paul Giamatti, and (in a weird caricature of Max Baer) Craig Bierko. But the film was released in early summer, when the public wanted lighter entertainment, and it died at the box office. Then Crowe's nasty involvement in a hotel tiff dealt it the final TKO.

9 *The Constant Gardener* (Fernando Meirelles). UK, color. Some crucial scenes seem to have ended up on the cutting-room floor in this film version of the angry John LeCarré novel that accused the world's pharmaceutical companies of criminal activity in AIDS-infected Africa. But there is still plenty to stimulate the mind, the heart, and – just possibly – the conscience, and Ralph Fiennes and Rachel Wiesz (AAS) are perfect as the oddly matched lovers.

10 *Brokeback Mountain* (Ang Lee AA). US, color. In a year when virtually all of the above-mentioned films met with some resistance from critics, there was a breakthrough with *Brokeback*, a critical and popular success based on a short story by Annie Proulx about two ranch hands who fall in love. Heath Ledger gives a beautifully controlled performance, but Jake Gyllenhaal seems at sea in an underwritten role, and we are not entirely convinced that the passion between the two is real. (We *are* convinced about the misery.) Partisans of *Brokeback* were outraged when the Best Picture Oscar went to *Crash*.

Contending for tenth place were *Downfall* and *Good Night, and Good Luck.*

2006

1 ***Letters from Iwo Jima*** (Clint Eastwood). US, Japan, color. The second of two Eastwood films released in 2006 about one of the most costly of all US victories in the Pacific during World War II. (The first of the two films, *Flags of our Fathers*, dealt largely with American responses to the celebrated photograph of the raising of the flag at the battle's end.) In *Letters*, Eastwood, working with a Japanese actors speaking in their own language, deals sympathetically with the enemy army, with their cruel codes of honor, their valor, and their despair. It was an artistic achievement comparable in many ways to Homer's portrayal of the enemy Trojans in the *Iliad*, and to Aeschylus's depiction of the invading Persians in his *Persae*. *Letters from Iwo Jima* seemed to bring the more heavy-handed *Flags of our Fathers* into clear focus. The American Film Institute called the diptych "the greatest cinematic work of this (i.e., the twenty-first) century".

2 ***United 93*** (Paul Greengrass). US, color. Two 2006 films dealt with the terrible events of September 1l, 2001. Oliver Stone's partly fictional and surprisingly non-political *World Trade Center* was an honorable tribute to heroism, but both critics and public preferred *United 93*, a scrupulously fact-based recreation of the hijacked flight that, thanks to the collective action of its passengers, self-destructed rather than crash into the White House or the nation's capital. Greengrass, the English director of the estimable *Bloody Sunday* (2002), has no use for phony suspense

or sentimentality. His film moves breathlessly from the flight's cabin to various civilian and military control centers, and stops abruptly, not with a crash but with a questioning, empty frame. I cannot describe the feelings I had as I left the theater.

3 *The Queen* (Stephen Frears). UK, color. Frears may have had to invent more in this account of the royal family's response to the death of Princess Diana than Greengrass did in his account of the crash of United 93. But invention of this high order is the soul of wit, and there hasn't been a movie this witty in a long time. There is a deliberately cartoonish quality to the performances of Michael Sheen as Tony Blair, James Cromwell as Prince Philip, and Alex Jennings as Prince Charles. That leaves Helen Mirren as the Queen to explore the situation in depth -- and Mirren compels us to understand, to like, even to love the tradition-bound woman facing overwhelming social changes she never anticipated and of which she could hardly approve.

4 *The Departed* (Martin Scorsese). US, color. Scorsese, back on familiar ground with this mean-streets-of-South-Boston shoot-'em-out, seems poised, at the time this is going to press, to win his long overdue Oscar at last. All the familiar Scorsese elements are working here at fever pitch and with a new complexity. Matt Damon and Leonardo DiCaprio deftly play two undercover moles, one secretly working for the Irish mafia, the other for the police. Jack Nicholson is allowed a self-indulgent performance that strains credulity, but Mark Wahlberg, Martin Sheen, and Alec Baldwin are eminently convincing in other roles. Be forewarned: this one is foul-mouthed and blood-soaked beyond anything previously released in commercial cinema.

5 ***Pan's Labyrinth*** (Guillermo Del Toro). Spain, color. One of the year's three shocking, cinematically accomplished movies from Mexican directors. Del Toro, hitherto known for horror films, tells the tale of a young girl who flees from the excesses of the Spanish Civil War into a fantasy world that - we ought not to be surprised - is almost equally nightmarish. Surprise follows gruesome surprise as the tension mounts. An exotically imaginative think-piece for adults. Definitely not for children.

6 ***Children of Men*** (Alfonso Cuarón). UK, color. Cuarón, another Mexican, transfers to the screen P.D. James's apocalyptic novel of a world in which no children have been born for eighteen years. In an England brutalized by violence, despair, and incomprehensible government decisions, suicide is available via a drug named, from *Hamlet*, Quietus. Clive Owen expertly plays the marathon role of an ordinary man heroically attempting to save one illegal immigrant -- a Figi woman who is miraculously with child. (Cuarón released his movie on Christmas Day). A fierce, terrifying film. With Julianne Moore and Michael Caine.

7 ***Babel*** (Alejandro González Iñárritu). US, color. Iñárritu and his fellow Mexican, screenwriter Guillermo Arriaga, once again (as with *Amores Perros* in 2001 and *21 Grams* in 2003) tell several interlocking stories. This time the theme - the random effect of global politics on individual lives and families – is grander, and the movie-making more sensational, but as we move quickly from Morocco to the US to Japan to Mexico, a sense of *déjà vu* seeps into the film. What saves it is an almost tactile sense of landscape and by some extraordinary performances. Brad Pitt and Cate Blanchett play the Americans.

8 ***Dreamgirls*** (Bill Condon). US, color. Movie version of the Broadway success based on the careers of Detroit's soul music sensations, Diana Ross and the Supremes. Unlike *Chicago* a few years back, this is a real musical, in which talented people sing, dance, and act up storms of emotion. When plump Jennifer Hudson sings her "I Am Telling You I'm Not Going", the movie audience explodes in applause as if they were watching a show on Broadway. With Jamie Foxx, Beyoncé Knowles, and Eddie Murphy.

9 ***The History Boys*** (Nicholas Hytner). UK, color. Another stage success, filmed with the same cast that played it in London and New York. Only about half as effective as it had been in the theater because director Hytner "opened it up" just where Alan Bennett's literate and compassionate comedy-drama needs the now-oppressive, now-liberating atmosphere of the classroom to make its full effect. Nonetheless, there is good acting all around, with a couple of delicious reenactments of scenes from beloved films of the forties. Movie audiences found the explicit homosexual content harder to deal with than had the theater public.

10 ***The Curse of the Golden Flower*** (Zhang Yimou). China, color. This most expensive movie ever made in China is also the most opulent spectacle any country has put on the screen to date, a splashy computer-enhanced exercize in excess that is required viewing even as it makes one long for the relative simplicity of director Zhang's earlier successes. The *Lion in Winter* story is acted to the operatic hilt by veterans Chow Yun-Fat and Gong Li.

Contending for tenth place were *Flags of Our Fathers* and *World Trade Center*.

THE TEN BEST FILMS OF OUR YEARS

THE GOLD RUSH

U.S., 1925. Written, directed, and produced by Charles Chaplin. With Charles Chaplin (the Lone Prospector), Mack Swain (Big Jim McKay), Tom Murray (Black Larsen), and Georgia Hale (Georgia). United Artists.

For some people the best scene in *The Gold Rush* is the opening - the iris-in on the hundreds of gold seekers struggling upwards through the snow, and the first appearance of Charlie shuffling along a frozen mountain path, alone and blissfully unaware that a bear is following him. Others prefer the scene where Charlie arrives at Black Larsen's cabin, is ordered to leave and can't make it out the front door for the force of the wind. Or the scene where Larsen and Big Jim, struggling for the rifle, inadvertently aim it at Charlie, no matter which way he runs to escape it. Or the scene where a starving Charlie cooks and eats one of his boots. Or the scene where Big Jim, raving with hunger, imagines Charlie is a chicken and starts after him with an axe. Or the scene at the Monte Carlo Dance Hall, where Georgia, beautiful and bored, longing to meet "someone worth while", turns to face poor petrified Charlie and doesn't even see him. Or the scene where the girls visit Charlie in his cabin - and Georgia returns for her gloves, and finds him sitting in all the feathers from the pillow he has torn up out of sheer joy. Or the scene where Charlie, dreaming he is entertaining the girls, makes the bread-rolls dance on the ends of the forks. Or the scene where Charlie, assuring Georgia he will make her rich, is unceremoniously whisked out the door by big Jim. Or the scene where Charlie and Big Jim awake to find their cabin teetering on the edge of a precipice, and make a hairbreadth escape after a series of agonizingly suspenseful mishaps. Or the final scene on shipboard, where Georgia proves her love for Charlie, unaware that now he is a very rich man indeed.

What Mark Van Doren said of *Hamlet* we can easily say of *The Gold Rush*, too: "All the scenes are good and relatively to the play as a whole each one in its turn is best." And this is so, not because *The Gold Rush* is a marvel of construction (that's about the one good thing it isn't), but because every sequence in the picture is a new demonstration of the comic skill of a uniquely gifted artist operating at the peak of his powers. And even as the comic effect in every scene is cumulative, so the overall effect is grandly cumulative. We come to see, as scene after scene makes its point, that this little fellow has his own little Hamlet's view of the world. Life is an endless series of almost impossible challenges: nature tests him through hunger and cold and raging storms; his fellow human beings trip him up and laugh at him or - worst of all - ignore him completely; even the brute beasts pursue him and take his food and bring his pants down. In the great frozen world, men kill one another out of greed or passion, or are killed by elemental forces, dropping in the snow from exposure or falling to their deaths in avalanches. And yet Charlie survives, sometimes triumphantly, out of some last-minute resourcefulness, more often simply hanging on for dear life, with a tenuous grasp on some outlandish object that has happened by to rescue him.

In every scene there is some comic business with a prop - a door or window, a plate or a knife, Charlie's own bowler hat, shabby coast, baggy trousers and cane, the icicles on the rafters to provide water for the coffee, the shoe laces that serve nicely as a side-dish of spaghetti for the boiled boot. Like any mime, he makes his own whatever comes his way; like only the greatest of artists, he confers a new reality on the objects within his vision. And he survives - ringed about by a sort of magic circle fashioned out of his relationship to his surroundings.

He belongs with the immortals because his art is comic and tragic at the same time. Comic essentially, because it depicts society through many characters on many social levels, and offers immediate solutions, and keeps its audience detached, and raises laughter. But tragic too, because it sums up the human condition in one man, and suggests some universal meaning, and involves its audience, and moves it to (perhaps too sentimental) tears.

The real miracle in *The Gold Rush* is this: the funnier Charlie is, the more we sense the tragic dimension in the comic business. The one heightens the other. When we are laughing the loudest, we also sense most strongly the pity and fear - of hunger as he nibbles away at the boot, of loneliness as he makes the rolls dance, of poverty every time he affects his elegant nonchalance in inelegant surroundings, of persecution every time he faces savage opposition from man or the elements. Mozart achieves grander tragicomic effects with three characters (Don Giovanni challenging the statue of the Commendatore while Leporello cowers under the table), Shakespeare is more comically savage with two (Falstaff, whom we love, proving his valor to himself by stabbing the corpse of Hotspur, whom we loved). But Charlie does it alone. It may not be so complete an illumination as Mozart's or Shakespeare's, but it's there, it's funny and touching at the same time - and I'm not sure it's to be found in the work of any other of the silent movie clowns, for all their special gifts.

We can almost say that Charlie's art is more of the cinema than that of any other actor in movie history. What, after all, establishes this little man's relationship to his world? His silent reactions, his movements. In the hundred situations in *The Gold Rush*, Charlie says nothing. He only moves. There is no verse, or song, as a clown out of Plautus might have, no quips, no color or fancy camera work such as serve today's movie comedians. All Charlie needs are moving pictures.

THE PASSION OF JOAN OF ARC

1928, France. Directed by Carl Theodore Dreyer. Written by Carl Th. Dreyer and Joseph Delteil. Cinematography by Rudolph Maté. With Renée Falconetti (Joan), Eugène Silvain (Bishop Cauchon), Maurice Schutz (Nicolas Loyseleur), Antonin Artaud (Jean Massieu). Societé Générale des Films. Original title: La Passion de Jeanne d'Arc.

In 1924, shortly after the canonization of Joan of Arc, the newly discovered documents of her trial were published. Carl Dreyer, interested in the subject, read the records and was strangely touched by the recorded words of the nineteen-year-old Joan. They were charged with a wisdom beyond her years and an insight beyond the learning of the professors and ecclesiastics who sat in judgment over her. Dreyer's life ambition, to make a film on Jesus, was never realized. But in *The Passion of Joan of Arc* he did make the most impressive of all religious films; he used the actual words of Joan and her judges to mirror the passion and death of Jesus himself.

Dreyer's Joan is tormented by soldiers, crowned and sceptered in mock royalty, struck in the face, spat upon by "the servant of the high Priest", unjustly tried and executed, with the charge against her nailed above her head. The parallels extend to the smallest details: the cemetery where, historically, Joan was asked to deny her mission is shown in the film as Pilate's Lithostratos (stone pavement), and we see not only the cobbled square but, as the English commander Warwick becomes Pontius Pilate, we see the helmets of his soldiers ranged as so many cobblestones at his feet.

Dreyer had more than sufficient reason for this approach. Joan's trial, at least the final stages of it, actually took place during Holy Week. The bishops and priests who interrogated her came to their task from the altars where they had read the four gospel accounts of the passion of Jesus, the mystery they were renewing that week in their liturgy.

Dreyer rightly chose to stylize his account of the trial and execution. In his *Joan* we look from the fifteenth century back to Jesus and forward to every human being subjected to injustice. While the priests in *Joan* appear in the timeless robes of their religious orders, the English soldiers wear World War I helmets. Joan herself is clothed as anonymously as any prisoner, and her hair is cropped. Not only is this closer to the real Joan, who had to dress as a man to live among soldiers, but it avoids such specifics as Ingrid Bergman's 1948 page-boy bob - effective then, a hopeless anachronism now. When Dreyer's Joan is sentenced to life imprisonment, the rest of her hair is cut off, with twentieth-century scissors, like a novice's or a convict's. By the end of the film, this shorn and sexless Joan has become every victim of every war and every prison camp. Not surprisingly, the film was denounced by some French nationalists for avoiding any reference to the patriotic aspects of Joan's life. It was, perhaps expectedly, banned in Britain for several years, and for decades it existed only in severely cut prints.[1]

The Church too demanded cuts - and indeed the sexual element in the courtroom scenes is hardly understated. The chaste Joan is surrounded by celibate male judges who tower obscenely over her, while she answers their rational, pragmatic but often perverse questions with clear-minded womanly responses that are instinctively right. If eventually her judges reduce her to something sexless, hers is the real victory. She becomes more spirit than flesh. And this is Dreyer's special victory too: Joan's story is a drama of the spirit, yet, with great artistry, he writes it in terms of flesh, in relentless close-ups of faces. His film is written in pores, creases, warts and wrinkles, in sweat, tears, and blood, in erupting mouths, sputtering lips and great, imploring eyes, all set against glaring white backgrounds. And the faces are without makeup.

One effect of this, according to Béla Balász, is to destroy space: "Fifty men are sitting in the same place all the time in this scene. Several hundred feet of film show nothing but close-ups of heads, of faces. We move in the spatial dimension of faces alone. We neither see nor feel the space in which the scene is in reality enacted. Fierce passions, thoughts, emotions, convictions battle here, but the struggle is not in space." And rightly so. This is a battle for Joan's soul, an intensely spiritual drama in which we are permitted, for long segments, to see nothing but flesh.

Years after, Dreyer made this statement: "The human face is a land one never ties of exploring. I know of no greater experience than to witness, in a studio, the expressions which form, under the mysterious power of inspiration, upon a sensitive face. It is possible to see the poetry of the heart become animate."

And there is a curious effect in all this typage of faces. The judges appear gradually to be imprisoned in their heavy flesh, and Joan to transcend hers. Everyone feels this as the film unreels. Subtle lighting has something to do with it, and sensitive performing, and camera angle and movement. A good deal of the time we look down on Joan, as she backs away to right or left, and upwards at the judges as they lunge forward. The camera will zoom in diagonally on a white background which is suddenly filled vertically with a great, rising, accusing face, or pan across a row of heads as across some oversized stone frieze in a medieval cathedral.

Some critics have objected to the zooming camera, and in particular to a shot near the end of the film, when the camera all but somersaults observing the English soldiers driving the crowds off to the execution. The effect is extreme, but at least it fits with a series of visual motifs in which circular shapes (the cowls and tonsures of the priests, the helmets of the soldiers, the many arches, the omnipresent wheels, including a spiked instrument of torture) signify the forces of oppression.

An effective use is also made of triangular patterns. A sympathetic young priest (played by Antonin Artaud, later the founder of the "Theatre of Cruelty") is twice photographed beneath an inverted triangle; the Trinitarian symbol pointing down to his head seems to suggest the action of grace. Joan's face appears against a similarly inverted triangle formed by her bedstead - and then there is a cut to Warwick against the walls and ceiling, his face at the top angle of a triangle on its base. The abrupt reversal suggests the denial of grace, at least of such grace as Warwick, playing God, can dispense. So, too, the clerical face preaching to Joan in the cemetery lurches across an angled, grace-denying pulpit. However we account for them, these are intended, studied effects, as are the circular *and* triangular motif of the sweeping arc described by the priest who places the prisoner's round, three-legged stool on the floor of the torture chamber.

Apart from visual patterns, Dreyer makes clear and beautiful use of symbols, most notably in the flock of birds that settle on a high cross as Joan mounts the pyre and clasps a crucifix to her breast. The birds leave the cross as Joan's cross is wrested from her. They fly overhead she suffers, and fly to heaven as she dies. Twice, at pivotal moments for Joan, the cross is blotted out. A cruciform shadow thrown by a window pane on her prison floor vanishes when an inquisitor enters to trick her and shuts out the light. A distant cross on a steeple, seen from a grave shaft, is obscured by a skull tossed up by an unseen gravedigger. After each of these symbols, Joan weakens; fear of death becomes stronger than her dedication to her purpose.

The climax of the film is done almost entirely in symbols. After Joan recants, the crowd celebrates what it regards as her victory in carnival acts, contortions, and grotesqueries that seem to comment on the cruelty of her world. Their dances are intercut with close-ups of Joan in prison, being shorn of her hair, watching the little crown she has woven out of straw swept up, as so much trash, with the shavings. It is out of this complex of symbols that this silent-movie Joan is moved to withdraw her recantation and choose the ultimate victory - martyrdom.

The same choice - spirit over flesh - is made by the people sympathetic to the martyr. Even before Joan makes her choice, one of the crowd is bound hand and foot and drowned - though we only see his sacrificial act in the reflecting water, for his martyrdom is to signal hers. Then at the close of the picture, when all the people side with Joan, they are brutally clubbed and maced by the English soldiers, and the penultimate image we see, as the drawbridge is raised against rebellion, is a corpse hanging on a distant scaffold. This grim finale has no basis in history; it is intended to state once again the uncompromising message of the film: when the spirit triumphs, the flesh must inevitably suffer. The final image is of the cross and the stake, both standing erect, in the same frame.

Dreyer shows, in this closing sequence, that he has thoroughly mastered and assimilated the techniques of montage. It is own horizontally moving, sharply angled version of the Odessa steps sequence in Eisenstein's *Potemkin*, all the more shocking for its being the last, summary statement of the film. Another remarkable set piece of montage occurs in the torture chamber: we see, in a series of quick shots à la Eisenstein, the spiked wheel from the side, cranked by the torturer; the wheel front-on, its spikes gleaming; Joan's terrified face; the pen dropping from the hand of a horrified scribe; and the face of the chief inquisitor, Bishop Cauchon, growing slack. In one astonishing moment, the surface of the wheel's rim changes from convex to concave and threatens to fall on us.

The Passion of Joan of Arc was a truly international effort. Dreyer himself was a Dane; his acting company mainly French, from the Comédie Française; his set designer (Herman Warm) a German who had worked on *The Cabinet of Dr. Caligari*, and his leading camera Man (Rudolph Maté) a Hungarian born in Poland. These different traditions blended in a work of remarkable unity of style. As one of the company noted, "It was a film made on the knees." All involved worked with dedication and fervor, and in few films has this intensity been so surely communicated to the viewer.

But the guiding force is surely Dreyer's. Falconetti appears to be a great actress at the height of her powers. Actually, she had had no previous experience before the camera. Dreyer found her in "a little boulevard theater whose name I have forgotten. She was playing there in a light, modern comedy, and she was very elegant in it, a bit giddy, but charming." He screen-tested her - without makeup - and found in her face what he wanted for Joan. Falconetti submitted completely to his uncompromising demands, worked with endless patience, suffered through to a single triumph, and was scarcely heard of again.

With gentle or ungentle persuasion, Dreyer seems to have got his way with the others as well. Rudolph Maté seems here to be the most skillful cinematographer of the silent screen. Actually, it was Dreyer who suggested and demanded the close-ups, the searing whites, the "frog perspectives". Maté had worked with Karl Freund photographing *Variety*, and later he did good work for Korda, Hitchcock and Lubitsch, but he ended up directing spear-and-sandal epics and photographing Loretta Young on TV. Hermann Warm, who had always insisted that a film should be "painting in depth" - something his work on *Caligari* almost was - built expensive stylized expressionist sets for Dreyer, then saw next to nothing of them appear on the final prints, where almost everything he saw was faces in close-up. *Joan* wasn't painting in depth; it was sculpture, monumental portrait sculpture, in motion. Warm's sets were largely reduced to circles and triangles, cornices and triglyphs to set off Dreyer's frieze of faces.

Some legitimate criticism can be and has been directed at *Joan*. The conflict is one-sided. Dreyer does something, but not enough, with the emotion that tore Cauchon in two directions, while the zooms and angled shots of Warwick and the other oppressors exaggerate what are already somewhat overstated performances. As for Joan, we know all to surely that the historical Joan wasn't always in tears. She was spunky, hard-headed, and commonsensical in the courtroom, where she laughed and even sang at times. And though she did faint from fear in the torture chamber, she first assured her judges that it was all going to be for nothing - she would simply take back any statement she made once the ordeal was over. George Bernard Shaw gave us, in his own words, a "queer fish" of a Joan, but he was closer to the record when he had her relapse with a brash, "Give me that writing", and then had her tear it up. Dreyer, aiming at a universal statement, oversimplifies.

But the basic problem, and the ultimate irony, in *Joan* is simply this: it is a silent film based almost entirely on words. All the pictorial inventiveness, all the marvelous faces cannot obscure the fact that it is the recorded words of Joan and her judges that propel the film along its agonizingly slow-moving course. The picture cries out for sound, yet in its very expressionism is silent cinema.

Ironically enough, Dreyer wanted to use sound but he did not have sufficient funds for it (just as he never found the backing for his life of Jesus). But then, if he had had sound he might not, almost surely would not, have given us those memorable effects with the camera. *Joan* is a film poised between the silent and sound eras. It seems to sum up all that went before: editing for dramatic purposes (*The Birth of a Nation*); the star performance, in which a character's relationship to the world is established by silent reactions (*The Gold Rush*); distortion of physical reality to express an inner vision (*The Cabinet of Dr. Caligari*); unity of style imposed by an uncompromising director (*Nibelungen*); moving camera (*The Last Laugh*); profuse use of symbols (*Variety*); set pieces of montage (*Potemkin*). But with every viewing over the years, it seems to me to have surpassed all of those predecessors.

GRAND ILLUSION

France, 1937 (American release: 1938). Directed by Jean Renoir. Written by Jean Renoir and Charles Spaak. Cinematography by Christian Matras. Music by Josef Kosma. With Jean Gabin (Maréchal), Erich von Stroheim (Colonel von Rauffenstein), Pierre Fresnay (Captain de Boeldieu), Marcel Dalio (Rosenthal), and Dita Parlo (Elsa). Realisations d'Art Cinématographique. Original title: La Grande Illusion (The Great Illusion).

Some forty years ago, in a symposium on "Films of Peace and War", Arthur Miller made this statement, which is more true today than ever:

> I have one thought about pictures on war, which is that the danger is to present war in such a way as unwittingly to give heroism in battle an inspiriting connotation. This is difficult to avoid, regardless of one's intentions, and the only movie which comes to mind which succeeded in this respect was *Grand Illusion*.

In any case, the problem today is not one of debunking war or extolling peace but of presenting, if indeed it is possible, the subtle machinery through which international accord can be effectuated.

Grand Illusion makes the most honest and intelligent effort of any film I have seen to present "the subtle machinery through which international accord can be effectuated." It was made in 1936, when there still seemed to be time to appeal to the basic humanity of the Germans. Jean Renoir drew on his own memories of personal experiences in the first war, and made a last-ditch effort to do so. But it was too late for pacifist pleas. And *Grand Illusion* did not address itself to the new kind of nationalism - Nazism - that was on the march. All the same, it was banned in Germany and Italy, halted in mid-reel in Vienna, and, when the Nazis finally occupied Paris, all the prints were confiscated. Goebbels called it "cinematographic enemy Number 1".

Grand Illusion is one of the great films, and also one of the most carefully understated. It is an anti-war film with no battle scenes, a film about World War I that never shows the trenches, a prison-escape film without suspense, and eventually a romantic idyll with no sentimentality. It is filled with situations wherein another director could get big effects very easily. Think of *Paths of Glory, The Bridge on the River Kwai, Stalag 17, The Great Escape, The Defiant Ones* - each admirable in its way, all obviously indebted to *Grand Illusion*, all "improving" on it with rigged emotion.

Renoir is not interested in twitching bodies or irony or sentimentality or suspense. ("I hate the sanctity of suspense," he says. "It's left over from nineteenth-century Romanticism.") Renoir is interested in people - in their common humanity, in their complex relationships to one another. So, like Orson Welles, he all but dispenses with the close-up, which isolates a person in the frame. Like Welles, he has no special interest in montage, which determines how we must react to the characters. He also avoids - and here he is unlike Welles - such dramatic devices as camera angles and shadows. He is leisurely, unintense, the artist concealing his art. He refuses to dramatize with his camera. Renoir wants his men to speak for themselves. So he fills his frame with figures (a sort of in-depth method without the showiness), bathes everything in a clear radiant light (he must owe something of this to his father, the painter Pierre-Auguste Renoir), and he pans across most of his scenes to allow us to see, without editing, the reactions of as many people as possible. Above all he provides his film with a novel's density, a richness of theme and image, and levels of meaning as the characters interact.

Renoir's Germans are acutely observed, but they show no stupidity, brutality, or cowardice; his aristocrats are closely scrutinized, but there is no absurdity about their adherence to outmoded military codes and *noblesse oblige*; his commoners are shown to be blunt and plain-spoken, but not dull or dishonest or unfeeling. In an imperfect world, Renoir looks unflinchingly at the good qualities. How else are we to survive?

In *Grand Illusion* we see the twilight of the long age of European Christendom (that knightly era of which men like the German von Rauffenstein and the French de Boeldieu are the last survivors) and the rise, troubled but full of hope, of the classless democracies (the new world which men like the Jew Rosenthal and the commoner Meréchal will create). We are invited to reflect that nationalism, feudalism, and class structures have sometimes served men well and have produced some beautiful things. But they have also divided men into arbitrary positions and taught them to kill one another in defense of those positions. *Grand Illusion* searches for some reality to replace the glorious but largely illusory and sometimes even destructive ideals of the past.

In his searching, Renoir concentrates on the ordinary things - how men think and speak and eat and pray and make love. The whole tissue of the film is made of these human actions used almost as metaphors for communication and division. Language, tradition, culture, and class-systems have been barriers when they could be bridges. Their divisive force is only illusory.

From the opening frame, where we see Maréchal in the French canteen, bent over a phonograph, humming "Frou-Frou" and dreaming of his Josephine, the metaphors begin to work. Music, for example. Only superficially a barrier, music is a great international language. So Maréchal's boulevard song is neatly contrasted with the Strauss waltz played on the phonograph in the German canteen in the next scene. The musical traditions are distinct, but the Strauss waltz cheers the French prisoners as they dine with their German captors, even as "Frou-Frou" still exudes its fragile charm when Maréchal plays it on a German harmonica in German solitary. Another *chanson* cuts across national lines at the prison entertainment, though the German officers are not sure how to react, and all four faces respond in different ways.

As the film unreels, music continues to be a shifting metaphor for what unites rather than divides. The English prisoners begin the *Marseillaise* at the news of a French victory; the French prisoners use a prison-bursting strain from Gounod's *Faust* (a French variant on a German masterpiece) to communicate secrets before the very ears of the Germans. Martial music cuts across all national lines, so much so that a French prisoner burns his trousers on the ironing board listening to German drums and fifes. The fifes may seem to divide the French prisoners along class lines: "I hate fifes", says the aristocratic Boeldieu. But this is only a matter of tradition and taste, and largely illusory. Boeldieu can confer an aristocratic dignity on the fife by using it to enable the lower class prisoners to escape: "I adore the flute," he says, and leads the

Germans off the track of the chase, like the those German tales of the Pied Piper and Prince Tamino in *The Magic Flute*, executing the most stylish trills in the neatest drill style. Finally when the escaped gentile and Jew fall into a childish quarrel, it is a nursery song, first played by Boeldieu as he enabled them to escape, that reunites them.

Language too is only superficially a barrier. It can divide vertically, along national lines: Maréchal hasn't enough skill with language to tell an incoming English prisoner that the French have begun digging a tunnel, and he nearly loses his mind in solitary where he hears only German. Language can also divide horizontally, along class lines: after eighteen months of comradeship, Boeldieu still calls Maréchal *vous*. But language can also unite: Maréchal falls in love with the young German widow, not in spite of, but because of the language differences (the Frenchman's "Lotte hat blaue Augen" is the most tender and telling moment in the film). Latin becomes a medium whereby the Russians can teach their complex language to the French, and English is a common ground whereon the German Rauffenstein and the French Boeldieu can speak without their less educated officers and common soldiers understanding. Education in languages and literatures can individualize men: Maréchal has never heard of Pindar; Boeldieu isn't interested in the study of Pindar because lexicons get in the way of his aristocratic life-style; Rauffenstein, with a characteristic German deference to all things intellectual, sighs, "poor old Pindar" when he sizes up the cranium of the ordinary Frenchman who is attempting to translate the Greek poet. The point is thereby made that our hope of understanding among the masses of men lies first in recognizing the common bond of the ordinary, not the extraordinary. So the Russian prisoners burn the crate of books sent them by the Tsarina, and curse her for thinking to feed their minds but not their bodies.

Taste in food is a great divider: Boeldieu prefers to dine at Fouquet's; Rosenthal knows the barman there, and gets special under-the-counter services; Maréchal knows it only from the outside, and prefers a bistro; the actor among the prisoner regards it only a place to perform in; the teacher doesn't know it at all - when in Paris he eats at his brother-in-law's (yet it is he who complains when the expensive wine from Fouquet's is used to revive the actor nearly asphyxiated in the tunnel). But eating is also a bond that can unite - both vertically, along class lines (Maréchal is welcomed back from solitary by every Frenchman: "Is there anything to eat? I'm hungry."), and horizontally, along national lines (a German officer cuts Maréchal's meat for him when his arm is in a sling). In a homely variant on Christmas communion, little Lotte asks to eat the Infant Jesus, carved out of potatoes for her *chèche* by the Jew Rosenthal. And Maréchal bites into a ripening apple before finding the courage to kiss his German Eve.

Religion need not be a barrier: the lowly Christmas celebration brings German and French, Christian and Jew together. Religion has always meant special things to different classes: Rauffenstein, an elegant Christian gentleman, feels within his rights quartering luxuriantly in the fortress chapel, and Boeldieu dies there, with the last sacrament as something eminently his own by right and heritage. But religious and racial differences may be surmounted: Maréchal simply isn't interested in the Senegalese prisoner's drawing of "Justice pursuing crime": he remains absorbed in his concentration on the plan of escape to that international haven, Switzerland. Ought he to avenge past wrongs? No. His instinct is towards brotherhood and understanding. His last exchange with Rosenthal ("Goodbye, dirty Jew"... "Goodbye, meathead") is beyond malice and bigotry.

The most delicately stated of all the metaphors of division in *Grand Illusion* has to do with sex. How remarkably varied are the responses of the French prisoners to the arrival of a carton full of feminine apparel. Boeldieu isn't remotely interested in participating in the theatrics for which the clothes have been provided; Maréchal is only interested in what real women would look like in the dresses; Rosenthal knows all the facts and figures about the new fashions; the actor is reminded of "going to bed with a boy". The teacher, certain he has been cuckolded, is soured on all women. Sniffing at the new styles, he retorts, "See what they'll do when we're not around to watch them? They go nutty." (This seems, for the moment at least, to be more true of the men.) Then a young prisoner appears, the first to have tried on one of the dresses. "Wait," says Maréchal, "leave us with our illusions." As it happens, the boy is strangely convincing. He tries to shrug off the fact, asking to be reassured that he looks "funny". But a deep silence settles over the group (and Renoir gives us a long pan across the faces.) As each man is alone with his private thoughts, we see how fundamentally united they are, not just in the common longing for a real woman but in a common humanity shared with all women. Sex is nature's division of the human race (and every Frenchman will hasten to add "*Vive la différence!*"), but the common ground of humanness lies deeper still.

The metaphor is continued throughout the film. For an hour and a half, we explore humanity in terms of one sex. The only women we see are the old crones who look sadly on the young Germans drilling for their deaths, and the nurse who checks the time and turns off the oxygen after Boeldieu breathes his last - and these brief glimpses of woman as angels of death are more than the prisoners ever see. To them, women are inaccessible and almost illusory, distant as Rosenthal's Botticelli Venus, unreal as Maréchal's Frou-Frou and his "twenty-two nights of love". When he and Rosenthal escape, they sleep together for warmth and, frightened by a passer-by, don't realize at first that it is a woman. Only when Elsa appears in the stable door with her cow and lantern does woman appear as anything more than illusory. And with the appearance of Elsa we are ready at last for the final scenes in which all the metaphors of division (language, tradition, nationality, race, religion, food, and sex) begin to work as metaphors of unity.

In no film are the symbols so many, so unobtrusive, so rich in meaning and resonance. Monocles blind the aristocrats, both German and French, to their fellow soldiers, and link them to each other. White gloves become a barrier between Maréchal and Boeldieu because they bespeak a style, an elegance, a tradition that the commoner cannot know. Though Maréchal will never understand, Boeldieu must wear the gloves when he executes the escape manoeuvre; he is not sacrificing himself for a commoner and a Jew, he is performing his duty as an officer and a gentleman. Fittingly enough, it is the white-gloved hand of Rauffenstein that shoots him and closes his eyes in death. Boeldieu's life ends like the last flower at Wintersborn - with the snow falling and the watch ticking, even as his last gesture before falling in the snow was a quick, efficient glance at his watch to make sure that the escape had succeeded. Rauffenstein's life-style is spread before us when the camera pans across his chapel-bedroom - from crucifix to pistol and riding whip to champagne bottle and perfume sprayer, to mother's picture and volume of Casanova. At Wintersborn, Rauffenstein wears a brace that allows him to bend only at the waist; yet in his very first appearance we saw that his standards of etiquette put the same restraint upon him. He downs a quick cognac in his first and again in his last scene - and both swift, still, assured movements are the same. The brace was always there.

After several viewings of *Grand Illusion* over many years, I still find the performances of Erich von Stroheim, Pierre Fresnay, Jean Gabin, and Marcel Dalio beyond praise, and it is certainly superfluous to document their achievements here. The picture is clearly a personal statement by its director, whose life was saved in World War I by a flyer who was shot down and escaped his captors seven times. (In much of the film Jean Gabin wears the jacket Renoir had worn in the reconnaisance squadron.) *Grand Illlusion* is more important today than ever before - when black and white and red and yellow people are meeting and mating, and when another world war might mean the end of civilization. There is a special poignancy in watching the trains in *Grand Illusion* pull past the *Lagern* of World War I and thinking how very different were the *Konzentrationslagern* a generation later. Two statements made by Maréchal in the course of the film are called illusions by his fellow solders. One is "The war will be over in two months". The other, "Let's hope this war is the last." *Grand Illusion* couldn't prevent what was to happen in 1939. But in the new century, and the new millennium, we still need its calm insistence that war, like anything else that separates men, is an illusion we can banish with the light of brotherhood, that peace and understanding are the fundamental realities.

CITIZEN KANE

US, 1941. Directed and produced by Orson Welles. Written by Orson Welles and Herman J. Mankiewicz. Cinematography by Gregg Toland. Music by Bernard Herrmann. With Orson Welles (Charles Foster Kane), Joseph Cotton (Jedediah Leland), Dorothy Comingore (Susan Alexander), Ruth Warrick (Emily Norton), Ray Collins (Boss Jim Gettys), Everett Sloane (Mr. Bernstein), George Colouris (Walter Parks Thatcher), and Agnes Moorehead (Kane's mother). RKO Radio.

Citizen Kane may stand alone, in one respect, in all the annals of art. Is there another first work so assured, so deft in its techniques, of such sustained brilliance? Hundreds of poets, painters, and composers have given us masterworks in their mid-twenties, and a few of them have made lasting impressions with their first efforts. But with *Citizen Kane*, which Orson wells directed, produced, starred in and (partly) wrote at the age of twenty-four, we have a first work which is arguably one of the best (it has often been voted the best) in the whole history of its medium.

Welles was known previously for his work on the stage (an all-black "voodoo" *Macbeth*, a modern-dress *Julius Caesar*) and on radio (especially the notorious broadcast that sent New York City into a panic, *The War of the Worlds*). Invited by RKO to make a movie, and given pretty well *carte blanche*, he spent several months running off the film classics, German and American, and brought his experienced Mercury Players from radio to Hollywood's sets and sound stages. Joseph Cotton, Everett Sloane, Agnes Moorehead, Ray Collins, Ruth Warwick and Welles himself were all making their screen debuts, and in performances of astonishing presence. William Alland played the mousy reporter whose face we never see - and was the voice of the pompous March of Time newsreel as well. John Housman, who had helped Welles found the Mercury Theater, was also on hand - as long as he could stand his erstwhile protégé's brash insouciance.

Welles had a marvelous script - much of it the work of Herman J. Mankiewicz[2] - which told of a newspaper magnate's rise to power and inexorable slide into despair, and told it obliquely, first in newsreel and then through interviews with five biased observers. It was a sensational subject, because there were obvious parallels with the life of the still-powerful William Randolph Hearst. When the picture was completed, there was a good deal of intimidation from the powers that were, and also disappointment in some quarters that the treatment wasn't more scandalous, or more politically incisive. What *Citizen Kane* turned out to be, above all else, was a compendium of past silent and sound techniques, all brilliantly used and running in counterpoint to other narrative devices borrowed from radio, inexpensively produced with masterly special effects and sensational cinematography. The miracle was that everything interacted.

Perhaps it is worth noting first what Welles decided against - the close-up and montage. There *are* memorable uses of each, separately and in combination: the close-up of Kane's lips as he breathes his dying word, "Rosebud" is arrived at by a montage of

316

bizarre tracking shots and dissolves, as the camera probes deeper and deeper in the gothic Xanadu that shields Kane from the outside world. Welles' close-up gives the clue to understanding Kane, and his montage is a visual prelude to the whole film (which attempts to penetrate the many layers of a fabled life). But there are very few other instances of the two techniques in the two hours to come. It is as if, after this obeisance to Griffith and Eisenstein, Welles set out to establish himself as a third person in the cinematic trinity.

Welles' alternative to close-up and montage was "in depth" or "deep focus" photography. His cameraman, Gregg Toland, had developed a process whereby objects hundreds of feet from the camera would photograph as clearly as those within ordinary range. *Kane* was not the first picture to use the device. Toland had already tried it in John Ford's *The Long Voyage Home*, and almost certainly he was helped with it by Karl Freund, cinematographer of many of the German classics. Its dramatic possibilities had been developed in several works of Jean Renoir, and in theory it went as far back as the wedding scene in Erich von Stroheim's *Greed*, when a funeral procession passed in the street behind and below the newlyweds. The difference in *Citizen Kane* is that Welles shot scene after scene in deep focus, using it in effect to replace the classic innovations — close up and montage — of Griffith and Eisenstein. In a not untypical scene, the camera looks unblinkingly for long takes as Kane and his mistress Susan Alexander are confronted in their love nest by Kane's wife Susan and his political opponent Boss Gettys. The four players are ranged across the playing area, and as they play to one another we are acutely aware of the distances, physical and psychological, between them. There are no close-ups to force us to concentrate on this character or that, no editing processes to shock us, yet the scene is full of shock, and the faces are all clear and vivid - except when Welles, for dramatic emphasis, blanks them out. Moving himself and the others in and out of pools of light, he has no need to edit. Almost for the first time, the movies had caught the special feeling of a stage performance - players in spatial relationships to one another - and sacrificed nothing thereby.

The technique may not have been new, but the dramatic use of it was so brilliant that it amounted to an innovation. And the same can be said for dozens of other startling devices at work in *Citizen Kane*. Carl Dreyer had used ceilings for pictorial effect in *The Passion of Joan of Arc*, but nothing previous to *Kane* compares with the oppressive dominance of the ceiling of the *Inquirer* office as Leland, Kane's long-standing friend, asks to be transferred to another city. *The Passion of Joan of Arc* also had vertical, even cylindrical tracking shots, but nothing in it compares, for economy and irony, with the vertical shot in *Kane*, where the camera follows the curtain rising on Susan's opera debut - up, up into the catwalks, where the stage hands, we see, have refined critical tastes. Josef von Sternberg, in *The Blue Angel*, had tracked into a room, moved in close up to a face, and then pulled away when the scene was over; but was there ever a more outlandish invasion of privacy than Welles' camera slipping through the skylight of the El Rancho night club to seat itself with the reporter at Susan's table ("Who said you could sit down?" she asks.)? There was soft focus over part of the frame in E.A. Dupont's *Variety*, but nothing in *Variety* is so memorable as the dim vision of ghostly figures in wheelchairs at the end of Leland's hospital corridor, with Leland's clear profile in the foreground. And no split screen, not even in *The Birth of a Nation*, was so effective as Leland sitting in that hospital while his story fades in and out obliquely. As for flashbacks, Hollywood movies were full of them in the early forties; but flashbacks which told a scene from two or more points of view - apparently only Jean Epstein had done it before. And did he have anything like those scenes of Susan's opera debut in the dreadful *Salammbô*, shown first from Leland's vantage point in the critic's box, then from Susan's on the stage?

Citizen Kane is no less remarkable for its audial innovations. Again, not all of these were new. In René Clair's *A Nous la Liberté* there were off-screen sounds and voices, there was the sudden amplification of sound at dramatic moments, and sentences begun in one scene finished in the next. But nothing in Clair's witty concoction really prepared audiences for the scream of the woman outside the tent while within Kane listens to Susan's harsh and realistic words about love, or for the abrupt high-decibel screech of a cockatoo as Susan leaves Kane forever, or for millionaire Thatcher's "Merry Christmas" at the end of one scene, and his "Happy New Year", two decades later, at the beginning of the next.

And there are some uses of sound in *Citizen Kane* that are new to the screen, transferred by the Mercury Players from their radio performances: the overlapping sentences (in the newsreel room), the babble of voices, intentionally unintelligible (at Thatcher's press interview), the orchestrated silences (during the showdown at Kane's love nest), the orchestrated noises (as Kane demolishes the nursery). There is, in addition to Bernard Herrmann's sardonic musical score, a rather special use of "heard music" for irony: a broken down hurdy-gurdy plays Kane's campaign song as Leland leaves the New York office. And when Susan pleads from her sickbed never to have to sing again, the same distant barrel organ plays the "Una Voce" she never learned to sing.

The picture is at its most effective when the "new" devices of sight and sound interact (which is a good ninety percent of the time). In the scene where Thatcher comes to take young Kane away from his parents, we get a deep-focus playing area - the mother close-up, Thatcher medium, the father medium-deep, and in long shot, outside the window, the boy playing in the snow, and actually dominating the shot. The action is carefully plotted so that the spatial distances between the characters indicate their psychological relationships: the weak and guilt-ridden father closes the window on the boy, the ambitious mother resolutely opens it again. (The whole sequence is framed by two scenes in the Thatcher Memorial Library, with its mannish woman and womanish man.) Meanwhile the voices are as carefully arranged as in an operatic ensemble - boy soprano, contralto, baritone, bass. The soprano line, as always, dominates, until the mother's contralto, in a startlingly sudden amplification, silences it. At the close, the shot of the sled left in the snow is complemented by the sound of a distant train whistle, then sleigh bells, and we pass by the juxtaposition of sounds to the next scene - Thatcher attempting to win the boy's affection with a new Christmas sled.

Later we realize that this moment is the beginning of Kane's compulsion to rise to power and his attempt endlessly to compensate for the lack of affection in his life. (He wants his life to be, as he says to Thatcher, "everything you hate".) The laboriously sought secret of his life is right there in the scene with his parents. The inscription on the sled may be covered with snow, but the sights and sounds of the scene are enough to tell us what it was that made Kane self-destructively acquisitive and hungry for affection.

The quest for the meaning of the word "Rosebud" is a convenient narrative device but, it has often been objected, inadequate as a support for all the heavy plotting. And as this bit of "dollar-book Freud" (Welles' own phrase) has come in for more than its share of criticism, it might be insisted that "Rosebud" is not meant to be an explanation (the reporter says at the end, "I don't think one word could explain any man's life"), but only marks the childhood trauma that affected Kane for life.

And if Kane was, as Susan and Leland repeatedly assure us he was, looking only for love ("That's all he really wanted out of life"), then "Rosebud", with its sentimental and almost overtly sexual overtones, whispered first from lips in extreme close-up, is a more adequate symbol than most have been ready to admit. More adequate than Welles himself was wont to admit. When asked what contribution Mankiewicz had made to the script, Welles ungenerously replied, "Everything concerning Rosebud belongs to him."

A more serious artistic weakness in *Citizen Kane* is, paradoxically, one of its strengths - the despotic hand of Orson Welles directing. As the players move in and out of the melodramatically lit playing areas, lunging across oblique angles, mouthing their overlapping sentences, our every reaction is determined by the puppet master behind the camera, and at some point in the picture we begin to resent it, to feel manipulated. Yet Welles is in front of the camera too, the most conspicuous puppet of them all. And strangely enough, we *feel* for the man he plays and for the rest of the film's unlikely and unlikable people. *Citizen Kane* is rigged from start to finish, and yet it is a dazzling film and a moving experience.

Unfortunately Welles discovered too late that very few films could be realized in this brilliantly dictatorial fashion, and his often brutally unfair treatment of Citizen Hearst and his mistress Marion Davies brought him face-to-face with more opposition than he could handle - from Hearst and his minions, and from Louis B. Mayer, who wanted to buy up the negatives and prints and burn them. As a result Welles spent most of his life in fruitless attempts to raise money for his other projects, and his early promise sputtered out in a long line of *flops d'estime*. By the century's end, it was painfully clear that the story of the rise and fall of Charles Foster Kane was also to a remarkable degree the story of the lavishly talented Orson Welles.

THE BICYCLE THIEF

Italy, 1949 (American release 1950). Directed by Vittorio de Sica. Written by Cesare Zavattini. Based on a novel by Luigi Bartolini. Photography by Carlo Montuori. Music by Alessandro Cicognini. With Lamberto Maggiorani (Antonio Ricci), Enzo Staiola (his son Bruno), Lianella Carell (his wife Maria), and Vittorio Antonucci (the Thief). Produzioni de Sica. Original title: Ladri di Biciclette. UK title: Bicycle Thieves. Special Oscar for foreign film.

'What de Sica can do," says Orson Welles, "I can't do. The camera disappeared, the screen disappeared - it was just life." In *Shoeshine* (the film Welles was talking about) and in *The Bicycle Thief* (his masterpiece), de Sica took to the streets to capture on film the troubled but hopeful lives of post-war Italians. At least at first, he had only a single camera and no sound equipment at all. (The dialogue had to be dubbed later.) But he had that most histrionically gifted of peoples, the Italians, and they responded to his direction as no actors had responded before. What de Sica and a handful of other directors accomplished in the late forties in Italy was soon hailed around the world as a revolution in the cinema. Actually, it was not so much a revolution as a revelation of what a man could do with a camera.

There never has been a really satisfactory definition of neo-realism, as the movement came to be called. De Sica himself eventually rejected the term. If his was the "new", what was the old realism? Soviet cinema? Perhaps. The Russians had laid claim to screen realism twenty-five years before de Sica, and had made their mark with montage, with heroic camera compositions, and with collective heroes. The Italians, with new social statements to make, struck off in an opposite direction. Instead of montage, they aimed for as much continuity as a single camera would allow; instead of monumental shots of revolutionaries against clouds and sea, ordinary views of poor people in the streets of war-shaken cities; instead of one collective hero assembled from a congeries of individual shots, each individual man all but living before the camera the experiences of his own life.

In *The Bicycle Thief* Lamberto Maggioñani, who plays the father, left his job for two months to act for de Sica, then went back to work. Enzo Staiola, who plays his son in what is surely one of the most extraordinary performances ever given by a child, was a refugee. Lianella Carrell, who plays the mother, was enlisted when she interviewed de Sica on the radio. The young thief himself, who appears only briefly, had had some professional experience, but for the rest de Sica simply roped off areas of Rome with the help of the police and enlisted the services of passers-by.

The Rome in the picture is no tourist's Rome. We have to look hard to see any classic monuments, Baroque churches, or beautiful women. It was the Rome of the poor man that needed documentation. In 1948, twenty-two percent of the adult male population of Italy was unemployed, and many others had only part-time jobs. So de Sica set out to tell the story of a man who after a long period of unemployment gets a job posting bills, only to have stolen before his eyes the bicycle which is essential to his work. The quest for the bicycle in company with his eight-year-old son becomes the substance of the film. For all its intensely personal feeling, *The Bicycle Thief* has the look and feel of a documentary. De Sica was a great admirer of Robert Flaherty, and hoped that Flaherty's poetic approach to documentary could be applied to Italy's post-war problems in a quasi-fictional way, "to surmount the barrier that separates the documentary from poetry." He succeeded in almost every way. His neo-realist films were more persuasive than straight documentaries could ever have been (how much more effective to show the hundreds of bed sheets and bicycles in hock than to give statistics on poverty and unemployment!); they cost less money and they were far less liable to government intervention and censorship.

The only persistent and, I think, the only possible criticism leveled against *The Bicycle Thief* is that it is too carefully structured to be completely credible as "realism". It is based on a novel, and adapted by the finest of neo-realist writers, Cesare Zavattini. All of the post-war Italian pictures have good stories to tell; nothing sets them farther apart from the usual documentaries so much as that. But in *The Bicycle Thief* we get almost literary plotting. The thief is found in the street just after a clairvoyant has pronounced that justice will come "soon or not at all". The father becomes a thief himself and most ask forgiveness where he has not himself forgiven. Society is represented in careful synopses: a union that is interested in collectives, not individuals, a police office that reduces men to statistics, a church that dispenses charity for a devotional price, and locks its penitents in. The lost bicycle is a Fides (faith), and the long fruitless search for it takes place on Sunday (and in Rome, we are told, "it always rains on Sunday"). One hesitates to look further for fear of finding more symbolic overtones to work against the realistic and intensely human texture of the film. We don't really need this sort of thing when the actors in the streets are themselves so thoroughly convincing. In the closing scene, when the son's tears win forgiveness for his father, when the father weeps for shame that his son has seen him doing wrong, when, finally, the boy clasps his father's had, we don't want the additional ironies that can be secured by careful plotting.

It seems unfair, perhaps, to fault a movie for being too rich, too carefully done - indeed, too beautiful. But the fact remains, what we really carry away from *The Bicycle Thief* is all there in front of de Sica's camera, not in Zavattini's script. No *a priori* plotting is responsible for the effect of the moment where the father, in a sudden burst of anger, slaps his son. It might help an American audience to know that the Italian *paterfamilias* commands a special kind of unquestioning authority over his family - something that has given way since the war. (Fellini constantly elegizes on the theme.) But we don't really have to know even that. De Sica's pictures are enough to tell us how utterly lost *this* father is when *this* boy, who has known poverty and has learned to be self-reliant, reacts not like a child but like a little man. Losing his son's respect, this father feels unmanned in a way no American father, accustomed to a more casual obedience, can feel. And we can see it. What makes the scene even more extraordinary is that in it de Sica and his actors bring off that rare, inimitable moment in art - the instant blending of comic and tragic. We smile at the boy's delightfully adult reaction even while we feel the father's shock and shame. (A few moments in Chaplin's movies compare with it. Indeed, de Sica, himself a skilled comedian, regards Chaplin as the major influence on all film-makers.)

The neo-realist movement lasted only about ten years,[3] but its influence is still present in the work of the more affluent and cosmopolitan Italian directors of subsequent decades. Antonioni said, apropos of *The Bicycle Thief*, "I would have told more about the man, less about the bicycle." Actually, he has done almost that. His *L'Avventura* is a quest for a lost girl that tells us more about the searchers than the sought-for; it too passes through metaphoric situations, involves the betrayal of ideals. and reaches its ultimate resolution in the close-up of a forgiving hand, as the man who has done the fruitless searching (and, in a sense the stealing as well) weeps for shame. There are differences, of course. Antonioni sees everything with a Marxist and elegantly pictorial eye; every irony becomes a black-and-white image, and the resolution comes in a graphic reversal, with a white hand laid on a black head.

Closer to the neo-realist tradition is Fellini, who once worked with Rossellini on *Open City* and *Paisan*, and decades later still thought of himself as a neo-realist: "For me neo-realism means looking at reality with an honest eye - but not just social reality, also spiritual reality, metaphysical reality, anything man has inside him." His *La Dolce Vita* and *Fellini Satyricon* are both quests for lost innocence in the streets of Rome, and both bespeak Fellini's Christian outlook, as opposed to Antonioni's Marxist ethic.

It is interesting to note that when neo-realism began, with *Open City*, the two resistance heroes were a Communist engineer and a Catholic priest. The obvious suggestion in 1945 was that Italy's two political parties could co-operate in building for the future. The whole neo-realist movement was subsequently divided between the Communist socialists (Visconti, de Santis, Germi) and the Catholic liberals (Rossellini, de Sica, Castellani, Zampa). In subsequent decades, Antonioni and Fellini showed that the polarity was till there, and it has continued with the work of Pasolini, Bertolucci, Rosi and many others. But none of them has really surpassed the pivotal work of the man who, in *The Bicycle Thief*, captured reality and used it not just to plead for social reform but to enable us all to share in "the hope of the marvelous thing that is man".

RASHOMON

Japan, 1950 (American release 1951). Directed by Akira Kurosawa. Written by Akira Kurosawa and Shinobu Hashimoto. Based on two stories by Ryonosuke Akutagawa. Cinematography by Kazuo Miyagawa. Music by Fumio Hayasaka. With Toshiro Mifune (the Bandit), Machiko Kyo (the Woman), Masayuki Mori (the Husband), Takashi Shimura (the Woodcutter), Minoru Chiaki (the Priest), Kichijiro Ueda (the Prowler), Fumiko Homma (the Medium), and Daisuke Kato (the Policeman). Daiei. Special Oscar for foreign film.

Akira Kurosawa's *Rashomon* was the first Japanese film to attract attention in the West. It had been a popular success in Japan, though it was thought difficult and was not much liked by the critics. An Italian cinéaste saw it and insisted on its being sent to the 1951 film festival in Venice, despite the objections of its Japanese producers, who thought it would be completely unintelligible to Europeans. No one was more surprised than the Japanese themselves when it took the first prize, and went on to win critical acclaim all over the world, including the "best foreign film" citation at the Academy Awards. There was suddenly a demand for other finely wrought Japanese films. Mizoguchi's *Ugetsu* followed, and Kinugasa's *Gate of Hell*, and Kurosawa's own *The Seven Samurai*. But at first it seemed a lucky turn of fate that Japanese film had been discovered by the West.

Rashomon is adapted from two short stories ("The Rashomon Gate" and "In a Grove") by the twentieth-century writer Ryonosuke Akutagawa. It takes place in twelfth-century Kyoto during a period of anarchy and despair, before the capital city entered its golden age of faith and prosperity. Briefly, the film tells how a samurai and his wife are attacked in a forest by a bandit who rapes the wife and, presumably, kills the husband. We only presume, because the story is told four times - by the bandit when he is captured and brought to trial, by the wife at the trial, by the dead husband speaking through a medium, and finally by a woodcutter who witnessed the whole course of action in the forest. The accounts contradict one another, as each narrator looks to defend his/her own honor. All of this is set in a framing story: the woodcutter takes shelter from a cataclysmic rainstorm under the Rashomon gate in Kyoto, and relates the four accounts to a young priest who is losing his faith and to a prowler who is robbing corpses in the ruined city. At the close the three find an abandoned baby, which the prowler despoils and the woodcutter eventually takes home, restoring the priest's faith in mankind.

Kurosawa tells the two stories with photographic images that, once seen, are never forgotten: the pelting rain on the steps of the great, ruined Rashomon gate, the sun flashing through the forest leaves and glancing off the woodcutter's axe, the dragger dropping from the woman's hand as she is overcome with passion, the last backward-tracking shot as the woodcutter carries the baby towards and past the camera eye, revealing the priest standing under the ruined gate, etched now against a clear sky.

In this country at least, critical attention has always focussed on the central story - the shockingly contradictory accounts of the incident in the forest. Not the least of the revelations is that each of the three involved in the action claims responsibility for the death of the husband: the bandit boasts that he dispatched him handily in a duel, and at the wife's request; the wife testifies that she stabbed him in a paroxysm of despair induced by the reproach in her husband's eyes; the husband, speaking through a medium, insists that his wife cold-bloodedly commanded the bandit to kill him, but that he was spared and then took the honorable way out - harakiri. Each of the testifiers speaks directly into the camera; we are the judge. Even the woodcutter's story is suspect; he has to rearrange the events so that it will not be clear that he has taken the woman's valuable dagger. We are forced to ask which of the four is telling the truth, to wonder in the end whether there is any truth at all. (We are left far more perplexed than the reporter in *Citizen Kane*, who heard five biased reports of Kane's life, but found no great discrepancy of fact. In *Kane* at least the audience was given a clue at the end. In *Rashomon* each version reflects off the other, like the distorted mirrors in some insoluble Japanese puzzle.)

Parker Tyler, in his essay, "*Rashomon* and Modern Art", saw the film as a time mural, not unlike Picasso's Guernica; truth was fractured into four panels when the consciousness of the characters - their "moral identity in the social order" - was shaken by the terrible events; each character has reconstructed the incident, assuming guilt, and presumably lying, in an attempt to reassert his identity to himself and to the others. But if the sum total of these is meant, like the various perspectives in Picasso, to add up to what Tyler finds, "great beauty and great truth", I should think that Kurosawa would have indicated this in the framing story. Instead, at the Rashomon gate, the woodcutter contradicts

331

all three versions we have heard, the prowler laughs at them, the priest despairs of them. Surely there is a deeper meaning in the film, and it should lie in the framing story (which Tyler, *alio loco*, dismisses as "hollow").

First let us turn our attention to some of the details about *Rashomon* that puzzled Western audiences from the start. If the picture was never intended to be shown abroad, why is so much of it Western in style? Why, as the Japanese critics complained, is the acting so unrestrained, the language so abusive? Why, as students seeing this as their first Japanese film unfailingly note, is there no Noh, no Kabuki, no ceremony in this medieval costume picture. Why did Kurosawa ask his composer to "write something like Ravel's *Bolero*" for the wife's version of the events? Why does he permit the bandit to kiss the wife full on the mouth, when in 1950 Japanese distributors regularly excised such scenes from American movies?

The film is about the West, even if it was never intended to be shown there. And one clue to its interpretation is provided by an article by James F. Davidson, who was working in Japan for the U.S. State Department when *Rashomon* was first shown. It should be noted first that the two Akutagawa stories themselves say nothing about the happenings of 1945. (The author died by his own hand, aged thirty-five, in 1927.) But as Kurosawa and his script collaborator Shinobu Hashimoto have interlaid the two tales, we are surely invited to see the Rashomon gate as an image of the country that had just seen two of its cities reduced to ashes by American atom bombs, and the events in the forest as a microcosmic symbol of the destruction.

"I can't understand it," exclaims the woodcutter again and again.

"I have seen hundreds of men dying, killed like animals,' says the priest, "but I have never heard anything so terrible as this."

As Davidson persuasively argues, the at-first demure samurai and his wife represent traditional Japanese values, while the bandit, with his coarse language and gestures and his impassioned kiss (none of which are indicated in the original stories), is a Japanese caricature of a Westerner. As Kurosawa has rearranged the sources, both East and West tell their own glory-seeking versions of what happened before 1945.

But the key figures - and here we leave Davidson - may well be the woodcutter and the priest, since in Akutagawa they appear only in the "forest" story, as minor witnesses at the trial, while in Kurosawa they figure in both inner and outer stories. The final, woodcutter's version of the occurrence in the forest implies that Japan (the wife) had long lusted after Western values (the bandit), that each side (samurai and bandit) fought ingloriously in a senseless war, and for nothing. The priest's disillusionment reminds us that the Japanese in defeat had to re-examine their unquestioning belief in the emperor, whom they had held infallible and even divine. In 1945, defeat for Japan meant the questioning of every value and tradition on which the old order was based. It was indeed a crisis of faith.

Viewed in this way, the episode with the baby becomes the crucial event of the film. The prowler - almost as unrestrained in speech and movement as the bandit had been - despoils the abandoned child like any war profiteer. The priest instinctively runs to protect it. The woodcutter, repentant, takes it home to feed and care for it, though he has six of his own. The old order may have given way, but new values in the old tradition are emerging. Japan will survive its disgrace and defeat. Davidson notes, and it is very important, that at this point the music at last becomes traditional, and the woodcutter and priest bow with Eastern ceremony to each other.

Can Kurosawa have planned all this, without any real hope that the West would ever see his picture, or the East understand it? There is only the evidence of the original stories, showing what deliberate changes were made in the translation to film, and a few reticent remarks of Kurosawa himself, to imply that an allegory underlies the puzzle, that the occurrence in the forest is meant to explain what transpires in the pelting rain at the Rashomon gate.

Finally it should be said that Kurosawa's command of cinema is total, that the checkered patterns of the sunlight on the leaves of the forest are as eloquent an image of ambiguity, and the pelting rain on the ruined gate as devastating a picture of a world in chaos as the movies have ever given us, and that Toshiro Mifune, in a spectacular performance as the bandit, is by turns brutish, seductive, horrified, and cowardly - depending on who is telling the story at the time.

LAWRENCE OF ARABIA

UK, 1962. Directed by David Lean. Written by Robert Bolt. Cinematography by Frederick A. Young. Music by Maurice Jarre. Produced by Sam Spiegel. With Peter O'Toole (T.E. Lawrence), Omar Sharif (Sherif Ali ibn el Kharish), Alec Guinness (Prince Feisal), Anthony Quinn (Auda abu Tayi), Jack Hawkins (General Allenby), Anthony Quale (Colonel Harry Brighton), Claude Rains (Mr. Dryden), Arthur Kennedy (Jackson Bentley), José Ferrer (the Turkish Bey), and Donald Wolfit (General Murray). Columbia/Horizon. Oscar for best film, six others.

Every movie fan has a problem with the Academy of Motion Picture Arts and Sciences and its annual awards. How many times has this fan concurred with the Academy on its choice of best picture? Only twelve times in seventy-five years.

One of those films on which the Academy and I were in agreement was *Lawrence of Arabia*. It was the kind of picture - big, costly, money-making, prestigious - that wins Oscars almost as a matter of course and, almost as predictably, is dismissed, with sometimes withering scorn, by more than a few critics. Bosley

Crowther in *The New York Times* called *Lawrence* "laboriously large" and "barren of humanity"; its script was "overwritten" and "surprisingly lusterless"; it was filled with "a conventional lot of action-film clichés"; it was, "in the last analysis, just a huge, thundering camel-opera that tends to run down rather badly." Even critics who liked the film, and some who loved it, were agreed that, despite its more than three hours' running time, it failed to give a satisfactory explanation of the enigmatic man it had chosen as its subject.

The Academy, on the other hand, showered *Lawrence* with awards, and in this writer's opinion every one of them was richly deserved. Let me explain.

Best Cinematography: Still the high-water mark in thrilling color photography is Freddie Young's in the scene in *Lawrence* where Ali (Omar Sharif) first appears out of the desert, a swirling speck on the horizon, black and reflected black in the shimmering sands. As he rides towards the camera, the mirage, which at first he seems to be, clears: no longer reflected in the sand, Ali actually seems to diminish in size, till we see him and his heavily caparisoned camel in clear perspective, and then, as he emerges from the waves of heat, he grows larger again, the tassels on his saddle swaying and sinister - and suddenly we are jolted by an abrupt cut and deafened by the close report of a rifle shot. Photographically this is one of the great moments in movie history. And there are other blazingly incandescent desert scenes that are not only triumphs of technical skill and photographic art, but come to be a great metaphorical mirror for Lawrence himself.

Best Editing: For sheer excitement, there is no editing in any movie to surpass that in the triumphant sequence in *Lawrence of Arabia* wherein Lawrence, after crossing a searing desert called "the sun's anvil", discovers a man has been left behind and heads back on his camel into the merciless heat to rescue him. Intercut with virtuoso shots directly into the sun are angled views of the lost man tramping over a parched expanse of waste. We never see Lawrence finding him. Instead, we wait for a miracle with Lawrence's Arab boy, perched on his camel. The editing carefully establishes the direction of every movement. Eventually, the boy sights his master returning, with the lost man, and rides out joyously to meet him. The camera cuts back and forth, with forward tracking shots (as we look adoringly through the boy's eyes) and one climactic long shot (as the two camels race from different directions to center screen). Naturally the music swells. But the real excitement, the exaltation that all but brings the audience to its feet, comes from the editing - by Anne V. Coates and, in a rush of last-minute adrenalin (so as to finish in time for a command performance for the Queen), director David Lean himself.

Best Art Direction/ Set Decoration: How strange it was to walk once into the Alcazar in Seville and exclaim, "I've been here before!". It was some time before I realized that I'd seen it in *Lawrence*, in the scenes wherein John Box and his crew added minarets and domes to Seville to make us believe we were in Damascus. The same crew also converted Seville's Casino of the Teatro Lope de Vega into the town hall in Damascus where, amid savagely squabbling crowds, Lawrence's dream of a united Arab republic is forever shattered, and the two Arabs closest to him - young, high-minded Ali and old, close-minded Auda - make their theatrical exits from history's stage.

Best Musical Score: There is no movie theme so sweeping, so absolutely right for the tremendous vistas of desert sand, and so evocative when heard apart from the picture, as Maurice Jarre's for *Lawrence of Arabia*. And Jarre's subtler music for sunrises, dramatic climaxes, and moments of horrified introspection add powerfully to already powerful scenes.

Best Sound: We're talking here not about the high-tech quality of the sound, but its use for dramatic purposes. Consider the ominous creaking of the swaying supports of King Feisal's tent that foretells of the miracle Lawrence promises, goes forth into the desert to meditate on, and finally delivers - the storming of Aqaba. Consider the tolling of two huge ladles dangling from a Turkish army wagon, harbingers of doom for the unfortunate soldiers about to be massacred by Lawrence's cutthroat army. Consider even the cries of the camels throughout the picture, always presentiments of what is to come or, in the last scene, of what has happened. Consider too the studied use of silence in at least a dozen great sequences.

Best Direction: David Lean had the genius to take the young Peter O'Toole, new to the screen, and use his unconventional charm to bring to life a daring but unstable would-be messiah forced to face the ironies of history and his own shameful and shaming sado-masochism. (The terse, character-revealing dialogue by Robert Bolt was of course an invaluable asset here.) Lean also had the genius to use the desert as a great shifting, challenging, beautiful, and ultimately cruel image of the inscape of the strange man who excitedly entered it, was ennobled by it, eventually saw his inner self mirrored in it, and left destroyed by it.

Best Picture: As the producer usually picks up the Oscar for best picture, perhaps we should give Sam Spiegel the last word here - on the persistent criticism that the film never "explained" its hero. "David and I had wanted to make a Lawrence picture for <many> years. Here was a man of highly controversial character who became a legend in his own lifetime. The hardest problem in the conception of our film was to *transpose* the self-contradictions, not to *resolve* them." (Emphasis added) Yes, Lawrence remains unexplained right to the end. But hauntingly unexplained, as eventually we all are.

NOTE: *Lawrence of Arabia*, which demands and deserves to be seen intact on a large screen, was brutally cut for theatrical distribution in 1962, cut still further in 1970, and in the eighties was discovered to be rapidly deteriorating. Thanks partly to Martin Scorsese and Steven Spielberg, it was lovingly and painstakingly restored by Robert A Harris and re-released at the end of the eighties - when several critics who had not seen it in 1962 proclaimed it the best picture of 1989. A Los Angeles writer echoed my sentiments when he said, "It really does make you remember why you love movies."

8½

Italy, 1963. Directed by Federico Fellini. Written by Federico Fellini, Ennio Flaiano, Tullio Pinelli, and Brunello Rondi. Cinematography by Gianni di Venanzo. Music by Nino Rota. With Marcello Mastroianni (Guido), Claudia Cardinale (his Muse), Anouk Aimée (his Wife), and Sandra Milo (his Mistress). Cineriz. Original Title: Otto e Mezzo. Oscar for best foreign film.

8½ is so named because its director, Federico Fellini, had already made seven other movies and two episodes for anthologies. The episodes were for *Love in the City* and *Boccaccio 70*; the full-length films were *Variety Lights*, *The White Sheik*, *I Vitelloni*, *La Strada*, *Il Bidone*, *Cabiria*, and of course *La Dolce Vita*. That elaborate, brilliant, and flamboyantly vulgar film had been an overwhelming international success, though there were not wanting some critics who thought it empty and insisted that Fellini did not really understand himself, his country, his religion, or the art of making movies. How does one answer such criticism, and how does one follow up such popular success?

8½ is Fellini's answer to his public and his critics. It is neither defiant nor submissive, only a movie about making a movie after *La Dolce Vita* and 6½ others. And its leading character, Guido Anselmi, seems to be Fellini himself. For Marcello Mastroianni has, from all reports, imitated Fellini's walk and talk, and incorporated many of the famous director's mannerisms into his remarkable performance. He even sports the outsized, floppy fedora that is Fellini's trademark.

As the movie begins, we see Guido/Fellini trapped in his car in an underpass during a traffic jam, suffering and indeed suffocating while impassive faces - presumably those of his public and critics - stare silent and accusing. He has reached an artistic impasse, and this is his hallucinatory experience of it. He escapes (this too is seen in nightmare terms), ends up under medical care, and is advised to rest at a spa. There, as he plans his new film (which he hopes *will* say something important about moral honestly, his own life, "the Catholic conscience in Italy," and the future of mankind), he finds that his ideas simply won't come together. Moreover he is badgered at the spa by producers, actors, writers, hangers-on, wife and mistress - and most of all by memories of childhood. Sometimes we witness his fantasies, wish-fulfillments, projections, and day-dreams. Eventually, Guido's attempts to make the picture *become* the picture.

Obviously this is not a movie in which everything can be explained. Even the people who made it admitted that, from day to day and week to week, they hadn't the slightest idea what it was about. Fellini didn't tell them. In 1963, *8½* confused both audiences and critics. But its technical virtuosity was dazzling, and many came back a second or third time and found that more of the pieces fell together on each viewing. Some of it was clarified by exposure (that is the right word) to Fellini's next film, *Juliet of the Spriits*, which was *8½* in color for ladies. But as a starting point it is better to look back to the predecessor, *La Dolce Vita*. At the end of that film, a lovely young girl called to us from the seashore, but we couldn't hear her words. We only felt that here was something beautiful, natural, and unspoiled amid all the degeneracy and decadence. Fellini promised to make his next picture about that girl, and she appears in *8½* - rather too amply reincarnated in the bosomy person of Claudia Cardinale, dressed in white and assisting Guido at appropriate intervals as a sort of guardian angel and inspiring muse. According to John Russell Taylor (in *Cinema Eye, Cinema Ear*), she invites Guido to "a world without shame." And this interpretation works nicely among all the symbols and dreams, for the picture is at least partly about conscience and traumas and the search for innocence.

Guido constantly dreams about innocence. The loveliest scene in the picture is an almost Proustian remembrance of childhood in a great familial homestead, aglow with warmth, laughter, white sheets, and loving, maternal hands. This is the lost innocence that Guido tries to recapture at the Terminal Hotel, in a long bedroom scene with his mistress – unsuccessfully. The episode ends with a vision of his mother, dressed in black, washing the bedroom wall. Later, in the movie's most famous scene, Guido imagines a harem where all the desirable women he has known come together as one big happy family to satisfy his every whim - and this takes place in the same vast, warm, innocent homestead of his memories. This is more than a return to the womb; it is an attempt to find innocenee even in what Guido feels are his most shameful desires.

Why does he feel this shame? Guido remembers how, as a boy on the seashore, he watched the gyrations of La Saraghina, a mountainous madwoman - without shame, until the priests who supervised his early education turned it into something shameful. This early trauma, experienced under clerical repression, recalls the portrait of another artist as a young man. (And in *Juliet of the Spirits* the heroine's problems are seen to stem in large measure from her early schooling with the nuns.) Guido respects and fears, loves and hates his church (this is true in all Fellini films). He looks to it for guidance, and is pained to find that its representatives have the trappings of innocence but no understanding of it; they wear cassocks and read breviaries but can only speak in terms of mythological side-issues and pat confessional formulae.

There is no innocence, no answer to the contradictions in life, to be found in film-making either. This is the most shaming experience of all; Guido tries to be honest in the film he is making, but is made to feel himself a shameless exhibitionist. In testing actors for the roles of his father, wife, mistress, and La Saraghina he seems to himself nothing more than a heartless sadist. Eventually the movie he plans is abandoned.

Does he yield entirely to shame, then? No. In the wonderful closing scenes, he decides he must come to terms with the contradictions within him and without. He invites all the people who represent his memories and associations to whirl in a dance of life: "You creatures, I accept you, I love you... this confusion is me... accept me as I am."

Throughout *8½* the imagined seems to be more real than the real. There is a precedent for this in Italian drama - notably in Pirandello, who sent six characters in search of an author. But there had been nothing like *8½* before on film. Individual scenes may suggest Cocteau, Bergman, and René Clair, and the spa setting seems a wry variant on Renais' *Last Year at Marienbad*. In the music, Guido is characterized as that jack-of-all-trades, Figaro, the barber of Seville; the well-to-do matrons, the nuns, even the rebellions ladies in Guido's harem are Wagnerian Valkyries; the movie stars are Nutcrackers, and Guido's wife is a Blue Moon. All of these echoes and associations are the bits of brac-à-brac that haunt the author's subconscious - and that is the landscape we are exploring in *8½*. Appropriately, there are also quotes from other Fellini films: the carnival musicians from *La Strada*, the lonely, dim-lit piazza from *I Vitelloni*, the mind-reading act from *Cabiria*, the tender memory of his father from *La Dolce Vita*. Even Nino Rota's main musical theme is a sort of "fast camera" acceleration of his three-note motif from that previous film.

But there is a logic to the way that the images and personal associations are manipulated. A mention of Suetonius' life of Julius Caesar leads to a scene in the baths, where we see Roman faces and towels are draped like togas; as the mists swirl around the sweating bodies and we think of Dante's *Inferno* we see a lean, ascetic cardinal in his private mineral bath; he quotes three variants on *extra ecclesiam nulla salus* (a most unecumenical formula from the self-castrator Origen), and a window slants shut on Guido as if he were excommunicated - to the soft strains of "Blue moon, you saw me standing alone" - and we cut to a crowd gathered around an Indian ascetic who has "broken all endurance records" as we see, standing alone, Guido's long-suffering wife, dressed Nehru style: through all the years of Guido's infidelity, she has felt excluded and "broken all endurance records".

There are a hundred such associative links, and tracing them is endlessly fascinating: Guido is distracted from the cardinal's irrelevant chatter by a woman who looks like La Saraghina, and though he tries to listen to His Eminence he is carried off on the shameful childhood memory ("Memories," he says, "have so little respect"). But the memory was already operating in the bedroom scene with his mistress: Guido couldn't tell then why he had so little success with his love-making, but the guilt-dealing song of Saraghina on the sound track tells us - at least, on the second viewing.

Even those who find the accumulation of associations off-putting will concede that the movie-making in *8½* is first-rate. Take the close of the "Proustian" episode in the children's bedroom. In the tenderness of the recollection, we have almost forgotten that we were told that this was going to be a sort of ghost story prompted by a phrase a mind-reader had plucked from Guido's memory - *asa nisi masa* (i.e, *anima*). At the close of the scene, however, the feeling of the supernatural is at last conveyed, beautifully, as the camera slowly tracks, to a howling wind and one of Nino Rota's repeated four-note phrases, across the silent room to a crackling fire.

Or take the closing scene, where Guido casts an eye back over all his experience. In *Citizen Kane*, a man's life was summed up as the camera tracked over vast rooms filled with his accumulated possessions and settled finally on his boyhood sled, consumed by flames. In *8½*, the camera follows the boy himself - his black school uniform now turned an unashamed white - as he pulls the curtain on a giant scaffold staircase, down which all the people in his life descend; the boy plays a wistful tune on his pipe and gently directs the crowd off-screen. It is a triumphant close, resolving no only a tangled web of personal associations, but completing as well a carefully controlled pictorial scheme (of blazing whites and sinister blacks) and sound track (of allusive music and eloquent silences).

Ultimately *8½* is a classic film because it is that rare thing in art - a glimpse into the workings of the subconscious of an artist. Only a few artists - Thomas Mann and James Joyce come to mind - have allowed us this view, and attempted to describe the actual feel of creation. Watching *8½*, we share the exultation and frustration of the creative process with one of the geniuses of cinema. Perhaps only one other film of the sixties challenges *8½* for imaginative flights of fancy - Kubrick's *2001*. And didn't Fellini anticipate that space odyssey? What was the film Guido didn't make? Some sort of science-fiction thing involving a space mission, transcending politics, religion, past traditions. The very lobotomy Kubrick's astronauts practice on their spaceship's computer, HAL, defusing his logic and his memory - the evolutionary step Kubrick seems to imply man himself must eventually take - is what Fellini is about in *8½*.

CRIES AND WHISPERS

Sweden, 1972 (American release 1973). Written and directed by Ingmar Bergman. Cinematography by Sven Nykvist. Music by Frédéric Chopin and J.S. Bach. With Harriet Anderson (Agnes), Liv Ullmann (Maria), Ingrid Thulin (Karin), Kari Sylwan (Anna), Erland Josephson (the Doctor), Anders Ek (the Minister), Georg Arlin (Karin's husband), Henning Moritzen (Maria's husband). Liv Ullmann also plays, in flashback, the mother of the three sisters. Cinematograph/ Svenska Film Institute.

"It is early Monday morning and I am in pain". So begins Ingmar Bergman's *Cries and Whispers*. Agnes, a middle-aged woman suffering from cancer of the womb, records the sentence in her diary. She sits at her desk in a sumptuous, wooded nineteenth-century Swedish manor house in which baroque clocks tick and chime the irrevocable passage of the hours and the walls and furnishings are patterned in the richest red and crimson.

Agnes, dressed in white, is being attended in her final hours by three women, also dressed in white - her older sister Karin, a bitter woman trapped in a marriage with an appallingly unfeeling diplomat; her younger sister Maria, a sensuous, manipulative beauty who hardly acknowledges her little daughter and cheats on her weak husband; and Anna, the maidservant, a sturdy peasant woman who has lost her little girl and is utterly devoted to the suffering Agnes.

They are four figures in white within a red enclosure: Bergman has remarked, "Ever since my childhood I have pictured the inside of the soul as a moist membrane in shades of red." Virtually every dissolve in *Cries and Whispers* fades into that luxuriant, sinister color. (The cinematographer is, as with all the great Bergman films, Sven Nykvist.) This is Bergman's most painful, powerful, and moving work, and like most of his oeuvre it is for him a means of facing his perennial problem - the silence of God in a world that is overwhelmingly cruel to its creatures, who are in turn overwhelming cruel to one another.

Bergman feels, and asks us to feel, compassion for those creatures. In a rare moment when the estranged Karin and Maria are briefly reconciled, he covers their words with a moving passage from Bach - the saraband from a unaccompanied C-minor suite for cello - so as to voice his own deep feelings. He also uses Chopin - a sadly reflective A-minor mazurka - to underline the memories Agnes has of her dead mother, and Anna of her lost daughter. There is a lovely scene at the start of the film, when Anna, in her humble room, readies herself for a day's work, assumes an attitude of prayer by a candlelit window before a photograph of her and her dead child, bows her head, and says, "I thank Thee, dear Lord, for allowing me to awake well and cheerful this morning, after a good sleep under Thy protection, and for the enjoyment of a restful night. I beseech Thee also today and each day to let the angels watch over and protect my little girl, whom Thou in Thy unfathomable wisdom hast taken to Thyself in Thy Homeland. Amen." Then she blows out the candle, bites twice into an apple, gazes into the picture, and moves quickly past the empty cradle. Nykvist lights the scene as Vermeer might have. The apple calls up film memories of Dovzhenko's *Earth* and Renoir's *Grand Illusion*. The effect is sublime.

Such tender moments are rare in a film filled with wounded anguish. At the close, Maria and Karin re-establish the defensive distance between them even though the Bach cello sonata has told us and them that a reconciliation between them was possible. And in two hallucinatory flashbacks, introduced by red close ups, first of Maria, then of Karin (with the sound of cries and whispers in the distance), we see something of the terror and hate in the relationships the two sisters have with their husbands. Cruel, selfish Maria once sent for a doctor when her husband was away, attempted to seduce him, and, when her husband returned, refused to help him when in despair he stabbed himself. And also in the past, frigid, distraught Karin, humiliated by her husband when she spilt wine at the dinner table, slashed her vagina with a piece of the shattered glass and defiantly went to his bed and smeared the blood on her face. Perhaps these shocking, almost surreal scenes are only the long-held vindictive wishes of the two sisters: at the picture's end Maria's husband is still very much alive, and Karin's seems to have no memory of her self-mutilation. The scenes are nonetheless painfully chilling revelations of the two sisters' inner feelings.

And after Agnes dies, there is a similarly harrowing sequence involving the faithful Anna. Once again it is introduced by a red dissolve and the distant sound of cries and whispers, and once again it may be a revelation of inner feelings – those the servant has, but dare not publicly express, for each of the three sisters. Anna is wakened by stifled cries, finds the two sisters anguished but speechless, and discovers that it is the corpse of Agnes that is crying out, asking her to send Karin into her chamber. Karin enters, cannot cope with her dead sister's cries, and flees the room. Then the dead Agnes asks Anna to send Maria in; left alone with the corpse, Maria feels the hands touch her face, is caught in its embrace, and hurls herself away screaming. Finally, Anna enters the room unbidden, takes the corpse in her motherly, sheltering arms, and we get perhaps the most memorable shot in the film - the two bodies are startlingly arranged like the figures of the mother and the crucified in Michelangelo's Pietà.

These terrifying sequences stay fixed in the viewer's memory, but they are not the scenes that have made *Cries and Whispers* a film classic. There are three further scenes that are unequalled in Berman's output for poignancy, moments that I would count among the greatest moments in cinema history. The first of these is Agnes' death. Harriet Anderson gives a harrowing performance, all cries, whispers, and screams of pain until the ultimate release. More than one critic has seen elements here of Christ's crucifixion; the very position of the legs, when the sisters wrap the body, is startling and strangely moving.

In the second classic scene, the minister prays over the dead Agnes. At first it is a formal prayer, read from a book. The camera moves to Karin's face to Maria's and then to Anna's, and the bookish prayer seems to be speaking not to the deceased Anna, but to each of them in turn: "May your sins be forgiven", to Karin. "May your Father in heaven have mercy", to Maria. "May He let His angels remove from you the memory of your earthly pain", to the faithful Anna. Then the minister puts the book aside, kneels before the body, and addresses the dead woman in his own words - and it is as if the doubting, questioning Bergman were speaking:

Should it be true that you gathered up our
suffering in agony into your body,
Should it be that you bore with you
this hardship through death,
Should it be that you meet with God as
you come to that other land,
Should it be that you find His countenance
turned toward you then,
Should it be that you know the language to speak
so this God may hear and understand,
Should it be that you talk with this
God who hears you out,
Should it be so, pray for us.
Agnes, dear child, please listen.
Listen to what I have to tell you now.
Pray for us who have been left in darkness,
left behind on this miserable earth with
the sky above us, grim and empty.
Lay your burden at God's feet - the
whole of your suffering -
And plead with Him to pardon us.
Plead with Him that He may free us of our anxiety,
of our weariness, of our misgivings and fears.
Plead with Him that He may make sense
and meaning of our lives.
Agnes, you, who have borne your anguish
and suffering for so long,
Are most surely worthy of advocating our cause.

These are hardly the words one would expect to hear from a Protestant minister firm in his faith, with a conviction that there be no intercessor between God and the individual believer.

The minister rises and explains to the mourners, "Her faith was stronger than mine." It is Bergman speaking.

The third immensely poignant scene is the very last. Anna, who has been almost contemptuously dismissed by the family, is left alone in the house. She takes up the diary of the woman she has tended, the woman who has never received real affection from her mother or her sisters, whose adult life has been nothing but physical suffering, and who has just died a death of appalling pain. Anna opens the diary to an entry where the suffering Agnes records that, that day, she was able to sit up quietly in a swing with the two sisters who had treated her so badly, rocked by the housemaid who had nursed her so faithfully. This is the entry: "Suddenly all my pain was gone. The people I loved most in all the world were with me. I thought, 'This is happiness'. I can not wish for anything more. Now, for a moment, I can experience perfection, and I feel profoundly grateful to my life, which gives me so much."

One moment in all her life was all that the suffering Agnes had, but she thanked God for it, because it was "so much". One way to think of heaven is to think of it as that one moment so beautiful we want nothing more than to live in it forever, the moment of everlastingness that encompasses, remembers, explains, forgives, and gives happiness. Bergman may not have believed in such a moment, but here he has stated more beautifully than any other master of film the possibility of its happening.

"All of my films can be thought of in terms of black and white," he said, "except *Cries and Whispers*." Somehow I think that when he said that he had more in mind than Sven Nykvist's omnipresent crimsons and reds.

DAYS OF HEAVEN

US, 1978. Written and directed by Terrence Malick. Cinematography by Nestor Almendros and Haskell Wexler. Music by Ennio Morricone. With Richard Gere (Bill), Brooke Adams (Abby), Linda Manz (Linda), Sam Shepard (the Farmer),and Robert Wilke (the Farm Foreman). Paramount.

Days of Heaven confounded its audiences in 1978. The leading music critic of *The New York Times*, who for some reason was sent to review the film and clearly thought a movie house was a place for slumming, called it "intolerably artsy", a "farrago" made up of "all kinds of fancy, self-consciously cineaste techniques". The leading drama critic of *The Toronto Star*, another slummer at the movies, mistook the central situation as incestuous and, when she was made aware that it was not, lazily countered that the film then had to be even worse than she had first thought. Other critics complained that the astonishing beauty of *Days of Heaven*'s images detracted from those more important concerns, plot and character - as if observations Aristotle made about a different art form twenty-four centuries earlier ought to be

355

applied indiscriminately as rules to a movie today. The objections "self-indulgent" and "unintelligible" and "meaningless" have been applied to movies before, most notably when one appeared that demanded of its audience a new kind of response. *Intolerance* and *Citizen Kane* and *2001* forced us to watch, listen, and react in ways we had not known, or had forgotten we knew. They were important, evolutionary films. So is *Days of Heaven*.

Before we see any of the film's now famous shimmering skyscapes and landscapes, we are alerted to its possible meanings by the biblical title (from Deuteronomy 11:21, a passsage often read out at the ceremony of the blessing of the fields), by what seems at first to be singularly inappropriate water music ("The Aquarium" from Saint-Saëns' *Carnival of the Animals*), and by a series of sepia-toned photographs of immigrant life in early twentieth-century America. All of this should prepare us for what, in a moment, we see - a film of about the flawed nature of man set in an Eden of astonishing beauty under a God ready to punish wrong; a film replete with animal images and vistas of water, earth, air, and fire interacting metaphorically; a film about a changing America, its rootlessness, its sources of power and strength, its polyglot origins, its industrialization, and its failure as promised land. The last of the sepia photographs is a picture of a young girl, not much more than a child, with a thin, haunting face. She (the extraordinary Linda Manz) is to be our narrator.

The tale she tells is a re-enactment of *Genesis* 12.10-20: Abraham, driven by hardship into the land of Egypt, persuades his wife Sarah to say she is his sister. Pharaoh, taken by her beauty, receives her and Abraham into his house. Then the Lord sends a great plague to punish the deception, and Abraham and Sarah are sent away. Virtually every critic was unaware that the story that they were watching came out of the Bible. The man who wrote and directed the film was not disposed to make things easy for them.

Days of Heaven was made by Terrence Malick, a one-time lecturer in philosophy at MIT who during his student days at Harvard had worked summers in the wheat fields of Alberta, where almost all of the film was shot, but grew up in the Texas Panhandle, where the film is set. He had made one previous feature, *Badlands*, a picturesque, determinedly amoral and detached telling of the tale of teen-aged Dakota girl on the run with her serial killer boy friend, and it would be twenty years before he would make another, *The Thin Red Line*, which would set the World War II battle of Guadalcanal in a vast, impassive sea of grass.

The astonishing photography in *Days of Heaven*, which has been called by more writers than the present one the most beautiful films ever made, is the work of Nestor Almendros (the Spanish-born cinematographer who also worked with Erich Rohmer and François Truffaut) and perhaps the best American cinematographer of the seventies, Haskell Wexler (who took over behind the camera when Almendros had to leave the two-year filming to work on a project with Truffaut). Between them they turn undulating wheat fields into light and dark watery expanses, while Ennio Morricone's musical score does variations on that water music from "The Carnival of the Animals". The cinematographers also capture as never before or since flocks of bison, herds of horses, silently omniscient antelopes, scurrying rabbits, a light-limned coyote taking possession of a hill, whirring eagles, hawks in flight, geese, peacocks, quail, partridge, wild turkeys, and, with terrible precision, ravenous locusts looming fiercely in immense close-ups. At one marvelous moment, Morricone inverts Saint-Saëns' childlike watery melody and turns it from a small glistening cascade to a great sweeping melody that fills the soundtrack like a prayer to "the land which the Lord swore unto your fathers to give them as the days of heaven upon the earth."

This is a picture where earth becomes water and fire becomes air. When I first saw *Days of Heaven* projected on a large screen in seventy millimeter, its sounds and images literally took possession of my senses, and I thought to myself that no film in my experience - not Griffith, not Dovzhenko, not Renoir, not the Germans, not even *Lawrence of Arabia* - had such overwhelming sensuous power. Its images are richly poetic, altogether unforgettable, exalted in a biblical way. Its sounds are vivid, precise, always in eloquent counterpoint to the visuals. Not a single frame is extraneous to the story and its characters. Nothing is random. Terrence Malick's intelligent sensibility controls everything we see and hear.

Malick tells the story in short, thirty to ninety-second segments, with a minimum of dialogue. This is his most remarkable innovation. We are not allowed to react to the story in the usual way of narrative film. Our emotions are all but closed off. What we see is interpreted for us (even more than in *Badlands* and *The Thin Red Line*) by a voice-over commentary - a drawling, matter-of-fact, idiosyncratic, childlike analysis of virtually everything we see, spoken by a prepubescent, illiterate girl who is naïve and at the same time profound in her observations about good and evil, innocence and corruption, nature and culture, heaven and hell. As movement, color, story, music, and voice-over conspire together, the picture takes on metaphorical, not to say metaphysical meanings. The smallest detail - a lonely bird in flight over a sea of grass, a campfire showering sparks into the air, a sentinel scarecrow, a wineglass dropped in a stream with fish impassively swimming by - calls forth progressively larger meanings.

The viewer ought to lose himself in wonder at the constantly changing pictures that glisten and darken before him. But he cannot. His sense of discovery is more wonderful still. He wonders

358

what it means, for example, when, to grimly realistic images of Chicago steel mills and Chicago violence, the impassive little girl's voice comments, "Me and my brother, we used to do things together. We used to have fun. We used to roam the streets. There was people suffering with pain and hunger. Some people, their tongues was hanging outa their mouth..." This very American waif is by turns *prophetic* (as the trains bring the migrant workers to the lush Texas wheat fields, she proclaims: "The whole world is goin' up in flame. Flames will come out of here and there and they'll just rise up. The mountains are gonna go up in big flames, the water's gonna rise up in flames. There's gonna be creatures runnin' every which way, some of them burnt, half of their wings burnin'... The people that have been good, they're gonna go to heaven and escape all that fire. But if you've been bad, God don't even hear you. He don't even hear ya talkin'"), *realistic* (as she labors among the bales: "If you didn't work dey threw ya right outa dere. Dey don" need ya. Dey kin always get somebody else"), *sensible* (about the desolate young landowner: "He knew there was nothin' he could do. He was headin' for the boneyard, but he wasn't squawkin' about it... You're only on this earth once. And in my opinion so long as you're aroun' you should have it nice"), *opportunistic* (as her brother plans to marry off his common-law wife to the dying landowner so as to come into his money: "Some need more than they got. Others got more than they need. it was just a matter of getting' it all together"), *close to nature* ("I could be a mud doctor, checkin' out da earth underneath. I'd talk to the wheat patches"), *forgiving* (when the plan ends in destruction and death, and nature takes its toll in a plague of locusts: "Nobody's perfect. There was never a perfect person aroun'. Ya just got half-devil and half-angel in ya").

God and the devil, Abraham and Sarah. and the three angels of *Genesis* are all here (the latter as a barnstorming flying circus), all giving meaning to a new context. Shot after stunning shot preaches, not only the prelapsarian truth that water is earth and air is fire, but that good is not any more easily distinguished from evil than man from animals when they both are set in and against an immense pantheistic universe that can be both beautiful and cruel. Roger Ebert once asked himself what "the payoff, the message" of *Days of Heaven* was, and concluded that Malick knew "how a child feels when it lives precariously, and then is delivered into security and joy, and then has it all taken away again - and blinks away the tears and says it doesn't hurt." I think that says it nicely.

Ultimately, *Days of Heaven* does what a great work of art should do - it makes a personal statement about what the world is and what man's place in it is. And it does this in a way only a film and no poem or novel or opera or painting can - by using moving pictures. Pictures limned with color and imbued with the additional suggestiveness of words and music. But, first and foremost, pictures. Moving pictures.

ENDNOTES

[1] Few great films have had so tenuous a hold on survival. *Joan* was premiered complete in Denmark, but in France objections from both church and state resulted in cuts being made before its premiere there. The original negative was destroyed by fire. A second negative, assembled by Dreyer from alternate takes, was believed lost in another fire, and copies of it became increasingly worn and mutilated over the decades, while the film was reassembled (and its component parts rearranged) in various versions lasting little more than an hour. In 1951 a good print of the second negative was discovered in Paris. Then, in 1981, a beautifully clear print of the original Danish negative was discovered in a mental institution in Oslo and released in remastered form in 1985. It is used in the DVD release, fitted with an excellent commentary by Caspar Tybjerg and a musical score ("Voices of Light", by Richard Einhorn) that provides the film with a continuity it lacked in previous issues. It is now clear that Dreyer used his five reels to turn the story of Joan's passion into a classical five-act drama - the courtroom, the cell, the torture chamber, the abjuration and retraction, and the stake.

[2] Pauline Kael, in a famous 1971 article in *The New Yorker* (subsequently published separately), argued that the script of *Kane* is substantially the work of Mankiewicz. If she is right - and there are many reasons to believe she is - it is ironic that the only Oscar that Welles ever received, for co-writing the script of *Citizen Kane*, was for work that was partly, perhaps largely, that of someone else.

[3] The chief causes of this were official government disapproval and a re-organization of the Italian film industry that resulted in producer censorship. I refer the reader to George A. Huaco's *The Sociology of Film Art* (New York, 1965), a study to which this chapter is indebted.

LIST OF FILMS AND YEARS

À Nous la Liberté. 1932

Adam's Rib, 1949

Adaptation, 2002

Adventures of Robin Hood, The, 1938

Adventures of Tom Sawyer, The, 1938

Affliction, 1998

African Queen, The, 1951

Age d'Or, L', 1930

Age of Innocence, The, 1993

Alexander Nevsky, 1939

Alfie, 1966

Alice, 1990

Alien, 1979

All About Eve, 1950

All About My Mother, 1999

All of Me, 1984

All Quiet on the Western Front, 1930

All Screwed Up, 1976

All That Money Can Buy, 1941

All the King's Men, 1949

All the President's Men, 1976

Amarcord, 1974

America, America, 1963

American Beauty, 1999

American Graffiti, 1973

American in Paris, An, 1951

Amistad, 1997

Anatomy of a Murder, 1959

Anchors Aweigh, 1945

And the Ship Sails On, 1984

Andrei Roublev, 173

Anna Christie, 1930

Anna Karenina, 1935

Annie Hall, 1977

Aparajito, 1959

Apartment, The, 1960

Apocalypse Now, 1979

Apollo 13, 1995

Around the World in 80 Days, 1956

As Good As It Gets, 1997

Asphalt Jungle, The, 1950

Assault, The, 1987

Atalante, L,, 1947

Au Hasard, Balthazar, 1970

Au Revoir Les Enfnats, 1988

Autumn Sonata, 1978

Aviator, The, 2004

Avventura, L', 1961

Awful Truth, The, 1937

Babel, 2006

Babette's Feast, 1988

Badlands, 1974

Bailiff, The, 1969

Ballad of a Soldier, 1960

Ballad of Narayama, The, 1984

Bambi, 1942

Band Wagon, The, 1953

Barry Lyndon, 1975

Battle of Algiers, The, 1967

Beautiful Mind, A, 2001

Beauty and the Beast, 1991

Becket, 1964

Before the Rain, 1995

Being John Malkovich, 1999

Belle Epoque, 1992

Belle et le Bête, La, 1947 L

Bells of St. Mary's, The 1945

Ben-Hur, 1959

Best Intentions, The, 1992

Best Years of Our Lives, The, 1946

Bête Humaine, La, 1938

Betrayal, 1983

Beverly Hills Cop, 1984

Bible, The, 1966

Bicycle Thief, The, 1949

Big Business, 1988

Big Parade, The 1925

Big Sleep, The, 1946

Big, 1988

Birth of a Nation, The 1915

Black Hawk Down, 2001

Black Narcissus, 1947

Black Orpheus, 1959

Black Stallion, The, 1979

Blowup, 1966

Blue Angel, The, 1930

Blue Velvet, 1986

Body Heat, 1981

Bonnie and Clyde, 1967

Boot, Das, 1982

Born Yesterday, 1950

Boucher, Le, 1971

Boys N The Hood, 1991

Braveheart, 1995

Bread and Chocolate, 1978

Breaker Morant, 1980

Breaking Away, 1979

Breaking the Waves, 1996

Breaking Through the Sound
 Barrier, 1953
Breathless, 1961
Bride of Frankenstein, The, 1935
Bridge on the River Kwai, The,
 1957
Bridge, The, 1961
Brief Encounter, 1946
Bringing Up Baby, 1938
Broadcast News, 1987
Brokeback Mountain, 2005
Broken Blossoms, 1919
Bullitt, 1968
Butch Cassidy and the Sundance
 Kid, 1969
Cabaret, 1972
Cabin in the Sky, 1943
Cabinet of Dr. Caligari, 1919
Caché
Call Me Madam, 1953
Camille, 1937
Capote, 2005
Captain's Paradise, The, 1953
Casablanca, 1943
Cast Away, 2000
Central Station, 1998
Cérémonie, La, 1996
Charade, 1963
Chariots of Fire, 1981
Chicago, 2002
Chien Andalou, Un, 1928
Children of Men, 2006

Chimes at Midnight, 1967
China Syndrome, The, 1979
Chinatown, 1974
Cid, El, 1961
Cinderella Man, 2005
Cinema Paradiso, 1990
Citadel, The, 1938
Citizen Kane, 1941
City Lights, 1931
Claire's Knee, 1971
Close Encounters of the Third
 Kind, 1977
Closely Watched Trains, 1967
Collateral, 2004
Color of Paradise, The, 2000
Color Purple, The, 1985
Coming Home, 1978
Conformist, The, 1971
Constant Gardener, The, 2005
Conversation, The, 1974
Cool Hand Luke, 1967
Crabe-Tambour, Le, 1984
Crash, 2005
Cries and Whispers, 1973
Crimes and Misdemeanors, 1989
Crouching Tiger, Hidden Dragon,
 2000
Crowd, The, 1928
Crying Game, The, 1991
Curse of the Golden Flower, The,
 2006
Dances With Wolves, 1990

Darling, 1965

David Copperfield, 1935

Day for Night, 1974

Day of the Jackal, The, 1973

Day of Wrath, 1948

Days of Heaven, 1978

Dead Man Walking, 1995

Dead, The, 1987

Death in Venice, 1971

Death on the Nile, 1978

Decalogue, The 1990

Deep End, The, 2001

Deer Hunter, The, 1978

Defiant Ones, The, 1958

Deliverance, 1972

Departed, The, 2006

Detective Story, 1951

Diabolique, 1955

Diary of a Country Priest, 1954

Die Hard, 1988

Discreet Charm of the Bougeoisie, The, 1972

Divorce – Italian Style, 1962

Do the Right Thing, 1989

Doctor Zhivago, 1965

Dog Day Afternoon, 1975

Dolce Vita, La, 1961

Don't look Now, 1973

Double Indemnity, 1944

Dr. Strangelove, 1964

Draughtsman's Contract, The 1983

Dreamgirls, 2006

Driving Miss Daisy, 1989

Duck Soup, 1933

Duellists, The, 1978

E.T., 1982

Earrings of Madame D..., The, 1953

Earth, 1930

East of Eden, 1955

Eat Drink Man Woman, 1994

Eboli, 1980

8½, 1963

Eight Women, 2002

Emigrants, The, 1972

Empire Strikes Back, The, 1980

Enchanted April, 1992

End of the Affair, The, 1999

Enemies: A Love Story, 1989

Enfants du Paradis, Les, 1946

English Patient, The, 1996

Enigma of Kaspar Hauser, The, 1975

Entertainer, The, 1960

Erin Brokovitch, 2000

Europa Europa, 1991

Face to Face, 1976

Fallen Idol, The, 1949

Fanny and Alexander, 1983

Fantasia, 1941

Far From Heaven, 2002

Far From the Madding Crowd, 1967

Farewell My Concubine, 1993

Fargo, 1996

Fatal Attraction, 1987

Fellini Satyricon, 1970

Femme Infidèle, La, 1969

Field of Dreams, 1989

Finding Nemo, 2003

Fist in His Pocket, 1968

Fitzcarraldo, 1982

Five Easy Pieces, 1970

For Whom the Bell Tolls, 1943

Forbidden Games, 1952

Foreign Correspondent, 1940

42nd Street, 1933

Forrest Gump, 1994

400 Blows, The, 1959

Frankenstein, 1939

Freaks, 1932

French Connection, The 1971

French Lieutenant's Woman, The, 1981

From Here to Eternity, 1953

From Russia With Love, 1964

Funny Face, 1957

Gallipoli, 1981

Gangs of New York, 2002

Garden of the Finzi-Continis, 1971

Gaslight, 1944

Gay Divorcée, The, 1934

General, The, 1926

Georgy Girl, 1966

Giant, 1956

Gigi, 1958

Girl With a Pearl Earring, 2003

Gladiator, 2000

Glengarry Glen Ross, 1992

Glory, 1989

Go-Between, The, 1971

Godfather II, The, 1974

Godfather III, The, 1990

Godfather, The 1972

Going My Way, 1944

Gold Rush, The, 1925

Golden Coach, The, 1954

Gone With the Wind, 1939

Good Earth, The, 1937

Good Will Hunting, 1997

Goodbye Girl, The, 1977

Goodbye, Mr. Chips, 1939

GoodFellas, 1990

Gosford Park, 2001

Gospel According to Matthew, 1966

Graduate, The, 1967

Grand Hotel, 1932

Grand Illusion, 1938

Grande Bourgeoise, La, 1977

Grapes of Wrath, The, 1940

Great Dictator, The, 1940

Great Escape, The, 1963

Great Expectations, 1947

Great Santini, The, 1980

Great Ziegfeld, 1936

Greed, 1924

Green Pastures, The, 1936

Grifters, The, 1990

Hail the Conquering Hero, 1944

Hallelujah!, 1929

Hamlet, 1948

Hamlet, 1996

Hannah and Her Sisters, 1986

Harvest, 1939

Harvey, 1950

Hear My Song, 1992

Heartbreak Kid, The, 1972

Heaven Can Wait, 1943

Heiress, The, 1949

Henry V, 1946

Henry V, 1989

Here Comes Mr. Jordan, 1941

Hero, 2004

High Noon, 1952

Hiroshima Mon Amour, 1960

His Girl Friday, 1940

History Boys, The, 2006

Holiday Inn, 1942

Holiday, 1938

Home and the World, 1985

Hoop Dreams, 1994

Horse's Mouth, The, 1958

Hot Millions, 1968

Hotel Rwanda, 2004

Hour of the Wolf, 1968

Hours, The, 2002

House of Flying Daggers, 2004

House of Games, 1987

House of Sand and Fog, 2003

How Green Was My Valley, 1941

Howards End, 1991

Hud, 1963

Human Comedy, The, 1943

Hunchback of Notre Dame, The, 1939

Hustler, The, 1961

I Am a Fugitive from a Chain Gang, 1932

I Know Where I'm Going, 1947

I Never Sang For My Father, 1970

I'm All Right, Jack, 1960

Ikiru, 1960

Importance of Being Ernest, The, 1952

In America, 2003

In the Bedroom, 2001

In the Heat of the Night, 1967

In the Line of Fire, 1993

In the Name of the Father, 1993

In Which We Serve, 1943

Informer, The, 1935

In-Laws, The, 1979

Insider, The, 1999

Intolerance, 1916

Intruder in the Dust, 1949

Ipcress File, The, 1965

It Happened One Night, 1934

It's A Wonderful Life, 1946

Ivan the Terrible, 1947

Jaws, 1975

Jazz Singer, 1927

Jean de Florette/Manon of the
    Spring, 1987

Jerry Maguire, 1996

Joan of Arc, 1948

Ju Dou, 1991

Jules and Jim, 1962

Julia, 1977

Juliet of the Spirits, 1965

Julius Caesar, 1953

Kagemusha, 1980

Kaos, 1986

Kermesse Heroique, La, 1936

Killers, The, 1946

Killing Fields, The, 1984

Kind Hearts and Coronets, 1950

King and I, The, 1956

King Kong, 1933

King of Comedy, The, 1983

Kings Row, 1942

Kiss of the Spider Woman, 1985

Kolya, 1996

Kramer vs. Kramer, 1979

Kundun, 1997

Kwaidan, 1965

L.A. Confidential, 1997

Lady Eve, The, 1941

Lady Vanishes, The, 1938

Lady With a dog, 1962

Lamerica, 1995

Lancelot du Lac, 1975

Last Emperor, The 1987

Last Laugh, The, 1924

Last Picture Show, The, 1971

Last Seduction, The, 1994

Last Temptation of Christ, The
    1988

Last Year at Marienbad, 1962

Laura, 1944

Lavender Hill Mob, The, 1952

Lawrence of Arabia, 1962

Leopard, The, 1963

Les Miserables, 1935

Letter from an Unknown
    Woman, 1948

Letter to Three Wives, A, 1949

Letter, The, 1940

Letters from Iwo Jima, 2006

Life is Beautiful, 1998

Life Is Sweet, 1991

Life of Emile Zola, The, 1937

Lifeboat, 1944

Like Water for Chocolate, 1992

Lili, 1953

Lion in Winter, The, 1968

Little Foxes, The, 1941

Little Woman, 1934

Lone Star, 1996

Long Good Friday, The, 1982

Lord of the Rings: The Return of
    the King, 2003

Lord of the Rings: The Fellowship
    of the Ring, 2001

Losing Isaiah, 1995

Lost Horizon, 1937

Lost Weekend, The, 1945

Love and Anarchy, 1974

Love Me Tonight, 1932

Lust for Life, 1956

M*A*S*H*, 1970

M, 1932

Madness of King George, The, 1994

Magnificent Ambersons, The, 1942

Magnolia, 11999

Maltese Falcon, The, 1941

Man Escaped, A, 1957

Man for All Seasons, A, 1966

Man of Aran, 1934

Man of Marble/Man of Iron, 1981

Manchurian Candidate, The, 1962

Manhattan, 1979

March of the Penguins, 2005

Marius/César/Fanny, 1948

Marquise of O..., The, 1976

Marriage, Italian Style, 1964

Marty, 1955

Mary Poppins, 1964

Master and Commander: The Far Side of the World, 2003

Mean Streets, 1973

Meet Me In St. Louis, 1944

Member of the Wedding, The, 1952

Memento, 2001

Memory of Justice, The 1976

Mephisto, 1982

Merchant of Venice, The, 2004

Metropolis, 1926

Midnight Cowboy, 1969

Mildred Pierce, 1945

Million Dollar Baby, 2004

Million, Le, 1931

Miracle of Morgan's Creek, The, 1944

Miracle Worker, The, 1962

Miracle, The, 1991

Mister Roberts, 1955

Moby Dick, 1956

Modern Times, 1936

Mon Oncle Antoine, 1971

Mon Oncle d'Amerique, 1980

Mona Lisa, 1986

Monsieur Vincent, 1948

Moonstruck, 1987

Morgan!, 1966

Mother, 1926

Moulin Rouge, 1952

Mr. Deeds Goes To Town, 1936

Mr. Hulot's Holiday, 1954

Mr. Smith Goes to Washington, 1939

Mrs. Doubtfire, 1993

Mrs. Miniver, 1942

Mulholland Drive, 2001

Munich, 2005

Murder on the Orient Express, 1974

Mutiny on the Bounty, 1935

My Beautiful Laundrette, 1986

My Best Friend's Wedding, 1997

My Big Fat Greek Wedding, 2002

My Darling Clementine, 1946

My Fair Lady, 1964

My Father's Glory/My Mother's Castle, 1991

My Left Foot, 1989

My Man Godfrey, 1936

My Night at Maud's, 1970

My Uncle, Mr. Hulot, 1958

Mystic River, 2003

Nanook of the North, 1922

Napoleon, 1927

Nashville, 1975

National Velvet, 1945

Network, 1976

New Land, The, 1973

New World, The, 2005

Nibelungen, Die, 1924

Night at the Opera, 1935

Night Must Fall, 1937

Night of the Hunter, 1955

Night of the Shooting Stars, The, 1983

Night to Remember, A, 1958

Nights of Cabiria, 1957

Ninotchka, 1939

No Way Out, 1987

Norma Rae, 1979

North By Northwest, 1959

Nosferatu, 1922

Notorious, 1946

Nun's Story, The, 1959

O Brother, Where Art Thou?, 2000

Obsession, 1976

October, 1927

Odd Man Out, 1947

Official Story, The, 1985

Oklahoma!, 1955

Oliver Twist, 1951

Oliver!, 1968,

Olympia, 1939

On the Town, 1949

On the Waterfront, 1954

Once Upon a Time in America, 1984

One Flew Over the Cuckoo's Nest, 1975

Open City, 1946

Ordet, 1957

Ordinary People, 1980

Orpheus, 1951

Osama, 2004

Out of Africa, 1985

Out of Sight, 1998

Out of the Past, 1947

Outcast of the Islands, 1952

Ox-Bow Incident, The, 1943

Padre Padrone, 1977

Paisan, 1948

Palm Beach Story, The, 1942

Pan's Labyrinth, 2006

Passage to India, A, 1984

Passenger, The, 1975

Passion of Joan of Arc, The, 1928

Pather Panchali, 1958

Paths of Glory, 1957

Patton, 1970

Pawnbroker, The, 1965

Perceval, 1978

Persona, 1967

Philadelphia Story, The, 1940

Philadelphia, 1993

Pianist, The, 2002

Piano, The, 1993

Pickpocket, 1963

Picnic, 1955

Picture of Dorian Grey, The 1945

Pinocchio, 1940

Pixote, 1981

Place in the Sun, A, 1951

Places in the Heart, 1984

Platoon, 1986

Pledge, The, 2001

Postino, Il, 1995

Potemkin, 1925

Presumed Innocent, 1990

Pretty Woman, 1990

Pride and Prejudice, 1940

Prime of Miss Jean Brodie, The, 1969

Prince of the City, 1981

Private Life of Henry VIII, The, 1933

Prizzi's Honor, 1985

Promesse, La, 1997

Psycho, 1960

Pulp Fiction, 1994

Pygmalion, 1938

Quartet, 1949

Queen, The, 2006

Quiet Man, The, 1952

Radio Days, 1987

Raging Bull, 1980

Raiders of the Lost Ark, 1981

Raining Stones, 1994

Ran, 1985

Rashomon, 1951

Rear Window, 1954

Rebecca, 1940

Red and the White, The, 1969

Red Desert, 1965

Red Rock West, 1994

Red Shoes, The, 1948

Red Sorghum, 1988

Reds, 1981

Remains of the Day, The, 1993

Return of Martin Guerre, The, 1983

Reversal of Fortune, 1990

Richard III, 1956

Rise of Louis XIV, The, 1970

Road to Perdition, 2002

Robin and Marian, 1976

Rocco and his Brothers, 1961

Roman Holiday, 1953

Romeo and Juliet, 1954

Ronde, La, 1951

Room at the Top, 1959

Room With a View, A, 1986

Rosemary's Baby,1968

Rosenkavalier, Der, 1962

Ruggles of Red Gap, 1935

Rules of the Game, The, 1950

Run Lola Run, 1999

Russian Ark, 2002

Sabotage, 1937

Sabrina, 1954

Sacrifice, The, 1986

Salaam Bombay!, 1988

Salvador, 1986

San Francisco, 1936

Saturday Night and Sunday
   Morning, 1961

Saving Private Ryan, 1998

Scenes from a Marriage, 1974

Schindler's List, 1993

Search, The, 1948

Searchers, The, 1956

Secrets and Lies, 1996

Seduction of Mimi, The, 1971

Sense and Sensibility, 1995

Separate Tables, 1958

Seven Beauties, 1976

Seven Brides for Seven Brothers,
   1954

Seven Samurai, The, 1956

Seventh Seal, The, 1958

Sexy Beast, 2001

Shadow of a Doubt, 1943

Shakespeare in Love, 1998

Shakespeare Wallah, 1966

Shall We Dance?, 1997

Shane, 1953

Shawshank Redemption, The,
   1994

She Wore a Yellow Ribbon, 1949

Sherlock, Jr., 1924

Ship of Fools, 1965

Shoeshine, 1947

Shooting Party, The, 1985

Shop on Main Street, The, 1966

Short Cuts, 1993

Show Boat, 1936

Sideways, 2004

Silence of the Lambs, The, 1991

Silence, The, 1964

Simon of the Desert, 1969

Simple Plan, A, 1998

Since You Went Away, 1944

Singin' in the Rain, 1952

Sleeper, 1973

Sling Blade, 1996

Smiles of a Summer Night, 1957

Smoke, 1995

Snow White and the Seven
  Dwarfs, 1937
Soldier's Story, A, 1984
Some Like It Hot, 1959
Song of Bernadette, The, 1943
Sons of the Desert, 1934
Sophie's Choice, 1982
Sorrow and the Pity, 1971
Sound of Music, The, 1965
Sound of Trumpets, The, 1963
Sounder, 1972
Spanish Prisoner, The 1998
Spellbound, 1945
Spider's Stratagem, The 1973
Stage Door, 1937
Stagecoach, 1939
Stalag 17, 1953
Star is Born, A, 1937
Star Is Born, A, 1954
Star Wars, 1977
State Fair, 1945
Sting, The, 1971
Story of Adele H., The, 1975
Story of Women, 1989
Strada, La, 1956
Strangers on a Train, 1951
Strawberry Blonde, The, 1941
Streetcar Named Desire, A, 1951
Stunt Man, The, 1980
Sullivan's Travels, 1942
Summertime, 1955
Sunday, Bloody Sunday, 1971

Sundowners, The, 1950
Sunrise, 1927
Sunset Boulevard, 1950
Superman, 1978
Sweet Hereafter, The, 1997
Sweet Smell of Success, The, 1957
Swept Away, 1975
Swing Time, 1936
Syriana, 2005
Tale of Two Cities, A, 1936
Talented Mr. Ripley, The, 1999
Taxi Driver, 1976
Tender Mercies, 1983
Terms of Endearment, 1983
That Hamilton Woman, 1941
That Obscure Object of Desire,
  177
Thelma and Louise, 1991
Thèrése, 1986
Thief of Bagdad, The, 1924
Thief of Bagdad, The, 1940
Thin Red Line, The 1998
Third Man, The, 1950
39 Steps, The, 1935
Three Brothers, 1982
Three Kings, 1999
3 Women, 1977
Tight little Island, 1950
Time for Drunken Horses, A,
  2000
Tin Drum, The, 1980
Titanic, 1997

To Be Or Not To Be, 1942
To Have and Have Not, 1945
To Kill a Mockingbird, 1962
Tokyo Story, 1972
Tom Jones, 1963
Tootsie, 1982
Top Hat, 1935
Topkapi, 1964
Topsy-Turvy, 1999
Touch of Evil, 1958
Trading Places, 1983
Traffic, 2000
Treasure of the Sierra Madre, The,
    1948
Tree Grows in Brooklyn, A, 1945
Tree of Wooden Clogs, The, 1979
Tricolor: Blue, White, Red. 1994
Trouble in Paradise, 1932
True Confessions, 1981
Truman Show, The, 1998
Turning Point, The, 1977
Twelve Angry Men, 1957
21 Grams, 2003
Two English Girls, 1972
2001: A Space Odyssey, 1968
Two Women, 1961
Ugetsu, 1954
Ulysses, 1967
Umberto D., 1955
Umbrellas of Cherbourg, The,
    1964
Under the Sun of Satan, 1989

Unforgiven, 1992
Uninvited, The, 1944
United 93, 2006
Unmarried Woman, An, 1978
Usual Suspects, The, 1995
Vanishing, The, 1991
Variety, 1924
Vera Drake, 2004
Verdict, The, 1982
Veronika Voss, 1982
Vertigo, 1958
Virgin Spring, The, 1960
Vitelloni, I, 1957
Wages of Fear, The, 1955
Wanderer, The, 1969
War and Peace, 1956
War and Peace, 1968
Watch on the Rhine, 1943
West Side Story, 1961
Whale Rider, 2003
When Father Was Away on
    Business, 1985
White Men Can't Jump, 1992
Who's Afraid of Virgina Woolf?,
    1966
Wild Bunch, The, 1969
Wild Child, The, 1970
Wild Strawberries, 1959
Winged Migration, 2003
Wings of Desire, 1988
Winslow Boy, The, 1950
Winter Light, 1963

Witness, 1985

Wizard of Oz, The 1939

Woman in the Dunes, 1965

Woman of the Year, 1942

Women in Love, 1970

World of Apu, The,

Wuthering Heights, 1939

Yankee Doodle Dandy, 1942

Yellow Submarine, 1968

Yi-Yi, 2000

Yojimbo, 1962

You Can Count On Me, 2000

You Can't Take It With You, 1938

Z, 1969

Zelig, 1983

Zero de Conduit, 1947

Zorba the Greek, 1964

Made in the USA
Las Vegas, NV
06 May 2024

89600678R00225